VIABLE ECOLOGIES

CULTURE, PLACE, AND NATURE
Studies in Anthropology and Environment
K. Sivaramakrishnan, Series Editor

Centered in anthropology,
the Culture, Place, and Nature series
encompasses new interdisciplinary social
science research on environmental issues,
focusing on the intersection of culture, ecology,
and politics in global, national, and local contexts.
Contributors to the series view environmental
knowledge and issues from the multiple
and often conflicting perspectives
of various cultural systems.

VIABLE ECOLOGIES

*Conservation and Coexistence
on the Galápagos Islands*

∽∾∾

PAOLO BOCCI

University of Washington Press
Seattle

Viable Ecologies was made possible in part by a grant from the Samuel and Althea Stroum Endowed Book Fund.

Copyright © 2024 by the University of Washington Press

Earlier versions of chapter 1 and 5 appeared, respectively, in "Tangles of Care: Killing Goats to Save Tortoises on The Galápagos Islands," *Cultural Anthropology* 32, no. 3 (2017): 424–49; and "Planting the Seeds of the Future: Eschatological Environmentalism in the Time of the Anthropocene," *Religions* 10, no. 2 (2019): 125.

Composed in 10.8/15.5 pt Minion Pro

All rights reserved. No part of this publication may be reproduced or transmitted in any form or by any means, electronic or mechanical, including photocopy, recording, or any information storage or retrieval system, without permission in writing from the publisher.

Photographs by the author. Maps by Ben Pease.

UNIVERSITY OF WASHINGTON PRESS *uwapress.uw.edu*

LIBRARY OF CONGRESS CATALOGING-IN-PUBLICATION DATA

Names: Bocci, Paolo, author.

Title: Viable ecologies : conservation and coexistence on the Galápagos Islands / Paolo Bocci.

Description: Seattle : University of Washington Press, [2024] | Series: Culture, place, and nature | Includes bibliographical references and index.

Identifiers: LCCN 2024014089 | ISBN 9780295753430 (hardback) | ISBN 9780295753447 (paperback) | ISBN 9780295753454 (ebook)

Subjects: LCSH: Ecology—Galapagos Islands. | Galapagos Islands—Environmental conditions.

Classification: LCC QH198.G3 B63 2024 | DDC 508.866/5—dc23/eng/20241002

LC record available at https://lccn.loc.gov/2024014089

♾ This paper meets the requirements of ANSI/NISO Z39.48-1992 (Permanence of Paper).

When we talk about biodiversity loss—I'm slightly troubled by the word "loss" because we have not lost these species.... We have destroyed them or we've destroyed their habitats. It's not a sixth mass extinction event that we are precipitating, it's a mass extermination event.

CHRIS PACKHAM / *naturalist, 2023*

I'm tired of being resilient.

RAMIRO, FARMER / *whispering at a 2014 meeting on agriculture and climate change*

Contents

Foreword *by K. Sivaramakrishnan*   ix

Preface   xiii

Acknowledgments   xvii

Introduction   1

ONE Escape Goats   29

TWO Unplanned Plan(t)s   51

INTERMEZZO I / ENCOUNTERING ILLEGALITY   75

THREE Uncertain *Vivir*   79

INTERMEZZO II / CULTIVATING BELONGING   101

FOUR Minor Thriving   105

FIVE Native Farming   129

Conclusion   147

Notes   155

References   161

Index   185

K. SIVARAMAKRISHNAN

∾✕∾

Foreword

Since the visit of Charles Darwin in 1835, the Galápagos Islands, off the coast of Ecuador, have been of key importance to biodiversity preservation. Many islands, especially in the tropics, became the subject of the earliest discussions around biodiversity conservation both in the colonial period of intensive European expansion in the new and old worlds, and then in the twentieth century, when biodiversity became a central concern of environmental scientists and activists.[1] This fine study by Paolo Bocci is based on these islands, which were subject to a century of intensive extractive activity before being targeted for conservation in part because of the legacy of Darwin's influential discoveries there.

By the late twentieth century biogeographers and conservation biologists began in earnest to document the tremendous destruction of biodiversity in tropical and other small islands. However, the actual global investment into species conservation was often directed to large terrestrial projects in the rainforests, wetlands, and hilly terrain of the Asian borderlands; the flatlands of the African savannah; and river ecosystems that were the lifeblood of large plains. Notably, biodiversity research was likely to be sequestered in its chosen field sites in small island societies or places like Hawaii. The Galápagos Islands that come into view in this study are a location where both research and conservation activity were undertaken.

As has happened in many places targeted as protected areas, notably in the aftermath of colonial rule, conservation has alienated large tracts of land from local livelihoods. In doing so, conservation programs have cast these local economies and societies as inconvenient to the cause of species conservation. People living around parks and protected areas have been criminalized when they contend for use of the lands taken for species conservation. Regional economies are then transformed by international x *Foreword*

traffic in conservation scientists and tourists, who then become a staple of the local economy and efforts by regional governments to create revenue streams for conservation efforts.

As Bocci shows, some of these processes played out in the Galápagos, but he finds an alternative vision in the efforts of Galápagos residents and the idea of *buen vivir* advanced in recent Ecuadorian government policies toward stewardship of land and protection of endemic species. He documents practices of living on the land while conserving nature or, to use terms that are more common these days, finding ways to sustain both human and nonhuman lives by taking a more-than-human perspective on life on earth. He writes about policies of progressive environmental intent that served to marginalize local rights and environmental struggles, participatory conservation as an ideal exerting a disciplining force on environmental ideas and political action. Here, too, as conservation programs recognized the need to involve residents in their mission, such people became subjects of a new kind of government by conservation that sometimes appeared to accommodate their aspirations but rarely consulted their values, beliefs, or knowledge.[2]

When conservation was a bounded enterprise of experts and governments directing their efforts toward the protection and reproduction of desired species, it was custodial and exclusionary.[3] Bocci traces the kinds of conservation science and policy that emulated such exclusive approaches in the Galápagos. These strategies underwent reform to incorporate local farmers and other rural residents as it became clear conservation needed to extend beyond the physical limits of the parks to the fields of farmers, especially in the fight against what were considered invasive species, such as hill raspberry (*Rubus niveus*).

As Bocci shows, with a bias in favor of endemism, restoration ecology took prominent place among scientific perspectives, resulting in the imposition of violent conservation programs. By contrast, local people found ways for multiple species to thrive, such as by keeping the goats identified as an invasive species and targeted for reduction and containment. Some endemic species found ways to coexist with recently arrived plants. The focus on native plants and forms of life inevitably resulted in restrictive policies relating to migration, the social impact of which is treated extensively in the latter part of the book.

Resilience and adaptation, terms currently much in use in environmental science and in planned responses to social-ecological disruption induced by climate change, take on a whole new meaning in the later chapters of this sensitive ethnography. Farmers reveal their commitment to their own livelihood and a more capacious notion of flourishing that includes the endemic nature with which they coexist. And, as Bocci shows, conservation ideas and values seep into the local imagination of multispecies coexistence, creating a multilayered sense of *buen vivir* as the exchange between local ideas and imported ideals becomes thicker and better informed by values, beliefs, and aspirations on either side.

Along the way, Bocci proposes his notion of *viable ecologies*, suggesting a program and spirit of action that makes conservation more pragmatic and imagines human thriving as an essential part of nonhuman flourishing. In writing about these aspects of the growing relationship between farmers and conservationists, he is inspired by some of the best work in multispecies anthropology but remains rooted in the politics of realizable futures.[4]

It is worth noting that in this case the locals are themselves migrants from earlier waves of settlement when the Galápagos Islands were targeted for various extractive activities. In that sense they too are caught up in contentious debates around natives and non-natives, and who can be included in a future where everyone might thrive together in mutually supportive relations. *Viable ecologies* are then forged not so much by rediscovering some Indigenous stewardship of the land or restoring control to people earlier unsettled by conservation. They emerge when human and nonhuman cooperation is built painstakingly on mutual respect and a more imaginative notion of belonging in the land, a process felicitously referred to by Wes Jackson, three decades ago, as becoming native to this place.[5]

In *Viable Ecologies*, Paolo Bocci advances a pragmatic and socially inclusive politics of conservation that recognizes that more-than-human approaches to the environment can be culturally and politically diverse and subject to change in the very socio-ecological conditions in which they form and flourish. In this endeavor he brings forth valuable perspectives from the small island societies at the heart of both earlier conservation efforts and the development of conservation science. He shows that these small islands, on the frontline of the emerging climate change crisis, may show the way forward.

NOTES

1   Key works on this subject include Richard Grove, *Green Imperialism: Colonial Expansion, Tropical Island Edens and the Origins of Environmentalism, 1600–1860* (Cambridge: Cambridge University Press, 1996); and Michael Lewis, *Inventing Global Ecology: Tracking the U.S. Biodiversity Ideal in India, 1947–1997* (Athens: Ohio University Press, 2004).

2   Conservation as a form of politics of sovereign power and local discipline has been explored in books such as Paige West, *Conservation Is Our Government Now: The Politics of Ecology in Papua New Guinea* (Durham: Duke University Press, 2006); Arun Agrawal, *Environmentality: Technologies of Government and the Making of Subjects* (Durham: Duke University Press, 2005); Pamela McElwee, *Forests Are Gold: Trees, People and Environmental Rule in Vietnam* (Seattle: University of Washington Press, 2016).

3   Dan Brockington described this as the fortress approach in his book, *Fortress Conservation: The Preservation of the Mkomazi Game Reserve* (Bloomington: Indiana University Press, 2002).

4   The work of Sophie Chao, *In the Shadow of the Palms More-Than-Human Becomings in West Papua* (Durham: Duke University Press, 2022), particularly comes to mind in this regard, among a plethora of books that have wonderfully explored and expanded the field of multispecies anthropology.

5   Wes Jackson, *Becoming Native to This Place* (Lexington: University of Kentucky Press, 1994).

Preface

I write this preface in the fall of 2023, when CO_2 emissions, average global air and ocean temperature, biodiversity loss, and subsidies to fossil fuel industries have—much like the yearly profits of the latter—all reached record highs. Greenhouse concentration is now higher than it has been since the mid-Pliocene, seven million years ago. A summer of heat waves, fires, oceans reaching 100 degrees, and a portion of Antarctica the size of Mexico failing to refreeze does not even offer the grim consolation that we have reached the much-feared new normal: it will, in fact, get much worse. Meanwhile, the diversion tactics of oil industries and their enablers multiply, from neocolonial land grabs through carbon market schemes to vacuous climate pledges set in distant 2050 or absurd technofixes such as solar radiation management and carbon capture.

Climate change is accelerating the already vertiginous rate of species extinction, now already two to four orders of magnitude higher than baseline extinction (Ceballos and Ehrlich 2023). Ecologists predict that soon climate change will surpass habitat destruction as the main driver of biodiversity loss. Both are caused by humans, and both are on the rise. Ecological concerns have broadened from endangerment of individual species within bounded ecosystems to defaunation and extinction on a planetary scale; from, in the words of Deborah Bird Rose, "double death"—the compromised ability of a species or territory to recuperate from mounting loss (Rose 2004)—to "triple death," in which one earth function cannot compensate for the deficit of others, and earth systems as a whole verge on collapse.

As the climate crisis worsens and the planet drifts, with calculated inaction, toward uncharted boiling waters, the temptation to consider the Galápagos an exception might become more pronounced than ever.

xiv *Preface*

(Commenting on the unprecedented temperatures of the 2023 summer, UN Secretary General António Guterres warned that "the era of global warming has ended; the era of global boiling has arrived," United Nations 2023.) These islands enjoy a worldwide reputation for featuring exceptionally well-preserved and unique ecosystems. This archipelago six hundred miles off the coast of Ecuador still hosts species that have evolved for millions of years in near-complete isolation, prompting illustrious visitors such Charles Darwin to describe the islands as "a world within itself" and, since the early advocacy for local conservation, the world's last natural laboratory of evolution (Darwin [1839] 2001, 87; Quiroga 2009).

However, construction of this archipelago as an exclusive site for conservation was not a natural occurrence. Instead, it was itself the result of competing uses of the islands from being a source of tortoises for pirates in the seventeenth and eighteenth centuries to becoming the site of mostly unsuccessful projects of extracting lichen, guano, or cane sugar (even fish exports) lasting until the early twentieth century. International pressure to protect the Galápagos coalesced then, as influential natural scientists mostly from Europe and the United States insisted on the need to preserve the islands where they believed Darwin, who had visited the islands in 1835, discovered the theory of natural evolution. Both the Galápagos National Park and the Charles Darwin Station were founded in 1959, on the hundredth anniversary of the publication of *The Origin of Species*. Since then, conservation policies have welcomed tourism as a reliable source of funding, while worrying about local residents' impact on the islands' unique species. The selective concern about humans is reflected in the park's fundamental policies: the park has jurisdiction over 97 percent of the archipelago, restricting human settlements to the remaining 3 percent. On the other hand, the park has never enforced a cap on tourists, against all scientific recommendations and even despite recent national pledges to the contrary (UNESCO 2023).

This approach has led to a booming tourism industry of three hundred thousand people a year, steady growth of the local population to thirty-five thousand, and increasing anthropogenic pressure on fragile species and

Preface xv

ecosystems. The promotion of tourism and neglect of subsistence activities such as agriculture are not just discursive, as they contribute to the current state of the islands: on average, about 50 percent of hotel rooms are empty, although new hotels are always being built (Benitez-Capistros, Hugé, and Koedam 2014). Meanwhile, in the rural highlands, invasive species cover an acreage almost double that of crops (Laso et al. 2020).

Poor governance, social inequality, and social strife have led to several at-risk declarations, both by Ecuador and UNESCO, followed by corrective measures. This book describes a broad suite of policies and initiatives that brought together two heterogeneous but key currents of environmentalism: the scientific framework of coupled socio-ecological systems and the revolutionary political manifesto of *buen vivir*. As both concepts called for a new form of local participation, I use them as an opportunity to shift the dominant focus from the protected areas to the rural highlands of the inhabited islands (Santa Cruz, Isabela, San Cristóbal, and Floreana). While these measures fell short of their promises, residents responded by demanding changes, leveraging the aspects they deemed promising, or carving out a space of autonomy where, for example, they could cultivate the land—and a distinct form of caring for the islands—outside of state prescriptions. Their practices and motivations, this book contends, hold political significance as they invite us to reconsider the goals, actors, and beneficiaries of old and new conservation plans.

Restoration as a conservation practice is, however, not going away. In fact, we are in the UN decade (2020–30) dedicated to it, since "restoration is one of the most important ways of delivering nature-based solutions for food insecurity, climate change mitigation and adaptation, and biodiversity loss" (UN Environmental Programme 2021, 7). Ecosystem restoration is viewed as a crucial means of increasing the capacity of carbon storage, a sine qua non condition to the goals of halving greenhouse gas emission by 2030 and limiting global warming to below 2°C and preventing the loss of one million endangered species along the way. An examination of the assumptions undergirding this practice is essential.

Rather than an escape from the global environmental crisis, then, the

Galápagos provide a cautionary tale: attempts to save the environment must interrogate human involvement, beyond the posture of detached stewards in its endless variations, ranging from a self-appointed role as saviors of wild nature to techno-solutionists and would-be Mars colonizers. Not quite the end of the world, then, the Galápagos can offer a new beginning.

Acknowledgments

Many people have helped me during a decade of conducting research and writing this book. This book, then, is not an island—or, if it was, it benefited from the myriad streams of contributions reaching its shores, nurturing and sustaining it for years.

I am first and foremost indebted to the people of the Galápagos Islands: farmers, park rangers, field researchers, guides, longtime settlers, or first-generation residents. They conversed with me, opened the doors to their houses, and guided me on farms, in woods, and along trails on celebrated or hidden terrains. They offered me water, food, and shade, giving me a chance to sharpen my questions and, over time, understand the *parte alta* in its social and ecological complexity and beauty. Teresa and Enrique took care of me and my wife in more ways than I can describe. I value our friendship immensely and still regret politely declining to eat the goat knee they once baked for us. Esperanza and José welcomed me repeatedly at their house in the highlands. I cherish the memories of hearing their old-time stories about hunting and fishing during lazy Sunday afternoons, resting after my culinary experiments with pasta and foraged *Lycopersicon cheesmanii*, small endemic tomatoes. In my first week of fieldwork, Mark, Joel, and Katy gifted me with a table and a mattress for my empty apartment, and then talked to me about the islands, from evolution of the flightless cormorants to the latest news about the mayor's corruption, almost every day until I left. The Angermeyer, de Roi, Devine, Cruz, and Carrión families taught me about the Galápagos now and many decades ago, giving me perspective and, truly, the gift of seeing the islands through their eyes, even if in glimpses. Thanks to all the other farmers, too many to list here, who showed me their land and talked about their crops, pests, hopes, and fears. Thanks especially to the farmers and other residents lacking proper xviii *Acknowledgments*

visa authorization who over time entrusted me with their stories. Pati, Andrew, Roberto, Washington, Jadira, and many other friends lifted me up during many episodes of fieldwork-related despair. Thanks especially to Monica, Ulises, Gonzalo, and Ramiro for the daily company, support, and unforgettable moments we spent together on the islands.

The Charles Darwin Foundation and the Galápagos National Park provided crucial logistical support and intellectual nourishment. I am especially indebted to Heinke Jäger and Gonzalo Rivas-Torres, both plant ecologists, who brought me to their research sites in the park, taught me about changing ecological communities, and even let me have a go at some endemic plant counts. Thanks also to Patricia Jaramillo, Christophe Grenier, Emmanuel Cleder, Josselin Guyot-Téphany, Daniel Orellana, Noemi D'Ozouville, George Heimpel, Javier Andrada, Pedro Cantero, Esteban Ruiz-Ballesteros and the other ecologists, biologists, geologists, hydrologists, and geographers whose research has informed mine. Discussions with Victor Carrión, Sebastian and Carolina Cruz, Karl Campbell, Gonzalo Banda-Cruz, Linda Cayot, Christian Lavoie, Godfrey Merlen, Richard Knab, Swen Lorenz, César Viteri Mejía, Veronica Toral, and Peter Kramer helped me understand the history, future, and scope of conservation measures on the islands. A heartful thank-you to Dannis Rueda, now director of the Galápagos National Park, for supporting this research from its early days, and to Wilson Cabrera and the other park rangers of the Department of Terrestrial Ecosystems whom I met many days at 5:30 am at the entrance of the park on our way to the highlands. The regional director of the Ministry of Agriculture (MAGAP), Jimmy Bolaños, and his state agronomists welcomed me in their offices for a mutually beneficial collaboration. Thanks to Normania Coello, Luis Cango, Hernan Simbaña, César Vinueza, Rene Ramiréz, Angeles Prado, Vilma Calvopiña, and Paulina Couenberg for the endless conversations and long days together in the field. And thanks to César for letting me borrow your second pair of rubber boots on more than one muddy occasion.

A fellowship from the Social Science Research Council in 2010 introduced me to an eclectic and fun cohort of graduate students in geography, political science, geography, history, law, and anthropology who were

Acknowledgments xix

interested in the environment. I thank organizers Peter Perdue and Steve Harrell, as well as Angelo Caglioti, Caterina Scaramelli, Zachary Caple, Samuel Dolbee, Nate Ela, David Fedman, Jenny Goldstein, Tim Johnson, Laura Martin, Maria Taylor, and Greg Tahler, for comments on my research and for sharing research projects, some which are now published books—with more to come. The Planetary Collapse / Academic Success (PCAS) writing group that Greg, Maria, Nate, and I created in 2021, despite its tragicomic name, helped me considerably in completing a first draft of this book.

Margaret Wiener had the arduous task of guiding my early research despite many pivots, doubts, and changes of mind over the years. Rudolf Colloredo-Mansfeld graced me with his humor and trenchant insight every time I sought his invaluable advice. Peter Redfield spent many hours going over drafts of dissertation chapters or research articles, always encouraging my passion for writing. Townsend Middletown and Neel Ahuja offered support and guidance during the first writing and publishing efforts of this research. Arturo Escobar taught me about conservation and development in South America as well as social movements' struggles for epistemic and world alternatives, which have inspired my analysis of the people and places in this book. Todd Ochoa's scholarship and teaching opened me to an appreciation for new studies of complexity and multitudes. Jim Peacock maintained his unwavering support for my research over the years; Elizabeth Hennessy helped me get started doing research on the Galápagos; Paul Schissel engaged in (too) many conversations about anthropological theory extending well into the night; Dragana Lassiter was always available to help; Marios Antoniou welcomed me at his place to discuss our projects; and Andrew Ofstehage organized a helpful writing group. Last but certainly not least, I thank Amelia Fiske, as she agreed to share and revise each other's drafts for years, and Vincent Joos for our indestructible bond of mutual support in our research projects and careers.

Questions, suggestions, and feedback I received at talks and papers I presented at conferences and workshops helped me clarify different parts of this project. Special thanks to James Scott and Harriet Ritvo, Julie Archambault, Vered Amit, Kregg Hetherington, Bill Durham, Bruce Barnett, xx *Acknowledgments*

Matthew James, and Lauren Urgeson. Jerry Zee deserves special thanks for the grace and intelligence with which he helped me think about this research. Jerry, you continue to be a source of inspiration for both your scholarship and your generosity. Leslie Maxwell, Rene Caputo, Lindsey Smith, Mike Dimplf, Miranda Welsh, Brenda Baletti, Kevin Casey, and Chris Shreve at Duke University provided a stimulating environment for research, teaching, and activism. In addition to discussing politics and research almost daily for the five years while we were colleagues, Nathan Kalman-Lamb crucially encouraged me to publish this manuscript despite many outside challenges. I am not sure this book would exist without his friendly exhortation. Louise Meintjes and Anne Allison in the Anthropology Department helped me with this project at very different stages but with the same brilliance and kindness. Dance professor Ava Vinesett and lead drummer Richard Vinesett welcomed me as a guest musician in their African dance classes for many semesters. Their class served as a brilliant reminder of the inexhaustible force that comes from a collective and the importance of always making or being immersed in one. Finally, thanks to my students at Duke University, many of whom shared with me the commitment to creating more just social and ecological communities. At IBM, Sean Warsaw carved out some time so that we could compare notes on our self-inflicted task of completing a manuscript outside our day job.

Funds from Duke University (Faculty Research Grant, 2018, 2019; TWP Competitive Research Grant, 2018, 2019), the University of North Carolina at Chapel Hill (Mellon Dissertation Fellowship, Institute for the Study of the Americas, 2016; Dissertation Completion Fellowship, UNC-CH, 2016; Off-Campus Dissertation Fellowship, UNC Graduate School, 2014; Tinker Fellowship, 2012; CV Starr Scholarship, 2010), and the Social Science Research Council (Dissertation Proposal Development Fellowship, 2012) made possible a cumulative twenty-one months of fieldwork and allowed me to devote several summers to writing. The Galápagos Science Center and Universidad San Francisco de Quito assisted me with the lengthy process of obtaining and renewing a one-year visa for the Galápagos. At the University of Washington Press, Lorri Hagman, Caitlin Tyler-Richards,

Shivi Sivaramakrishnan, and two anonymous reviewers provided thoughtful and attentive peer and editorial support.

Andrea Ricci listened in from afar about my fieldwork challenges and offered the idea of small tweaks (*giro di vite*) to encourage me to find small improvements wherever possible, which helped tremendously during the hardest times of this research. Despite the distance, I knew that Paola Ceresetti and Sara Ferrari were always available to talk. My parents-in-law always showed interest in this project, even revising a lengthy NSF dissertation grant before submission. My parents cared deeply about this research and followed closely its progression (and a few stalls), mostly from afar. When they visited us, they helped me and my family in concrete and labor-intensive ways, showing in an exemplary manner how actions best express love and support. I also thank my mother for her lifelong teaching on not being afraid to ask questions, even at the cost of exposing yourself, and my father for approaching any intellectual project with method. My beloved paternal grandmother passed away in the middle of this project. I miss calling her from two oceans away or, at her house, hearing the melody of her voice in the kitchen while I wrote upstairs.

I dedicate this book to my wife, Dietra, who has been alongside me since the inception of this work, weathering the ups and downs of my academic life with patience, balance, and more patience still, and to Giulia and Simona, our *bambine strepitose*: you are our present, future, and beyond. I can't wait to see how you will improve your personal copies of this book with drawings and other important messages.

VIABLE ECOLOGIES

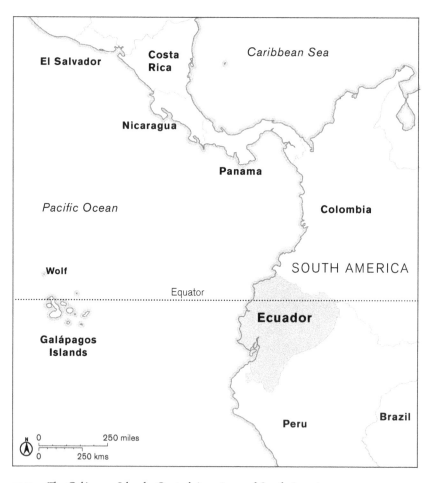

MAP 1. The Galápagos Islands, Central America, and South America.

Introduction

During my first stay on the Galápagos, I met Carlos Carrión, the director of the Galápagos Invasive Species Fund (Fundo Para el Control de las Especies Invasoras Galápagos, FEIG), in his office on Santa Cruz Island, the most populated of the four inhabited islands of the archipelago. FEIG is a trust that manages international funds for local conservation projects, which often require partnerships across public and private institutions—like the Galápagos National Park and the Charles Darwin Foundation—and international donors. Given the undisputed and ubiquitous image of the Galápagos as the last natural laboratory of evolution in the world, these conservation projects put a strong emphasis on restoring ecosystems and protecting native species. Carrión was a crucial person I wanted to interview for my research, which I initially framed around the increasing challenges of managing invasive species and the resultant paradox of needing more human intervention in a site that was supposed to have none.

His office was in Puerto Ayora, the biggest town of the island and the archipelago. NGOs and international environmental organizations such as the World Wildlife Fund, Conservation International, Island Conservation, and of course, the Charles Darwin Foundation all have headquarters there. His heavily air-conditioned room, a sign of financial possibility on the islands, immediately confirmed that I was in the office of an important person on the islands. Born on the Galápagos at a time when the islands had only a few thousand people and very limited connections to the mainland, Carrión nevertheless became an economist and even undertook postgraduate studies in Madrid. In the early 1990s, he became the director of the highest authority on the Galápagos Islands (now the Consejo de Gobierno). The way he treated me was expected: polite but understandably harried. Perhaps for both reasons he invited me to join him at a meeting with

2 *Introduction*

MAP 2. Protected and nonprotected areas in the four inhabited islands of the Galápagos archipelago.

farmers in the highlands slated to start imminently. Given that this was my first week on the Galápagos Islands, I knew little about the highlands and accepted eagerly. He ushered me outside the building and hailed a taxi. Twenty minutes later we reached a small school in Bellavista, a highlands village where the meeting was taking place.

Away from the sun-stricken, dusty streets of the coastal Puerto Ayora, clouds covered the sky over Bellavista. Before we reached the school, it began to drizzle. Farmers filled a dark, unadorned room, speaking softly among themselves or waiting in silence. They wore heavier clothes than people in town, with long pants or skirts and long-sleeve shirts, and were dressed more cheaply, their clothes discolored and frayed. Attired too formally, I was in a room where residues of mud sketched a mosaic of footprints on the floor, bringing inside some of the landscape at the heart of the meeting.

The Galápagos National Park had called the event to announce a new conservation initiative for the highlands that, for the first time, would bring together farmers and park rangers. A park official from the Department of Land Ecosystems sat behind a table with three public officials: the mayors of Santa Rosa and Bellavista, the two parishes of Santa Cruz's highlands, and a representative from the Puerto Ayora municipality. These public officials spoke before the park representative, seemingly to preempt any skepticism among the farmers about the park's proposal. The official from Puerto Ayora gave a brief, rather standard speech. The talks of the two parishes' mayors were different: with a loud voice, holding the microphone too close to his mouth, Señor Loyola from Bellavista seemed to almost beg farmers to join the project. Struggling to find refined words, he tried to compensate by raising his voice and talking even more. Growing more uncomfortable, he continued anyway, his voice absorbed by the apathy of the audience.

The project, the park representative then explained, building on the little momentum created by the previous speakers, was to tackle hill raspberry (*Rubus niveus*) in an integrated fashion, by clearing contiguous rural and park areas. Innocuous on the continent, *Rubus niveus* (*mora* in Spanish) is invasive on the Galápagos. Bearing small, bitter fruit, *Rubus niveus* grows in thick groves that stifle native vegetation in the highlands. Although the park had long conducted periodic control efforts, results had been poor, ostensibly due to the abundance of *mora* on farms adjacent to the park. To tackle this problem, the park wanted to intervene also in the rural areas. The Pilot Plan for the Control of Hill Raspberry (Plan Piloto para el Control de la Mora, simply called Plan Piloto) proposed to clear an area one hundred meters (about 330 feet) wide—fifty meters on each side of the park's border—and several miles long. This limited intervention would test whether such an integrated approach would be effective in keeping *mora* at bay. If successful, the park intended to adopt it on a broader scale and extend it to other invasive species.

4 Introduction

After limiting its efforts to protected areas for decades, in 2013 the Galápagos National Park was experimenting with conservation measures that would extend to the human areas. The park marked this shift by adopting the increasingly popular socio-ecological system (SES) conservation framework, which allows for comprehensive study of feedback loops traversing protected and nonprotected areas. And after decades of nominal involvement with locals but in practice few opportunities for collaboration, the park decided to directly include them. At the meeting, the park representative announced that they were going to provide herbicide to farmers, who in exchange would uproot *mora* from designated areas on their farms. Meanwhile, park wardens would clear *mora* from the corresponding park area. After all, the park representative remarked, both farmers and the park shared a common interest in eliminating this invasive plant, whether for economic or ecological reasons.

This type of mutually beneficial collaboration, in which the park directly recruited residents in a conservation effort, deliberately articulated one of the main tools of President Correa's agenda, citizen participation (*participación ciudadana*). Under the self-proclaimed revolutionary plan of *buen vivir* (2007–17), the government had recently committed to recenter politics away from the sole goal of economic growth (with its negative social and ecological consequences) toward the well-being of citizens and ecosystems (SENPLADES 2009). Ecuadorian citizens would be both the recipients and the actors who were ultimately responsible for producing (*actuar*) the revolution. Together, the scientific and political framework of SES and buen vivir, respectively, reframed conservation on the Galápagos around the principles of ecosystems services (what nature provides to society) and, as shown at the meeting in Bellavista, renewed citizenry (what society—here, farmers—ought to do for nature).

Innovative or even revolutionary though it may have been, Plan Piloto proved less ambitious than what farmers had expected: the beginning of a new relationship aimed at sharing and addressing pressing issues of all parties. The park had invited the farmers from Santa Cruz to the meeting, but it eventually made clear that the pilot project would enroll only fifteen farms that border the park in one specific sector of the highlands. More

Introduction 5

disappointingly even, the areas within the farms where Plan Piloto proposed to intervene were not the ones where farmers needed help the most. The portions of their farms bordering the park, the highest in elevation and often unlevel, were least productive, if at all. With little mechanization as a result of a park ban on heavy agricultural machinery and minimal profits in agriculture on the Galápagos, cultivating such difficult land — or ridding it of unwanted species — made little sense. These areas had long been unproductive anyway, regardless of *mora*'s presence or absence.

Unconvinced by the limited scope of Plan Piloto, they nevertheless cared a great deal about *mora* and other invasive species. "To the present authorities of the municipality, the parishes, and the park; fellow Santa Cruz farmers and the other people who honor us today with their esteemed presence at this important meeting," a farmer offered as a preamble once the floor was opened to questions and comments. "Why will only fifteen *compañeros* receive help, when most of us deal with *mora*? Last week I tried to clean up half a hectare to plant potatoes. I protected myself with thick pants and long-sleeve shirts, but in the end I got fever anyway, because of the thorns. I had to spend the next day in bed and could not work at all. . . . I beg you to reconsider: we all need help to farm!"

The attendees also questioned whether this plan would result in improved farming conditions or just less work for park rangers tasked with maintaining the park's highland ecosystems. To the park's proposal of continuous control of hill raspberry with no mention of a plan to get rid of the species, a farmer respectfully disagreed. He looked uncomfortable when he was handed the microphone and held it unsurely, with the microphone leaning sideways toward his shoulder rather than pointing at his mouth. But his voice grew firm when he stated that, if all farmers joined forces with the park, *mora* could be eradicated from the island. "If we all use one hundred milliliters of Combo [a herbicide] per hectare, cultivate the cleared land with pasture or crops, and repeat the clearing [*limpieza*] every three months, it is my humble estimation that, by virtue of a combined effort that, as the park representative just announced, would finally bring together farmers and the authorities [the park and the local office of the Ministry of Agriculture], we could eliminate the hill raspberry (*nos deshaceremos*

6 Introduction

de la mora) in less than a year." He concluded seriously, "With the help of God, we can do it." To him, mentioning God added gravitas, rather than invoking actual divine powers. For the park official, the latter reason would have probably made more sense. "Thanks for your comment," he offered imperturbably, his answer showing the training in public relations he had likely received at the park. "But we know that currently we cannot eradicate it, nor do we have the capacity to involve everyone right at this moment. But we need everyone's help to protect both the park and farms, even if the park at this moment does not have the funds to support everyone. It is only with perseverance and. . . . " The room suddenly filled with protests, drowning out the speaker.

"*Ve?*" (Do you see?), *economista* Carrión told me amid the confusion. To him, things had been exceedingly clear since the beginning. I thought he was going to sit with the presenters, but instead he stood at the back with the audience, behind the last row of plastic chairs. There, he greeted all the farmers, with either a kiss or a handshake, as they entered the room. Earlier, he had told me about his proud identification as a *colono*, an early settler. He was a member of one of the few families that, for decades, survived on the islands without electricity, primarily thanks to farming, well before the advent of tourism and isolated from the continent. His remarkable career in conservation had not altered his or the farmers' understanding of where he belonged, nor his belief that an honest dialogue with residents about their livelihood and conservation goals—which the park increasingly promised but never fully delivered—was a necessary condition for the future thriving of the islands. *Economista* Carrión was wearing formal clothes, the fold of his impeccably ironed slacks connecting his leather shoes to his formal shirt in two straight lines, in striking contrast to the farmers' working clothes. Yet Carrión looked at home: farmers approached him with confidence, their calloused hands lingering in his hand, as a formal greeting turned into a conversation between friends.

Unfortunately, things were anything but clear to me. For a proposal that was quite specific in its geographical scope, time frame, and objectives, farmers advanced a broad range of requests: to address an invasive ant species that bites ferociously during the harvest of citrus fruit, the need for water during the increasingly long summers, the exorbitant price of fertilizers, bureaucratic impediments to hiring workers from the mainland, the need for competent training on how to regenerate the soil, and so on. Along with demands, farmers also noted the positive effect of their labor in the highlands, which politicians, scientists, and park officials had long failed to notice. Clearing the land of invasive species, keeping soil erosion in check, and tending to both cultivated and native vegetation, farmers argued, served to maintain both the park and the farms. At the very least, one participant reflected, farmers are often among the first to notice changes in the highlands because they live in the area, and "that must account for something." My puzzlement at the meeting continued despite my best efforts to pick up on the cues that *economista* Carrión gave me. As farmers repeatedly urged the park to engage with the rural highlands beyond Plan Piloto, he would lean over and look at me intently, eyebrows lifted, to remark the obvious implications of what was unfolding before us. His silence was deliberate, expressive, aimed at letting the full significance of the event speak for itself.

"See?"

∽∽

As much as I tried, I could not see. Only over time did I grapple with farmers' commitment to a composite flourishing of the Galápagos — what Carrión on that afternoon was delighted to see and urged me to consider. Two subsequent years of fieldwork (2013–14) taught me that, at that meeting in Bellavista, those farmers tied together aspirations for a better life for their families and for the future viability of the highlands. Farmers not only claimed that their presence and their need to secure a livelihood were legitimate and indeed necessary for local society but also argued for their role in the ecological care of the islands. Carrión occupied a unique position from which he could appreciate the chasm between farmers and the park thanks to his intimate knowledge of both sides, drawing on his biography as a *colono* as well as decades of professional experience in international conservation. At stake in the meeting in Bellavista was not just an approach to invasive hill raspberry but how the park limited farmers

8 *Introduction*

to a role as helpers, not equals, in ensuring conservation, albeit under the promise of a new form of collaboration. In the eyes of many farmers, conservation plans, traditional or pilot, continued to fail on that score. Instead, farmers felt they could play a significant role in supporting humans and nonhumans across the highlands as a whole, rather than simply watching protected spaces wilt over the park's fence.

INVASIVE SPECIES, UNWANTED PEOPLE

Agriculture on the Galápagos is at once an overlooked and misrepresented aspect of the islands' socio-ecological systems. This archipelago often conjures images of marine and coastal life, although it also features high land and volcanoes reaching above 1,700 meters (5,580 feet) and encompassing five climatic zones. What locals call *la parte alta*, which I refer here as the highlands, corresponds to the humid zone ranging from about 400 meters to 1,200 meters. Above that elevation, the climate reverts to dry as the short, treeless vegetation captures little moisture and trade winds grow stronger. The human areas, which are only outside the Galápagos National Park, occupy a small portion of each of these zones, except for the highest one, which is only in the park. The two lowest climatic zones, littoral and dry, contain the only towns of the archipelago, where restaurants, hotels, travel agencies, and gift shops drive employment and immigration. The transitional zone, mostly park with some urban sprawl in the nonprotected areas, gives way to the humid zone, with its water, shade, and organic soil, where most of the initial settlers chose to live and where farms are still located today. Although most of the population resides in the coastal towns, the largest percentage of human areas is in the humid areas.

For decades, scientific and conservation literature has consistently discussed agriculture on the Galápagos as a cause of habitat fragmentation, the introduction and propagation of invasive species, and undocumented immigration (González, Montes, and Rodríguez 2008; Graham and Cruz 2007; Jäger, Crespo, et al. 2018). Policies related to local agriculture had mostly reflected the assumption in these reports that agriculture posed a threat to conservation. Instead, Plan Piloto, soon followed by other local policies, abandoned that premise and included farmers based on arguments about the ecological benefits derived from strengthening local food production, such as reducing biosecurity threats from pathogens and invasive species that may arrive with food imported from the mainland (Guzmán and Poma 2013). Yet this book shows that farmers' positive contribution goes beyond these considerations, which conservation plans have at least nominally started to consider. In growing food, farmers cultivate ties to a place that conservation and tourism have long treated as inhospitable to humans, all the while making the archipelago the destination of an ever-growing number of tourists. Local farmers' agriculture becomes, then, also culture, distinct from the one promoted by conservation and a tourism industry that is largely preoccupied with denying its existence as such by insisting on the image of deserted islands. In their refusal to comply with the role assigned to them in the *Plan Piloto*, farmers gestured toward an alternative form of coexistence based on mutual dependency, care, and accountability sustained over time.

Viable Ecologies centers on the experience of farmers and other recipients of environmental plans on the Galápagos Islands during the decade 2008–18. Starting in 2008, the Ecuadorian state began to recruit citizens, species, and ecosystems on the archipelago in accordance with the political goal of buen vivir and the conservation objective of fostering a resilient socio-ecological system. However, residents enacted modes of caring for and living on the islands only in partial connection with such state plans. While the state was busy recruiting—in fact, producing—codified societal and natural subjects (lawful citizens, native species, and socio-ecological systems), alternative forms of socio-natures started to emerge. As social and ecological crises deepened over time, these forms began to hint at a different approach to conservation on the islands that is worth examining. In this perspective, I aim to show not conservation failures per se, but rather the struggles for alternative socio-natures that emerge out of the fissures in official political and ecological configurations. It is through these apertures that I seek to recover the political significance of marginalized actors in pointing to an alternative (to) conservation that is not idealistic and unmoored but rather viable and already taking place.

HUMANLESS CONSERVATION

The Galápagos Islands might look like one of the last places on earth where one might investigate whether local residents can have a positive role in safeguarding the environment. The islands are several million years old, yet humans reached their shores only five centuries ago (in 1535) and have established permanent settlements for less than two (since 1832). Straddling the equator six hundred miles west of mainland Ecuador, the archipelago is composed of thirteen large islands, only four of which have human settlements, and over a hundred islets. Since 1959, almost 97 percent of the archipelago has been under the auspices of the Galápagos National Park, where no human can reside. These islands also host one of the world's biggest marine reserves, covering 53,000 square miles, half the size of continental Ecuador, which strictly regulates tourism and local fisheries while banning commercial fisheries. Relative to the area covered by the park and the marine reserve combined, humans live in less than 0.01 percent of the archipelago.

Such drastic conservation measures are motivated by Galápagos species' high endemism—that is, the number of species that are found only there. This term is distinguished from "native species," which refers to species that are also found elsewhere through natural distribution. The Galápagos' unique biodiversity is determined, first, by their isolation. These islands emerged through a series of volcanic eruptions near two diverging tectonic plates, Cocos and Nazca; consequently, the islands were never attached to the mainland. At an average rate of one species per ten thousand years, most species have colonized the islands by hitching on logs or drifting along two westward marine currents, the cold Humboldt Current from southern Chile and the warm Panama Current from the north, depending on the season. Other plant seeds and insects have reached the Galápagos' shores swept by the strong westward Walker trade wind. Due to isolation and lack of mammal predators, species composition in terrestrial ecosystems is highly unusual. For instance, native terrestrial animals are predominantly reptiles and birds, and not mammals, which are represented only by bats and the rice mouse. Native vegetation, too, mostly consists of bush and shrub species—with the notable exceptions of the deciduous incense tree *Bursera graveolens* (Sp. *palo santo*), the *Scalesia* family, and the *Opuntia* cactus—lacking the many species of tall trees found on the mainland.

In addition to the challenging ecological conditions of volcanic islands, species have adapted to harsh climatic conditions and significant variability. Usually, the Walker system moves air and surface water along the equatorial line from South America toward Southeast Asia, causing abundant precipitation and even higher sea levels (up to twenty-four inches!). The cooled air returns east, descending over the west coast of South America and producing arid climatic conditions in the low-elevation zones of the Galápagos. This powerful wind pattern is temporarily reversed during an El Niño–Southern Oscillation (ENSO) event. During such events, a period of unusually strong winds and, consequently, cold and dry air (La Niña) is followed by one during which hot air and water flow back eastward to the Galápagos, causing up to ten times higher annual precipitation (El Niño). Ecological communities on the Galápagos are believed to be the most impacted by ENSO of any site. As a result of these periodic climatic extremes, Galápagos species have evolved remarkable characteristics, both behavioral and morphological. Climate change is making ENSO events stronger, more frequent, and longer lasting. This anthropogenic stressor, resulting in the increased endangerment of endemic species, has added urgency to the conservation agenda.

Despite the radical changes brought about by human colonization in the past century or so, the degree of species endemism on the Galápagos is still exceptional, estimated at 95 percent of its prehuman level (Bensted-Smith 2002). No other inhabited archipelago in the world has maintained similar levels of endemism, largely because of the late arrival of humans on the Galápagos. However, the accelerating pace of recent human colonization has not afforded local species enough time to develop defense mechanisms against humans and their portmanteau biota, nor against local and global anthropogenic stressors like pollution and climate change. High endemism and isolation have thus rendered the islands more vulnerable to human influence and made the imperative of conservation all the more pressing.

Reasons for conservation extend beyond arguments about the islands'

12 Introduction

biogeographical remoteness and draw on the image of an archipelago of unique importance to science. This image finds its mythological origin in 1835, when, three years after Ecuador took official possession of the archipelago, a seasick young amateur naturalist from the United Kingdom, Charles Darwin, visited the islands for two weeks. Contrary to popular imagination, however, Darwin arrived at his revolutionary theory of evolution years afterward, as he began to consider how populations of one species might evolve into separate species through adaptation to different environments, now known as allopatric speciation. Nonetheless, on the Galápagos he had failed to separate by island the specimens he collected, a crucial step in building the case for his theory, even though locals had informed him about differences in tortoise carapaces across islands. This myth of a sudden scientific epiphany contributed to later international efforts to conceive of the Galápagos as a special site for conservation and natural scientific research, though no major discovery has since taken place there (Sulloway 1982).

Local conservation and tourism, which started in the 1960s, have amplified the perception of the Galápagos as a place detached from the rest of the world (Bowman 1957; Mariscal 1969; Grenier 2007). Both domains have circulated photos conveying the tameness and singular look of animals such as giant tortoises and iguanas—coupled with a careful elision of any mention of local residents. Since its inception, conservation has designated tourism as its necessary counterpart, providing significant revenue for environmental protection of the islands (Eibl-Eibesfeldt 1959; Mariscal 1969; Bocci 2019). Conservation and tourism alike have promoted the image of a place where unique animals live undisturbed by humans, as if in a prehistoric world where, counter to the very tenets of Darwin's theory, things don't change.

Biogeographical, cultural, and political reasons have fused to portray the Galápagos as one of the premier places where tourists and scientists can find respite from the anthropogenic ecological degradation ever more apparent elsewhere. Against the backdrop of an increasingly connected, homogenized, and of late, ecologically damaged earth, the Galápagos stand as the exception: a site protected *from* the human species and its devastation, and a remnant of the prehuman past. The Galápagos' most iconic animal, the fifteen species of giant tortoises, encapsulate this story. Far from a rarity, giant tortoises were a common presence in both North and South America for millions of years before their population was decimated by indiscriminate hunting. Only remote islands like the Galápagos shelter this species and, to this day, present them to tourists, although omitting to tell the larger context of its continental decimation (Durham 2021). The Galápagos tortoises, the single biggest attraction in the islands and a source of great joy for tourists, are a reminder that the Galápagos constitute an *island* surrounded by extinction.

Sadly, a model of conservation premised on the assumption of the Galápagos' complete isolation has also driven tourism growth and its deleterious effects on fragile ecosystems. Attracted by the labor opportunities in tourism, mainland Ecuadorians immigrated to the Galápagos to escape unemployment and poverty. In the early 2000s, tourism was responsible for an economic boom: if the archipelago were an independent state, its growth rate would have ranked among the highest in the world (Epler 2007). In 2007, the Ecuadorian government and UNESCO deemed the islands to be in a state of crisis. In April, Ecuadorian president Rafael Correa declared the islands "at risk"; two months later, UNESCO included them in the list of "world heritage sites in danger" because of invasive species, poor governance, and the steep influx of people visiting and living on the islands. Today, over thirty-five thousand reside on the islands, and about three hundred thousand tourists visit the archipelago each year—with no limitation imposed by the park. Ultimately, the very success of the image of humanless islands has undermined the nexus of conservation and tourism, not only leading to escalating threats to the islands' ecosystems but also to putting in doubt the validity of this approach to conservation.

SOCIO-ECOLOGICAL *BUEN VIVIR*

Aware of this predicament, at the time of my fieldwork in 2013 the Galápagos National Park had begun to recruit residents as active allies. This book analyzes the tensions within this project in the context of two of the most influential paradigms in contemporary environmentalism: resilient socio-ecological systems (SES) in conservation and a radical political program enacted by the Ecuadorian government, buen vivir. SES, the preeminent conservation framework for protected areas today, enrolls local residents and nature alike in a single system touted as resilient. In conservation, resilience is the capacity of a socio-ecological system to adapt to change while maintaining its identity and functions. On the Galápagos, resilience refers to the archipelago's ability to respond to ecological stressors, such as pollution and invasive species, so that it can continue to deliver eco-system services to species, residents, and tourists (González, Montes, and Rodríguez 2008). Prior to espousing SES, the park showed limited interest in including residents beyond environmental education campaigns, such as the community-based conservation model that enjoyed wide international application in the 1980s and 90s. With SES, the park for the first time integrated protected and human areas in a formalized and ostensibly comprehensive way (Parque Nacional Galápagos 2014).[1]

The park's latest management plan (Parque Nacional Galápagos 2014), a comprehensive document that lays out conservation goals for the next ten years, framed SES as a tool that could ultimately ensure the composite flourishing promised by buen vivir—the second conceptual axis of this book. In 2007, the new Ecuadorian president, Rafael Correa, instituted a national assembly, which drafted the world's first constitution to inscribe "rights to nature" and promote Ecuadorian Indigenous knowledge and practices of multispecies coexistence. With buen vivir, Ecuador gained international popularity among environmental activists, academics, and even government officials. Under the aegis of the new constitution, the Ecuadorian government advanced a populist, environmentalist, and de-colonial political agenda decrying entrenched global structures. Its most spectacular proposal, the Yasuní ITT, asked the international community to compensate the Ecuadorian government for its commitment *not* to drill oil in the Ishpingo-Tambococha-Tiputini region, a small section of the Yasuní Indigenous territory and national park in the Amazon. Since then, buen vivir has entered in the vocabulary of both international cooperation and grassroots activism, with a powerful and evocative message encompassing a wide range of practices and political goals.[2]

Resilience in conservation and buen vivir in Correa's agenda were presented as innovative progressive tools to produce profound change. Both frameworks introduced considerations about complexity and uncertainty. Resilience in SESS famously challenged the model of an ideal static ecosystem that had informed conservation until then, thus introducing the need for adaptive management. The goal of buen vivir was no less daunting, if elusive. While, according to the government, buen vivir aimed to restore socio-ecological flourishing, it was also "a complex, alive concept, rooted in history and yet subjected to continuous resignification" (*un concepto complejo, vivo, no lineal, pero historicamente costruido y que por lo tanto estará en constante re-significacion*; SENPLADES 2009, 6). More promises than realities, both concepts began to recruit citizens and assign them a fundamental responsibility to participate in the realization of such goals.

In what the government aptly called the Citizens' Revolution (Revolución Ciudadana), the Correa presidency established citizens as a central figure of new politics and their participation as a crucial condition for building a new Ecuador. Correa's ascendency was initially supported by Indigenous and progressive movements, both embracing his promise that marginalized voices would become key actors of future political change (Accion Ecologica 2012; Zaldívar 2017; Vanhulst 2015). With Correa, then, participation served a progressive—in fact, revolutionary—mission. There were, of course, profound contradictions within Correa's plan, which critics labeled *neoextractivismo*, as it particularly increased reliance on the extractive industry to later fund a postdevelopment model of society organized around buen vivir (Gudynas 2009; Kothari, Demaria, and Acosta 2014; Riofrancos 2020; Hidalgo-Capitán and Cubillo-Guevara 2018; Caria and Domínguez 2016). Of interest here is how buen vivir, specifically the Citizens' Revolution, forged an intransigent model of citizenship that resulted in further marginalizing minority groups such Indigenous and environmentalists (Novo 2014, for Bolivia, cf. Postero 2017). With the establishment of the National Secretariat of *Buen Vivir* (Secretaría Nacional

16 *Introduction*

del Buen Vivir) in 2010, the Citizens' Revolution became an apparatus of surveillance and exclusion of any subject who deviated from governmental plans to expand extractivism, foreign investment, and centralized state control (Vanhulst 2015; Hidalgo-Capitán and Cubillo-Guevara 2018; Zaldívar 2017). In a telling instance, while President Correa enjoyed international acclaim for enshrining the rights of Mother Nature, or Pachamama, he outlawed, among others, the environmental group Pachamama, a collective of activists critical of the government's plan of oil extraction in Indigenous territories (Pachamama Alliance 2022; Des Informémonos 2013).

On the Galápagos, too, both buen vivir and resilience invoked but strictly codified local participation. In contrast to conservation's early preoccupation with maintaining or restoring a static nature, the park's latest management plan considered human presence as a given. Rather than setting the goal of eliminating any anthropogenic disturbance, the management plan called upon local actors to ensure that the Galápagos continued its functions as a complex socio-ecological system. Soon after, state actors such as the Ministry of Agriculture, the Galápagos National Park, and environmental NGOs, including the Charles Darwin Foundation and Conservation International, all began to involve residents as "partners in conservation." Ultimately, conservation became a responsibility of locals, who were asked to "recognize that the resilience capacity of marine and island ecosystems has limits that must not be exceeded" (Parque Nacional Galápagos 2014, 13). At the same time, however, the same institutions redoubled their efforts to limit locals' contributions to opportune forms of "participation" and manifestations of "resilience," while discouraging human and nonhuman presences that did not fit the plan for integrated conservation at the confluence of buen vivir and SES.

For instance, a 1998 special immigration law for the Galápagos, which restricted residency in the archipelago, began to be enforced more strictly at a time when the province announced the goals of achieving food sovereignty and buen vivir on the islands in its Plan for Island Good Living (Plan para el Buen Vivir Insular) This plan remarked on the importance of local agriculture and offered farmers subsidized loans and incentives to form associations. However, this policy framework did not address some of the most pressing obstacles to development of local agriculture: farmers' precarious residency status and land tenure. Further, the Plan for Island Good Living increased bureaucracy and state presence in the highlands, which led to the deportation of thousands of undocumented Ecuadorians on the islands back to the continent. This plan also reduced social and economic opportunities for those not yet caught by the police as well as those navigating the time-consuming and uncertain yearly process of renewing residency.

VIABLE ECOLOGIES

Counter to the islands' reputation, this book invites us to reorient conservation toward the goal of viable, rather than unpeopled or exclusionary, ecologies. This proposal by no means intends to negate the exceptional natural value of this archipelago. To the contrary, my appreciation for it only grew as I lived there. During my two years of fieldwork, I spent most of my days in the highlands of Santa Cruz, looking down at the muddy or rocky soil, the crops, and the various types of vegetation. At the end of the day, I would often return home on the back of a pickup serving as a collective taxi. A few curves past the last village in the highlands, the truck would gather speed, the wind blowing against my face and whistling past my ears. Soon the vista would open to the wide transitional plains running down to the city, around the bay, and then to the ocean, changing colors as the island's volcanic gradient continued its descent into deeper waters: azure, teal, aquamarine, indigo, and midnight blue. Stretching to the open horizon, all the way to the hazy contours of Santa Fé to the East and Isabela to the West, the windswept ocean brimmed with scintillas and tremors of light, both inviting and menacing in its vastness.

The view captured in a snapshot the geological, climatic, and biogeographic characteristics of the Galápagos and came alive through all my senses. Even after months of fieldwork, I never tired of the rush of emotions it provoked in me. For tourists arriving in the city, the vista probably confirmed their reason to be there: a pocket of rugged islands of spectacular, if austere, beauty in the middle of the Pacific Ocean. My experience with residents' quotidian struggle to make a living while attending to the highlands' ecosystems felt so different from what I expected incoming tourists searched for: a site devoid of messy entanglements between natural processes and human affairs. And yet, these two Galápagos are more connected than what I had long thought. Or rather, they should be more connected, given that, as this book submits, management of the islands for tourist consumption and scientific research needs to give way to more lasting and composite ways of caring for the islands.

I must tread carefully here. In reassessing the role of locals in conservation, the goal of this book is *not* to celebrate anthropogenic change, disregarding the salience of the Galápagos Islands' biodiversity and the reasons for their protection. Instead, rethinking present conservation efforts offers important sources for broadening the scope of what conservation might look like—and how it could work better. Combining critique and curiosity, I want to bring attention to types of thriving and remediation that are already happening outside state plans, whether in the midst of a mass eradication or in the quiet experimentation of a hidden farm.

These attempts produce what I theorize as viable ecologies. I take the etymological root of viable—*vita*, "life"—not at as a bio-political term describing what is governed by structural power (Foucault 2008) but instead as a lens capable of capturing what emerges at the margins and through continuous contestation of such power.[3] Unlike conservation biology's use of *viable*, which focuses on the survival of one species in relation to a fixed environment, *viable ecologies* thinks of the possibility of life as always relational and plural.[4] Attention to these forms of experimentation does not negate the influence of the official environmentalism enacted by state and international environmental agencies. For instance, residents in or around protected areas pose a significantly smaller threat, if any, than the one wrought by powerful outside interventions such as tourism and natural resource extraction, yet these communities are disproportionally targeted by conservation measures (Büscher and Fletcher 2020; Fairhead, Leach, and Scoones 2012; Fairhead and Leach 1996; Peluso and Watts 2001). At the same time, I lend ethnographic attention to the unexpected socio-natures that form alongside or even in spite of the dominant arrangements, exhibiting forms of vitality and viability otherwise hard to account for.

Viable ecologies, as this book understands them, are livable, rather than ideal, ecosystems. Considering and working toward livability sets a markedly distinct goal from the one of attempting to restore ecosystems to their historical baseline, inherently an arbitrary decision, while ignoring conservation's own effects on these ecosystems (Alagona, Sandlos, and Wiersma 2012). Viability emphasizes what works, but it does not assume this means being obvious or easy, including regarding our conceptual categories of right and wrong. *Viable Ecologies* treads on these uncertain terrains — ecological and otherwise. In my fieldwork, I followed the winding lines that different species traced in their old and new entanglements. Sometimes, I looked for spectacular vistas. From there, I contemplated the distilled, elemental scarcity of land biodiversity on an isolated archipelago like the Galápagos. More often, however, I gazed down at where I placed my feet, where particulars of the landscape revealed a much more complex story. I dodged the thorns of introduced bushes, worrisomely invading local ecosystems, as well as, sorely, my flesh. Searching for introduced edible fruits, I avoided endemic, poisonous ones. To brush off invasive, biting ants, I sat in the benign shade of toxic, endemic trees. In choosing what to engage with and what to avoid, what futures to anticipate or try to undo, I was not alone. Attention to emerging alliances across plants, animals, and humans outside tired interpretive schemas of humans and nature is a necessary mode of engagement in fragile and changing terrains.

In advocating for the role of viable ecologies on these islands, I highlight practical forms of coexistence away from conservation's focus on unpeopled nature but also from social sciences' limited interest in environmental issues beyond their most immediate implications to society (Biersack and Greenberg 2006). To obviate their own anthropocentrism, these disciplines have recently taken a renewed interest in nonhuman worlds and how these inform social spaces previously thought as human-only. Building on early contributions from environmental history, eco-feminism, and Indigenous scholarship, a broad range of social sciences (including anthropology,

20 *Introduction*

geography, sociology, and political science) and several interdisciplinary concentrations, such as science and technology studies and environmental humanities, have begun to bear witness to the intricate forms of ecological interdependence, troubling the category of species as a discrete unit of inquiry and even cultural assumptions regarding the very separation between biotic and abiotic factors (Chao, Bolender, and Kirksey 2022; Dooren, Kirksey, and Münster 2016; Haraway 2008; Povinelli 2016; TallBear 2017).

The newly coined multispecies ethnography in anthropology, as well as similar initiatives in other disciplines, has provided an aperture not only to ecological thriving and its celebration, but also to loss, injustice, and the fraught ethical relationships with them (Bocci 2017; García 2019; Fry, Marino, and Nijhawan 2022; Sideris 2020; van Dooren 2014; Chao 2022). Here, a more-than-human analysis of conservation and discussion of alternatives requires a fine-tuned understanding of a plurality of species and their interactions. Thus, this book treats each species it discusses less as a settled entity and more as continuous source of interrogation and surprise. This comes also from getting acquainted with the scientific understanding of these species. Alongside the proverbial hanging out with locals (here, local species too) prescribed by the ethnographic method, this book also benefits from long conversations with ecologists and conservation biologists, as well as my participation in their fieldwork and current debates in their disciplines (Geertz 1973). Studying endemic or invasive species, then, becomes less about embracing or outrightly condemning them and more about accounting for the complexity on the ground, including the impact of certain narratives—such as the labeling of native and invasive—on conservation and ultimately ecosystems (Lidström et al. 2015; Chao 2022; Robbins and Moore 2013; Subramaniam 2014; Favini 2023; Martin 2022).

CONTESTED ECOLOGIES

Viable Ecologies considers social and natural domains as always plural, intersecting, and becoming, and thus intervenes in debates about more-than-human assemblages. Assemblage, first theorized by Gilles Deleuze and Félix Guattari, was later applied by sociologists of science to formulate one of the first contemporary Western theories of nature-cultures (Callon 1984; Deleuze and Guattari 1987). This analytic allows us to look at other species and the environment with openness, beyond approaches that frame them as resources, whether material or symbolic, of human societies. Such theories have produced crucial insight on structural determinants but perhaps less on emerging, situated agency. Further, social sciences have long relied on codified frameworks for understanding not only the environment but also the people living in it. In Latin America, research has long detailed how forest dwellers and peasants resist powers that push them to the margins of economic opportunity and civic participation (Brass 2002). More broadly, *resistance* has been the dominant framework, whether in environmental justice or political ecology, of residents suffering from dispossession, degradation, and pollution. Grappling with the gravity and violence of such forces and their impact on local society, scholarship has often focused less on affirming ways of life that have always existed beyond resistance to structural power. Here, instead, broadening the scope of my inquiry to unscheduled aggregations of natural and social life allows me to find unexpected spaces of possibility. Residents' interventions on their farms or the highlands at large, sometimes long rehearsed, other times improvised or even desperate, exhibited more capaciousness, in both their everyday practices and future ambitions, than what was offered by the dominant framework of resistance.

Apace with the rising popularity of more-than-human assemblages, however, critiques have also been leveled against such methodologies and theories for delivering apolitical analyses. In the course of connecting actors, tracing unintended consequences, or celebrating the vitality of matter, these studies risk losing sight of powerful actors' unequal participation in messy hybrid social terrains (Jasanoff and Kim 2015). Similar critiques point to the superficial attention devoted to macro political and economic determinants (Bond 2022; Hornborg 2017; Malm 2016). Building on these critiques, I consider socio-natural webs less as flat assemblages and more as uneven sites of worlding, where "assembling the social" (Latour 2007) is always an ontological *and* political question (Escobar 2018; de la Cadena 2015). My goal is not to map complexity per se but to indicate how these webs produce sites of contestation and the emergence of alternatives. Tensions among competing socio-ecologies have political relevance, revealing the struggle over who holds the power to arrange, control, and participate in the sanctioned socio-natures (Blaser 2016; Braverman 2009, 2023; Pugliese 2020).

This book joins recent efforts, mostly from Indigenous scholarship and activism, to return conservation to fundamental questions about control of resources and knowledge production: Who gets to decide what is worth protecting? And which subjects, human and nonhuman, and territories can be sacrificed? Environmental scholarship about and by Indigenous communities, social movements, and farmers' collectives has reclaimed the political agency of marginalized groups. Pushing back against long-rehearsed discussions of environmental struggle split between documenting passive subjugation and advancing tenuous arguments about hope and individual responsibility, Indigenous and other critical scholarship has cast light on complex forms of power dynamics, ranging from refusal and resistance to resurgence and revitalization (A. Simpson 2014; Hoover 2017; Dhillon 2022; L. B. Simpson 2016; Carroll 2015; Goodyear-Ka'ōpua 2017; Puar 2017; Walsh 2022; Colloredo-Mansfeld 2009; Sieder and Cervone 2017). Embedded in these efforts are arguments about alternative forms of knowledge production: from the dominant Eurocentric paradigm based on separation from and domination of nature to paradigms built on relationality, responsibility, and kinship (Mignolo and Escobar 2013; Kohn 2013; Liboiron 2021a; Ferdinand 2021; Whyte 2017).

This political salience is captured not only by a focus on agency but also by lending attention to the forms of imagination that practices generate and with which they are imbued. Alternative forms of coexistence "renew perception [of] submerged perspectives [on] knowledge, vitality, livability" (Gómez-Barris 2017, 17; Thompson and Ban 2022). As a result, the choice of a more-than-human approach in this book is designed to make us care more, not less; to sharpen our sense of urgency and responsibility, not to dull them. In this vein, I treat conservation neither as solution nor as indictment, but as an intellectual, political, and even moral question worth examining. The importance of protecting the Galápagos, which this book does not question, requires substantial and sometimes uncomfortable examination of the status quo in conservation.

Specifically, my theorization of viable ecologies seeks to decouple conservation efforts from their pervasive antihuman bias. Mainstream conservation, which is dominated by international non-governmental organizations headquartered in the Global North, tends to worry a great deal about residents in biodiversity hot spots—mostly in the Global South (UN Environmental Programme 2021). At the same time, the tourism industry is left undisturbed, as if it were its own protected species. More broadly, this approach avoids questioning the macro political and economic system funding conservation.[5] The neocolonial element in conservation at the global scale, apparent in how it assigns blame and, conversely, the burden to steward, is hard to miss. Rather than providing a respite from the global political system, conservation maintains the same logic. Ecuador and Latin America generally are, unfortunately, prime examples of how extractive industries, as a crucial articulation of the global economy, and conservation share a common framework for treating the environment and people. Both protected areas and extractive sites (of oil, gas, and metals) are carved out of human and nonhuman territories as space of exception, where locals become interlopers and nature is assessed as a sum of discrete, quantifiable, and increasingly fungible units (Le Billon 2021; Enns, Bersaglio, and Sneyd 2019). Recently, the rapprochement between conservation and extractive industry has advanced, as the latter has moved away from resisting efforts to save nature to proclaiming itself, absurdly, an ally in such campaigns by committing to hollow and even nonsensical goals of "no net loss" or even "net-positive gains" measures for biodiversity and the climate (Apostolopoulou and Adams 2017; Otis 2023). In turn, these initiatives have resulted in placing more blame on local residents, migrants, and their livelihood.[6]

Conservation's reluctance to confront the underlying cause of the Galápagos' imperilment mirrors the inertia and even complacency of most official environmentalism at the global level vis-à-vis global issues such as biodiversity loss (in fact, the sixth mass extinction) and climate change (in fact, the climate catastrophe). Despite the incessant, often heroic activism of marginalized communities worldwide,[7] mainstream environmentalism avoids addressing demands for radical change, powerfully articulated along the two axes of decolonial and degrowth practices, and continues the managerial approach of resilience and market-based solutions to our environmental crisis. For his part, soon after gaining power in 2021, the right-wing president of Ecuador, Guillermo Lasso, expanded the Galápagos Marine Reserve as a sign of his commitment to environmental causes. At the same time, however, he signed more concessions for international mining, despite the mounting protests of local communities (and increase in assassination of activists) decrying the ecological and social devastation caused by this industry.

Despite the promises of mainstream conservation, world biodiversity has plummeted to the brink of a sixth mass extinction (Ceballos et al. 2015; Finn, Grattarola, and Pincheira-Donoso 2023). If cordoning off land while excluding residents or, at best, enrolling them as participants in mainstream conservation have not proven effective solutions, we need to direct our attention, and passion, elsewhere. *Viable Ecologies* presents the side of marginalized actors, yet without any illusion that they alone hold the key to addressing socio-ecological problems on the islands and beyond. Romanticizing locals or, worse, burdening them with the responsibility of solving problems not of their own making harks back to the same colonial legacy—now on full display in the selective engagement with Indigenous knowledge and ways of life—that Catherine Walsh and others aptly call epistemic extractivism (Walsh 2022; Santos and Menseses 2020; Tuck and Yang 2012). Instead, this book aims to cultivate new socio-ecological possibilities through an examination of nature and how to protect it on a site where these two issues are seemingly most settled. On the Galápagos, conservation's long-standing goal to return local ecosystems to near-pristine status aligns with the construction of the islands as a natural laboratory. This image invokes concerns about contaminants and a need to keep them out (Cetina 1999; Kohler 1994). What if conservation centered around what works rather than what does and does not belong? *Viable Ecologies*, then, is about the emergence of an alternative environmentalism in a time of emergency, one that does not rely on past knowledge, grapples with current as well as future threats, and is concerned with redefining society as much as protecting nature.

The Galápagos are often portrayed as a unique site at safe distance from global trends and troubles. Rather than an exception, and in fact due to the heightened commitment for conservation, the Galápagos are uniquely illustrative of an environmentalism that misses the point. On the Galápagos and elsewhere, official conservation evades crucial conversations and turns conservative. While the emergent, imperfect practices in the highlands that I discuss in this book hardly constitute a triumphant tale, they ask us to foster a new understanding of how to protect a precious archipelago not as an exception but rather, as the etymology of *ecology* (*oikos*) suggests, as we ought to do for our planet anywhere and as a whole: as our home.

ANOTHER GALÁPAGOS: WRITING AND METHODS

My writing in this book departs from the scientific canon—despite its ubiquitousness among publications about these islands. Given the prominent role of this archipelago in conservation and natural sciences worldwide, expectations for scientific literature about the Galápagos are as hard to ignore as the very volume of scientific literature about the islands. Woven into expectations about the Galápagos' ecosystems are assumptions about how to write about them. And yet I wanted to break away from the cycle of research recommending more research or producing a list of policy recommendations too often divorced from political reality. For over a decade, I have read those in reports by state and international organizations, conservation agencies, independent experts, and of course, academic publications about the Galápagos. Instead, *Viable Ecologies* aims to bring to life the Galápagos as more than a dispassionate object of inquiry. Along with arguments, it reaches and valorizes the intimacy and everydayness of human and more-than-human living in the Galápagos. By viewing the archipelago under a different light, as textured and alive, I hope to elicit new forms of care and thinking about its socio-ecological viability. While ethnography has long been understood as the writing of difference, ethnographic writing can also make *a* difference. Here, ethnographic writing contributes toward the theoretical goals of this book: to situate the readers in a less detached position, to alert them of ongoing contestations and alternatives, and to spark different imaginaries of forms of life on the at once familiar and strange microcosm of the Galápagos.

As evidence of planetary collapse mounts, environmental agencies tell us of the need of storytelling to grapple with, and care for, the damaged planet we inhabit. However, the same agencies insist on more of the quantitative same, continuing to keep at a safe distance contributions from the arts, the humanities, and critical voices. This book does not limit itself to a false mutual exclusion: while in close dialogue with the natural sciences, it participates in and argues for the relevance of other forms of thinking about the environment. Feminist science studies also inform my view of conservation as a continuous, unresolved, and at times controversial commitment (Lyons et al. 2017). But I also ask, What works? What is attainable? My goal is to reclaim our sense of collective responsibility and possibility from, equally, the perceived inevitability of the status quo and the escapist, fantastic, hypermasculine technofixes of late (from geoengineering to exoplanet colonization).

Viable Ecologies, in sum, is a more-than-human ethnography about out-of-place subjects. Their presence, let alone their voices, was not obvious and required time to attune to them. During a cumulative two years of fieldwork (2010, 2013–14, and 2018), I engaged in conversations of all types and duration (some one-off, other years-long) with farmers, ecologists, biologists, park personnel, and politicians.

I regularly participated in the monthly meetings of the four farmers' associations in Santa Cruz and, when possible, those in San Cristóbal and Isabela. I conducted open-ended interviews and a dozen focus groups with farmers on topics as diverse as invasive species, the market, farming traditions, and residency status. In addition, I interviewed the three directors (during the time frame of my fieldwork) of the provincial Ministry of Agriculture and Fishery (MAGAP) and over a dozen of the state agronomists working on agriculture in the islands. I also interviewed National Research Institute of Agriculture and Fishery (INIEP) agronomists and soil scientists conducting research on the islands and participated in their field trips. In Quito, I conducted follow-up interviews with the same INIEP researchers, and at MAGAP headquarters, I interviewed state agronomists working on buen vivir policies. In 2013 and 2018, I collaborated for a total of six months with MAGAP directors on ongoing projects to strengthen agroecology in the archipelago. For over four months in 2013, I participated in the daily work and field trips (*salidas de campo*) of MAGAP agronomists in Santa Cruz. I produced and presented two reports evaluating two plans for islands' buen vivir and agroecological practices.

To understand the ecological, political, and economic context of conservation and agriculture, I joined in field trips with Charles Darwin Foundation scientists and park rangers, as well with members of Conservation International (CI), Island Conservation (IC), and local conservation organizations (Fundar Galápagos, Mola Mola). I conducted repeated interviews with members of fishers' and artisans' associations, the director of the Institute for the Popular and Solidarity Economy (IEPS) of the Galápagos, representatives of the state bank (Banco del Fomento), the two directors and other officials of the Consejo de Gobierno, and mayors of the three coastal towns of Puerto Ayora, Puerto Villamil, and Puerto Baquerizo Moreno as well as the representative of the four parishes on these three islands. Further, I conducted multiple interviews with the director and other members of the Invasive Species Fund (FEI), the Galápagos National Park (PNG), the Charles Darwin Foundation (CDF), as well as international state and private donors visiting the islands.

The ethnographic nature of my research, however, does not lie in the number of people I talked to or the number of times I talked to them. Instead, in line with the long-term commitment and collaboration that should inform all academic research, I worked with farmers on their land, taught my own ESL version of English to their children, and more broadly, tried to help whenever possible, from assisting with accounting to speaking on their behalf to tourist agencies and cruises in order to find new markets—and sharing their hopes and frustrations along the way. It was thanks to the trust I progressively gained that, for example, I was able to understand and research the vulnerability of temporary and undocumented

28 *Introduction*

residents. This prompted me not only to modify my research but also to organize with these farmers to seek a political solution. My participation in their daily lives avoided some of the informant fatigue that compromises both research and conservation projects on the Galápagos. Crucially, this method permitted me to appreciate the cultural and political relevance of their practices and beliefs in enacting a form of viable conservation, which is at the heart of this book.

ONE

∾◦∿

Escape Goats

For over six decades, the Galápagos National Park has protected about 97 percent of the archipelago. Although tourists have access to limited areas of the park in guided tours, local residents are confined to the remaining 3 percent of the archipelago. Introduced animals such as goats, however, have cared little about such important demarcations between nature and culture. They have lived on the Galápagos throughout human colonization, since well before the first Ecuadorian colonies in the early 1830s (Latorre 1999). In fact, goats preceded any permanent human settlement there, since pirates brought them to the islands as early as the seventeenth century (Dampier 1699). Throughout the last three centuries, goats have been pirates' food, hermits' companions, a source of income for settlers, and a means of colonization. Early human-goat entanglement on the Galápagos is perhaps best illustrated with the story of Alexander Selkirk, an Irish sailor abandoned in Floreana for over four years by an English ship in 1807. There, he perfected the art of hunting goats by chasing them through thorny bushes and barefoot over lava rocks and grabbing them by the horns. Selkirk also surrounded himself with a multitude of cats that he fed, unsurprisingly, "with his Goats' flesh" (Porter 1815, 79). Sailors who later rescued Selkirk described him as "a man cloth'd in Goat-Skins who looked wilder than the first owners of them" (Porter 1815, 82). For their part, goats proved as successful as Selkirk and other fellow humans, if not better, at adapting to the rugged terrain of the Galápagos Islands. Goats benefited from an omnivorous diet, slow metabolism, efficient digestion, low water requirements, and a high reproductive rate. To early settlers, goats' adaptability appeared boundless, even uncanny: to survive during the dry season, goats even drank salt water from the ocean (Latorre 1999).

Once their population grew, goats transgressed ecological barriers that

30 *Chapter One*

ecologists considered impassable. In fact, crossing one such barrier provided the immediate justification for Proyecto Isabela (PI), the eradication project at this heart of this chapter. Perry Isthmus, a seven-mile-wide lava corridor between the Sierra Negra volcano in the south and Alcedo in the north, dramatically divides southern Isabela. Devoid of vegetation, this isthmus consists of bare lava of the sharpest kind, which makes walking extremely treacherous if not impossible for humans or animals. Perry Isthmus has thus created two tightly delimited ecological communities, technically termed "ecological islands," that have evolved separately for millions of years (Warren et al. 2015).

For more than a century, goats lived only in the south, the only portion of the island that has human settlements and where goats had been introduced. But in 1966, a park ranger spotted a few goats north of the isthmus, on the flanks of Alcedo, demonstrating their successful crossing of the thus far impenetrable lava barrier. Undisturbed, the population grew fast. In the early 1990s, park wardens who climbed Alcedo were dismayed to observe goats' effects on vegetation. Previously, wardens trekking up the scorched slopes of pumice pebbles would pass through low, dry shrubs and gray palo santo trees. Closer to the caldera's rim, endemic *Scalesia* trees dotted a landscape that hosted *Chelonoidis nigra vicina*, the largest population of Galápagos tortoises in the wild (de Vries 1984). Nestled in *Scalesia*'s branches, epiphytic ferns and orchids' leaves captured water particles in the air and condensed them on the ground. In these drip pools, tortoises drank and bathed. By the mid-1990s, all of this had disappeared. What a herpetologist described to me as the "impenetrable forest of Isabela's volcanoes" was completely gone. Goats' grazing had converted forests and shrubs into grassland. Lower humidity in the newly treeless landscape increased erosion triggered by the goats' hooves (Desender et al. 1999). Instead of trees and drip pools, there was a barren landscape and dust. Instead of tortoises, goats.

Although quite spectacular, the dramatic effects of introducing a new species in island ecosystems were not surprising: ecologists had observed islands' heightened vulnerability to biological invasions for more than a century. This observation confirmed a general law of ecological communities, which postulates that the latter arrive at equilibrium through a delicate balance of ecological mechanisms such as competition and the trophic chain. Endemic species on islands, which often live in less complex ecosystems—that is, with fewer species than those on the mainland—are less equipped to compete with new arrivals than their counterparts on the mainland. In a new setting, any mundane species could become invasive. As Charles Darwin observed, "Lighten any check, mitigate the destruction ever so little, and the number of the species will almost instantaneously increase to any amount" (Darwin [1859] 1909, 231). As a result, a disproportionate number of endemic species on islands have gone extinct compared to mainland species (Wood et al. 2017). On the other hand, islands' limited species count but higher endemicity has offered a clearer insight into population dynamics and ecological theory. Both Charles Darwin and Alfred Wallace, for example, relied on observation of endemic species on islands to build, independently, a theory of evolution, the foundational theory of modern ecology. Similarly, islands served a century later as an ideal setting for the theory of biogeography, concerned with the theoretical balance between extinction of local species and introduction of new ones (MacArthur and Wilson 2015). With exceptional levels of endemicity and limited exposure to anthropogenic pressure, the Galápagos proved an ideal site for invasive species like goats.

From an estimated three thousand in 1992, the goat population on Alcedo was believed to have risen to between fifty thousand and one hundred thousand in 1996. An eradication campaign in 1996 killed ten thousand, but that number was regained in only one year (Cayot 1996). Outcompeted, the *nigra vicina* tortoise subspecies had not died out, but it did face a concrete possibility of extinction. Goats were eating everything: all types of vegetation and even tree bark. After a trip to the volcano in 1992, a local biologist remarked on the difference between tortoises' rather clumsy mechanics of eating and the precise, voracious methods of goats. For these sure-footed mammals, eating had been sharpened by millennia of competition within their own species and against others (Merlen 1999). Goats place their front legs on tree trunks or even tortoises' shells to reach higher leaves, in an accidental yet revealing posture of defiant domination not unlike that of safari hunters posing on their trophies. *Nigra vicina*'s shells

32 *Chapter One*

had evolved with an arch above the neck to allow them to reach higher leaves, but goats hastily and unceremoniously dismissed this delicate line of evolution. Photos of goats on Alcedo led to international support for an eradication campaign. With eerie exactness, those images captured the unverbalized uneasiness about what appeared to be the ultimate affront: goats' opportunistic bipedalism and resemblance to humans, alike in our tendency to proliferate and trample nature.

The eradication project Proyecto Isabela was designed to bring about the solution to this problem. It responded to the urgent matter of the near extinction of *nigra vicina* by scaling up a conservation tool that had long been used to address ecologists' distress about the ecological changes that goats, other invasive species, and humans brought about on the islands. In the 1950s, the presence of alien species and "uneducated" residents alike provoked shock and fear among scientists visiting the islands, which prompted them to establish the Charles Darwin Foundation and the Galápagos National Park (Bocci 2019; Eibl-Eibesfeldt 1959). While cordoning off the vast majority of the islands proved more successful in controlling humans than goats, measures for eradicating the latter figured among the park's first interventions. Later studies estimated that goats, whose population continued to grow, threatened to drive to extinction around 60 percent of the Galápagos' 194 endemic plants (Lavoie et al. 2007, 194). Eradication seemed the only type of intervention to tackle an issue that would only worsen if left unaddressed. The park had learned this the hard way. In the early 1960s, fishermen introduced two goats on Pinta, a deserted island northwest of the archipelago. Only a decade later, the single pair had become more than forty-one thousand goats (Campbell et al. 2007)! To curb goats' inexorable proliferation, PI personnel concluded that only "eradication ensures a permanent solution with a single and final investment" (Lavoie et al. 2007, 10).

GOATS NOTWITHSTANDING

On my first trip to the Galápagos in 2010, I took a speed boat (*lancha*) from the island of Santa Cruz that crashed against a curled winter surf for over three hours before finally arriving in Isabela, the archipelago's westernmost inhabited island. European, fair skinned, and disastrously prone to seasickness (all like Charles Darwin), I was on Isabela to witness less natural evolution and more the aftermath of profound human intervention in nature. A few years before, Proyecto Isabela, the world's largest mammal eradication program, had targeted goats on the Galápagos Islands. A multi-million-dollar Global Environment Facility grant funded a multi-institutional effort involving the United Nations Development Program, the Galápagos National Park, the Charles Darwin Foundation, the Galápagos local government, and the Ecuadorian Ministry of Agriculture. Proyecto Isabela recruited thirty-eight hunters locally; weapons, veterinarians, hunting dogs, helicopters, and pilots came from all over the world. Together, they formed the most sophisticated and deadliest eradication assemblage ever attempted. From 2001 to 2006, Proyecto Isabela targeted the mammal that had denuded large swaths of vegetation and contributed to starvation among the endemic Galápagos tortoises: goats. Using helicopters as mobile shooting platforms, hunters killed more than two hundred thousand goats over an area of six hundred thousand hectares. Mangled by multiple shots, their legs stiff in death, goats' carcasses lay on the steep gradients of volcanoes and the immense lava plains, rotting under the equatorial sun.

Proyecto Isabela was a success, or so campaign personnel declared once it ended. After PI, conservationists moved on to other eradication projects, some of which I discuss in the next chapter. Nature guides began to tell the epic of goat eradication with the detached relief that one savors when reminiscing about past menaces. According to many on the Galápagos and even more abroad, goats were gone from the Galápagos. But as I walked down the sandy main road of Isabela's coastal town, to my shock I spotted a goat outside an unpainted, unadorned house. Tied to a frayed, discolored rope, it was grazing, unhurriedly, on a few leaves of grass sprouting on top of a pile of gravel. Quickly but carefully, I reached into my backpack for my camera and took a picture of the impossible presence.

It turned out that, although Proyecto Isabela had been successful, it had only targeted goats on northern Isabela, Santiago, and Pinta Islands.

34 *Chapter One*

Small goat populations remained on Santa Cruz, San Cristóbal, and southern Isabela, despite conservationists' recommendation to remove them. Once Proyecto Isabela ended, with all the logistics in place, its personnel insisted on moving to the logical next step: archipelago-wide eradication. Without complete eradication, the personnel argued, the possibility of goats reentering the eradicated areas would always be there, along with the nonnegligible risk of undoing much of what Proyecto Isabela had accomplished. Yet locals, who had protested Proyecto Isabela but could not stop it, successfully blocked the ensuing proposal for archipelago-wide eradication. As a compromise, the park later conducted several campaigns aimed at reducing the number of goats on the inhabited islands. However, hunters spared pregnant goats and young individuals, thus ensuring the survival of the goat population. Despite conservation's most cogent arguments and best efforts, goats still chewed on the islands. They just did it on fewer islands and in smaller areas. Why?

To answer this question, this chapter examines Proyecto Isabela as a technoscientific intervention that altered goats' sociality as well as their biology. Rather than marking a profound discontinuity (that is, by eliminating all goats), then, eradication inserted itself in the shared history of humans and goats on the islands. PI personnel deployed radio-collared goats to track hiding peers and, for the first time in the world, engineered sterile female goats with an exceptionally long estrus that could attract male goats for longer periods and thus lead to faster extermination. I then turn to a discussion of how hunters, goats, and the general population on the Galápagos opposed the eradication campaign. Not only did Proyecto Isabela prompt locals to reaffirm and even create new modes of engagement with goats, but the technoscientific practices of eradication created new forms of human-goat sociality.

As I will show, PI's downplaying of the role of goats in the ecological and social fabric of the Galápagos compromised its results. Counter to the promise of a "single and final" procedure, Proyecto Isabela unfolded in a more complicated manner. This contention challenges arguments about harmonious well-being in buen vivir and SES's formalized models of invasion, which framed this type of conservation intervention. The moral and technological aspects of Proyecto Isabela offer a first entry point into the tensions between sanctioned and local forms of caring for the islands.

OPPOSING FORMS OF CARE

Proyecto Isabela was an intervention into the matter of life and the flesh of death. The project exploited and intervened in the goats' sociality, and even their very bodies, in profound ways. Goats were studied, modified biologically, lured, pitted against each other, chased, betrayed, poisoned, and shot. Hunting techniques were devised to counter the goats' altered behavior as the campaign progressed. Goats were even enrolled in the campaign for their own death. Sterilized and fitted with radio collars, hundreds of so-called Judas goats led hunters to goats who had survived earlier phases of eradication and were looking for a new herd. Furthermore, in a procedure never attempted before, PI personnel injected hormones into a sample of sterile female goats to lengthen their estrus and render them attractive to male goats for longer periods. In effect, the campaign brought to life a new gender of goats to plunge their species into a localized annihilation. While many conservationists and ecologists had deemed its ambitious goal a chimeric fantasy, eradication in the targeted areas came about with the creation of an actual chimera (like the part-goat monster in Greek mythology). Rather than constituting a single measure, eradication demanded an unprecedented intervention into animals' bodies and sociality, as well as continuous "care."

I use the analytics of care to explain not only local resistance to Proyecto Isabela and alternative forms of interactions with goats, but also PI itself. On the one hand, care involves alternative forms of seeing and living with goats among farmers, fishers, and even some local PI hunters. On the other hand, I extend arguments on care's unpleasant, coercive, even violent side to understand eradication's motivations and modalities. Iconic species of the Galápagos Islands such as the endangered giant tortoises have been catalysts for conservationists' focused attention and intense forms of care (Santander et al. 2009). By eliminating goats to save endangered tortoises, PI's eradication followed from care for tortoises.

Whether in the context of humans in hospitals or animals in a farm or zoo, care has not always been viewed as kind. Work in animal studies, the environmental humanities, and science and technology studies has shown that measures to keep endangered animals alive can be ambiguous and even violent (Chrulew 2011; Hennessy 2018; van Dooren 2014). Here, I enter uncomfortable terrain to ask if care can kill. Care and eradication make an unstable and difficult marriage, given the habitual positive and negative connotations, respectively, of the two terms. Yet I argue that PI's engagement with goats, based on persistence, creativity, and endless reconfigurations of technological and multispecies assemblages, is best understood as a form of care. Such care unfolded through an open, though unequal, relationship between conservationists and goats, each constantly attuned to the response of the other.

Such forms of technoscientific care emerged in opposition to other practices of care for goats. Residents excluded from the tourism boom of the past two decades have particularly voiced their attachment to goats. Fishers and farmers have traditionally lived with, and hunted, goats. Before tourists came, everyone on the islands was either a farmer or a fisher or both. In the 1980s and 1990s, the nexus of tourism and conservation consolidated into a powerful political and economic regime (Ospina and Falconí 2007; Quiroga 2009). At the same time, fishers and farmers began to suffer from a double marginalization. Compared to tourism, their economic activities became less and less profitable; at the same time, new policies increasingly restricted their activities in the name of conservation. Even today, still at the periphery of the tourism industry, fishers and farmers consider themselves to be remnants of a past way of life on the islands. Their ties with goats are of a historical, cultural, and economic nature. And in response to Proyecto Isabela and the ensuing proposal for archipelago-wide eradication, locals' relationship also became political.

Scholars of humanitarian interventions have discussed how the moral imperative to save human lives often results in fraught practices of care. In instances such as conducting medical triage (Redfield 2013; Nguyen 2010) or rendering the suffering body legible to forms of state recognition (Ticktin 2011; Fassin 2012; Fassin and Rechtman 2009), the intent to do good likely produces uncomfortable situations, in which care "is accompanied . . . by practices of violence and containment" (Ticktin 2011, 6). Care in conservation is no exception: here I unveil the continuity between the care for a loved species (Galápagos tortoises) and the lethal taking care of another one (goats). A "logic of care" (Mol 2008) has extended the practices of tending tortoises to learning about and intervening with goats, with a goal of extermination. This continuum unsettles the moral distinction between caring for a species to which nature lovers and scholars alike subscribe comfortably, and killing (animal) others, which is generally condemned or ignored.

Taken together, care allows us to move from the heroism of a techno-scientific challenge to continuous engagement with a complex terrain, through moral dilemmas and practical complications and not away from them. Such engagement results in a much more demanding commitment (ecological and ethical) to a site than a priori statements for or against eradication, whether in the promises of conservation or the leveling critiques in environmental humanities (Rose 2008). Instead, this chapter urges us to be more careful when it comes to invasive species, native ones, and us humans. Exploring eradication ethnographically, this chapter shows the challenging ways in which we are implicated in animals' lives and deaths, and they in ours. Showing the world's most sophisticated eradication campaign to be a complex, contentious, and species-entangling practice of care illustrates this point.

KILLING GOATS

The clatter of helicopters is what Dona Carmela remembers most about the eradication campaign: "For two years we had the noise [of helicopters] over our head . . . from the town to the park, to kill goats. Two years! It was like a war!" Proyecto Isabela used helicopters on the expanses of volcanic landscape, with basaltic soil too brittle and areas too vast to be covered on foot. The Galápagos are volcanic islands with fierce sun, little water, and thick vegetation on rocky terrain or barren lava beds, depending on the altitude. Helicopters were but one aspect of the campaign. Mules carried hunters into the dense thickets above the arid coastal region. One hundred dogs from New Zealand and a few local ones trained in the Galápagos accompanied hunters. Outfitted with special boots to protect against the heat and sharp rocks, the dogs corralled goats into specific areas or found individual goats hiding in fissures. Semiautomatic shotguns, Benelli's M1 Super 90, came from Urbino, Italy.[1]

Targeted by a symphony of hunting techniques deployed in a concerted fashion, almost all goats were killed. Estimates suggested that nearly 99 percent of the entire goat population on Santiago and 90 percent on Isabela died. The remaining population, however, learned that humans, no longer allies in the islands' colonization, had become their enemies. The surviving goats lost their innocence and became *cautelosos* (wary): hiding in inaccessible caves, they made themselves undetectable (Lavoie et al. 2007). However, even a small number of individuals holds the promise of regaining the original population size and cannot be tolerated by an eradication campaign. On both islands, the surviving goats, now educated and suspicious, constituted a serious problem, as they eluded standard hunting techniques.

"In an effort to avoid educating animals, a systematic approach is needed," wrote PI field assistant and veterinarian Karl Campbell about this problem. Campbell proposed adding a further hunting technique to the human, canine, mule-assisted, and helicopter-based ones: hunters would capture hundreds of goats, fit them with radio collars, and release them onto Isabela's plains. Months later, these became the so-called Judas goats, the betrayers.[2] The reason for their success traversed species boundaries: goats, as Aristotle (2004, 64) wrote of humans, are social animals: their aversion to isolation would lead them to find their peers. Sending invisible signals to a satellite and back to the island, the radio collars would remotely tether goats to PI hunters armed with directional antennas, first, and rifles, second. Once the goats were found, hunters would kill all except the collared goats. Two weeks later, hunters would return. The collared goats were expected to have recovered from the previous massacre and found the strength, once again, to look for peers, to be gregarious, to hope for the future. On Isabela, this succession of shooting, allotted time for psychological recuperation, and more shooting went on for more than two years.

Unlike the biblical figure that inspired their name, Judas goats were not aware of the scheme in which they were protagonists, but the result was the same. Prevailing above everything, the herding instinct propelled eradication as inexorably as a natural force. Certainly, some unforeseen complications arose, such as when a Judas goat would find other collared goats rather than unmonitored ones. In that event, all but one of the goats would be killed, the radio collars retrieved, and the survivor monitored to lead to further killings.

Judas goats proved helpful but not decisively so. PI personnel realized that female Judas goats, once pregnant, would lose their sociality and thus stop leading PI hunters to other goats. Following the pregnant Judas goats, radio antennas would beep in a diminished cacophony. Helicopters flew longer distances only to find fewer goats. In the midst of an eradication campaign, the goats' pregnancy meant a respite for their species in more than one sense: not only by procreating new life but also by slowing death. Local extinction through Judas goats alone would occur too slowly and at too great a cost.

"I started then to think about how to improve this," Campbell explained to me in an interview. "What would be the perfect, ideal Judas goats?" He was thinking about a Judas goat that would search for and be searched for by other goats in perpetuity. What may sound like a Platonic quest for an ideal animal in fact unfolded in the realm of actual goats. Since veterinarians identified males searching for mates as the main driver of gregariousness, strategies to increase estrus were key. According to Campbell and his colleagues, the literature had established that "estrus duration may be increased by denying penile intromission during estrus"—admittedly rather impractical in the wild. The other known cause of a longer estrus is nymphomania, "a poorly understood condition often diagnosed as cystic ovarian disease." Campbell and his colleagues went on to reflect that "while nymphomaniac behavior would be desirable in Judas goat operations, it is unknown how to induce this condition" (Campbell et al. 2007, 14).

Campbell instead resolved to capture female goats, terminate any pregnancies, sterilize them, and inject hormone implants. As a result of a new procedure, estrus would last not for the typical twenty days per year but

40 *Chapter One*

for an astonishing one hundred eighty days. Since transportation to a veterinary camp would have been costly and time-consuming, Campbell operated on goats, one by one, on the scorched slopes of Isabela's volcanoes or the treeless volcanic plains of the lowland. Famous as the world's last natural laboratory of evolution, the Galápagos became less a site for observing gradual changes over time and more a setting for artificial and deliberate variations on matter: the making of a new goat. With a scalpel, anesthetics, and hormones, Proyecto Isabela recombined the elements of female goats into oversexualized individuals, devoid of the ability to bear life but with an irresistible talent for delivering death.

The more their instinct for gregariousness, a chief survival mechanism in normal times, prevailed over the landscape of death, the closer they came to eradication. The Judas goats, surpassing six hundred individuals, were thus divided: 33 percent fertile female, 33 percent male, and 33 percent sterile females with implanted hormones. Project personnel called the latter Mata Haris, after the famous Dutch spy working in Indonesia during the First World War (Carrion et al. 2011). Female spies are imagined to be attractive, after all, and definitely not entangled in the laborious, motherly business of pregnancy. Fusing the otherness of tropical exotics and alluring female deception, Mata Hari, the goats' third gender, performed 1.5 times better than the other Judas goats. With the creation and deployment of Mata Haris, Proyecto Isabela personnel achieved what many experts believed impossible. Care for the tortoises killed the goats. Nowhere in the world had a mammal eradication of such magnitude ever been attempted (Carrion et al. 2011). If achieving it seemed to be a chimera, the key to PI's success lay in the careful forging of an actual chimera, a monstrous goat.[3] The only way to create a chimera, then, was to make one.

MATTERING CARE

By looking at eradication as a continuous practice, my interpretation differs from both natural- and social-science approaches to this topic. The decision to execute Proyecto Isabela rested on the assumption that it was going to deliver a definitive solution to the ecological nuisance posed by goats. Literature on the virtues of eradicating an invasive species proliferates, like the species it promises to eliminate, in conservation biology. Invasion ecologists often portray eradication as "a cost-effective and theoretically neat solution to prevent future or current impacts of invasive species" (Wolff and Gardener 2012, 34). Eradication of a species results in fewer kills over time than do periodic population checks, thus offering both economic and moral advantages. As for the "theoretically neat" aspect, eradication ostensibly gets rid of the problem — the invasive species — once and for all: what could be neater than that?

Whether critical (Rose 2008) or in favor of eradication (Rolston 1999), work in the social sciences and humanities has similarly reflected on eradication as a fait accompli, thus sharing the assumption that eradication always works. Building on seminal work in environmental history (Cronon 2011, 1996), scholars have argued that these interventions often hinge on a rigid temporal divide that separates nature (in the past, to be reverted to) from culture — the time when European settlers arrived (Brockington 2002; Low 1999; van Dooren 2011). To be sure, the desire to eliminate all forms of anthropogenic nature motivated conservation on the Galápagos not too long ago: a World Wildlife Fund report (Bensted-Smith 2002) stated that conservation's goal is to return ecosystems to their state prior to the islands' discovery in 1534.

Environmental humanities scholars have mainly focused on the ethical dimension, or lack thereof, of invasive-species management (J. L. Clark 2015; Ginn, Beisel, and Barua 2014; van Dooren 2011). They have argued that the labeling of undesired animals as invasive species and the practices that target them as humane killing or euthanasia obscures the moral implications of conservation (J. L. Clark 2015; van Dooren 2011). While I second this line of critique, this chapter investigates not only what eradication stands for but also what it does. Anthropologists and others have long criticized conservation measures for ignoring the ways local societies inscribe species, endemic or not, in their cosmologies, livelihood, and everyday life (Carrier and West 2013; Comaroff and Comaroff 2001; Moore

2010; West 2006). In the same fashion, we should treat eradication not as a self-contained project but as an event that reconfigures multispecies assemblages.

As a sustained and sophisticated intervention in an animal species, goat eradication on the Galápagos was unprecedented in magnitude but not in typology of conservation intervention. The project's modulation of goats' bodies and sociality continued forms of intensive care directed toward saving the Galápagos tortoises—the species for which the goats were eliminated. As early as in the 1930s, long before the establishment of the Galápagos National Park's Giant Tortoise Breeding Center in 1965, San Diego zookeepers experimented with a suite of practices to help Galápagos tortoises survive in captivity. A San Diego curator urged keepers to "put tortoises to bed every evening to protect them from the cold and rain, since these animals are prone to respiratory ailments" (Hennessy 2013, 75). Other measures aimed at enhancing tortoises' fertility, copulation, and nesting behavior. Keepers opted for giving tortoises periods of sexual rest to increase fertility, while also finding the best surface in the corrals to enable male tortoises to assume the "proper position to achieve copulation" (Hennessy 2013, 75).

On the Galápagos, the park's breeding center has raised more than four thousand tortoises and released them into the wild over fifty years of continuous improvements. This result has come about through meticulous manipulation of tortoises' lives, including sexual arousal, copulation, hatching, nesting, rearing, socialization, and diet. Conservation measures have not been limited to promoting tortoises' healthy habits; they have also intervened in the matter of tortoises. For instance, as tortoises' sex is determined by the temperature of the egg, the center has kept two-thirds of the eggs at 29.5°C (for females) and one-third at 28°C (for males), which the park believes to be the optimal ratio for promoting population growth (Hennessy 2013). In this context, PI's tinkering with goats' estrus comes less as a surprise. On the Galápagos, as elsewhere, saving species on the brink of extinction requires great determination and continued effort (Hennessy 2013; van Dooren 2014). But so does the elimination of species posing an ecological threat. There is nothing inexorable about keeping one form of life alive or making another die. Both implicate humans, ethically and practically, in profound ways. Struggles to induce an invasive species' death are a continuation of those devoted to maintaining an endangered species: both demand certain types of care. Eradication should evoke the image of continuously attending to an open wound in the tissues of living biota rather than that of swiftly performing a surgical incision.

Achieving animal mass death, in other words, is a laborious business, and it shares this characteristic with its human counterpart—arguably the darkest chapter in human history. Adding to the grave moral considerations raised by systematic killing, scholars of genocide have reflected on the intimate imbrication between extermination and the tools of modernity in the hands of nation-states: a powerful bureaucracy, the rational division of labor, and increased reliance on technical measures (Bauman 2015; Feldman and Seibel 2005; Wolf 1999). Anthropologists and others have examined the necessary and at times complicated work to design a group within society as the part that must be excised and dispensed of (Hinton 2004; Fujii 2009). Eradication is also a practical event: whether it achieves its goal or not, it shapes society and nature, as well as the body politic and actual bodies. Touted as a one-off, efficacious way to deal with invasive species, eradication instead requires sustained, sophisticated, and extraordinary efforts, and it is always rife with the possibility of failure.

In showing the continuum between tending and caring for tortoises and intervening in and taking care of goats, I question not only the assumption of care's benevolent means but also its goals. Anthropologists and science and technology studies scholars have reflected on forms of care that take place in hunting (Nadasdy 2007; Willerslev 2016), eradication (Nading 2012; Wanderer 2015), and animal mass killing (Mol, Moser, and Pols 2010). John Law has uncovered the moral dilemmas of UK farmers and veterinarians responding to the foot-and-mouth epidemic in the spring 2001. For Law, care for the suspected sick bovine was, much like Ecuador's buen vivir, "a matter of good death" (Law 2010, 61).[4] Yet Proyecto Isabela presents a different scenario: care was instrumental in scaling up the number of dead goats, rather than delivering a good death. Caring for the tortoises' survival translated and extended into technologies to make

44 *Chapter One*

goats die: care's ability to reach and respond to the animal, as well as to gather knowledge about and harness control over it (see Giraud and Hollin 2016; Wanderer 2015) was subsumed under a logic of extermination. If care is the practical orientation that "attunes to the mortal bodies" (Mol 2008, 31), PI's care attuned to goats not to attend to their mortality but rather to exalt it, to make mortality thrive and contagiously proliferate.

RESISTING CARE

Eradication in the targeted areas finally occurred when all but the Judas goats were eliminated. In the end, hunters were dismissed; the targeted mammals and even the introduced hunting dogs were killed; and the helicopters and weapons were repackaged in boxes and shipped out of the islands. The project seemingly concluded as planned: by effacing any trace of itself and allowing "nature" to take center stage. Photos circulated by the park showed the rapid regrowth of vegetation on the rim of Alcedo. These images were juxtaposed with ones taken before the advent of goats on the volcano. "I would like to say that we have done what the world believed was impossible! . . . Goats are part of Santiago's history," PI's director exulted (Cruz, Harcourt, and Lavoie 2007, 56). Only their absence (and the erasure of the shared human and goat colonization of the islands) allowed goats to figure in the annals of Galápagos history. Goats' menace to endemic tortoises and ecosystems seemed nothing more than a parenthesis in the millions of years of placid unfolding of natural evolution, while Proyecto Isabela positioned itself as the best example of successful, if drastic, management of protected nature.

In fact, Proyecto Isabela did not resolve matters as unambiguously as its supporters claimed. Local resistance to goat eradication coalesced against the ensuing prospect of an archipelago-wide eradication but was already present during PI, as some of the hunters attempted to boycott it. The official publication about the campaign issued by the park proudly remarks that 95 percent of the hunters were Galapaguenos, a decision the program directors made not only to counter the common complaint on the islands that jobs are outsourced but also to coalesce local support behind the

Escape Goats 45

initiative (Cruz, Harcourt, and Lavoie 2007, 18). Yet among these hunters, even those most renowned for long-standing collaboration with the park, uneasiness with eradication spread. Miguel, an elderly farmer, told me about his son, a park warden, who felt troubled about killing so many goats: "During the weekend he would come to my house and, with the kids away during the afternoon siesta, say that he was tired of shooting goats. 'It's not why I chose to work in the park!' he would tell me." Miguel's son added, "After weeks of walking and shooting, I got fed up. I loathed killing goats, especially in Santiago." Carlos, another hunter, talked to me, almost embarrassed, about his experience with corralled goats in Santiago. His task was to shoot goats, one by one, for hours.

The dull repetition of killing, devoid of the fair rules of hunting and scaled up to the level of a massacre, understandably affected hunters. Yet there were other reasons for their defection. Because many hunters were local, their biographies had long been interwoven with rural land and the park's highlands, the tall grass of pasture, the narrow hunting trails *monte adentro* (in the mountains). "I was born and raised *en la parte alta* [in the highlands]," my friend Mauricio told me. "As a kid I learned to ride horseback; later, I looked after the cattle and started to hunt: goats, feral cattle, pigs, but mainly goats. I joined the [eradication] campaign for the money, but the idea that I will never be able to go with my kids on a friend's *lancha* [small boat] to Isabela and hunt goats for a weekend bothered me." While on a hike through the thick vegetation of the highlands, he once confided that during the goat population-control measures on Santa Cruz following PI, he and other hunters spared young goats and pregnant females. "We were okay killing goats, but eradication seemed like too much!" (*Matar sí, pero erradicar nos pareció demasiado!*), he told me. But he quickly added, "It is something we kept to ourselves." Other hunters revealed that even on Santiago they recorded some kills when in fact they had let goats go, until they were required to provide a piece of ear for each goat they killed, as evidence.

As another complicating factor, Proyecto Isabela took place during a tense period between the Galápagos National Park and fishers. To voice their frustration against catch quotas set by the park, fishers released goats on goat-free islands. A diving cruise once spotted a goat on Wolf, the most remote island of the archipelago, 120 miles from park headquarters on Santa Cruz. Two park rangers and a local photographer sailed there. One of the two rangers eventually shot the goat. They sailed back, against the westward wind and current in rough seas, for a seemingly interminable forty-hour journey. "It [the goat] was a message," the ranger who shot the goat told me firmly. For this reason, PI officials decided to leave Judas goats on the targeted islands longer than planned to alert the park to potential introductions. If there were goats, Judas goats would find them, sending their GPS location to the hunters. For fishermen, goats served as a message of protest against the park; in response, the park deployed Judas goats. Far from gone, goats became at once signified and signifier, message and messenger: fishers' symbol of rebellion and, for the park, a technology to further its policies.

Judas goats stayed on the islands for almost two years after PI had officially ended. Ironically, the project devoted to getting rid of goats intentionally left some on the ground. Because they were neutered, they could not increase the goat population. Yet their lingering presence symbolized a further departure from the image of eradication as a one-off, neat intervention. Surviving the most systematic and technologically advanced killing of mammals ever undertaken, Judas goats were left grazing in the wake of their own species' eradication, amid thousands of carcasses — sterile but useful.

The complication of Proyecto Isabela's aspirations was not only symbolic or human: during the campaign, goats' resistance added to human defections. James Scott (1985) has drawn attention to the minor modalities of protest in which oppressed people engage, whose significance, or even existence, long escaped historians' and often even their own oppressors' awareness. His book *Weapons of the Weak* masterfully describes the fragmented, uncoordinated, and diffuse ways in which peasants in a small Malaysian village expressed their dissent and acted against the status quo. Proyecto Isabela's official documentation, amid the dazzle of graphs and data, did not include acts of protest, human or caprine. Yet goats resisted by learning, escaping, hiding, and standing still (see also Hribal 2007; Wadiwel

2016). After all of the interviews and conversations about Proyecto Isabela, the most staying image I was left with was that of immobile goats eluding hunters under the vegetation, the noise of helicopter blades hovering above and reverberating all the way to the coastal town of Puerto Villamil on Isabela. For animals of prodigious agility, the decision to stop came only after learning from the infelicitous fate of those that moved. It was, indeed, the little available to them to resist—likely just to postpone—their elimination.

CARE FOR THE UNLOVED

By exploiting and altering goats' sociality and biology for the sake of their own local extinction while asking hunters to perform mass shootings, PI demands that we explore consequences and, indeed, forms of care that are uncomfortable. This departs from current anthropological understandings of multispecies care. In studies of public health campaigns against malaria or dengue, care informs the laborious, mundane, but necessary practices of everyday life in a more-than-human world. Attending to the lives of insects as dangerous vectors or plants as loved others, humans establish and maintain multispecies encounters through which they "explore what it entails . . . to be human" (Archambault 2016, 265). Two aspects of this type of multispecies care stand out: that it is about maintenance rather than change (Keller 2014; Nading 2012; Carr 2015) and that it is positively affective (Archambault 2016; Nading 2014). In the context of dengue prevention in Nicaragua, Alex Nading (2012, 572–73) describes "caring for the cisterns, water barrels, and containers" that larvae of *Aedes aegypti* might infiltrate as satisfactory and even delightful: "Looking for mosquitoes is not just learning, it's fun."

Though this literature's concern with care as practice is relevant to my account of PI, taking care of unwanted species such as goats involves, I contend, neither maintenance nor pleasure. Proyecto Isabela aimed at profound ecological changes and not a continuation of the status quo; its proponents even ventured to compare their initiative with the biblical event of saving species in Noah's ark.[5] Such messianic undertones illustrate PI's high stakes: to prevent extinction and restore ecologically degraded

48 *Chapter One*

ecosystems. This justified even eradication's most contentious measures, such as leaving dead goats on the ground. Local residents proposed instead to recover and sell some of the meat. Project personnel refused, for they wanted (in their own words) to "close the loop" of a nutrient cycle: via plants, goats extracted nutrients from the soil; if removed, these minerals and organic components would have been subtracted from the ecosystems. "It could be very destructive, like removing ten thousand trees from a rainforest," Campbell said. "Better to let the bodies decompose into the soil." A handful of goats were consumed by the eradication team, but not many. Allowing the carcasses to rot offered the only possibility, if slow and distressing, for returning the nutrients to the soil.

Against the goals of uncomplicated coexistence charted by the state-sponsored buen vivir, reflecting on how goats were "taken care of" points to the contentiousness of conservation: rather than "fun," eradication entailed guns (see Martin, Myers, and Viseu 2015). Recent work in animal studies has argued that conservation measures aimed at protecting endangered species are not always as irenic and uncontroversial as we have imagined—they can be ambiguous, coercive, and even violent (Kirksey 2012; Haraway 2010). Reflecting on practices for the insemination and breeding of endangered whooping cranes in the United States, Thom van Dooren (2014, 91) talks about forms of "violent care" whose goal of saving a species from extinction does not entitle us to disregard the ethical concerns raised by these practices (see also van Dooren 2011; Giraud and Hollin 2016, Parreñas 2018). This contentiousness of caring for an endangered species is further amplified when, to save a species, conservation advocates plan for the local extermination of another one. Far from harmonious, care sheds light on the distressing aspects of conservation and, broadly, the complications that emerge when humans intervene in the lives of animals, whether by sustaining life or laboring to thwart it (Shelton 2004).

CAPRINE HUMANITIES

"Goats have always been with us—they have helped us during all this time. I love raising goats. . . . The park cannot exterminate *that*, for sure!"

Rodrigo spoke to me with a grin showing at once disappointment and defiance, as he held the horn of one of his goats. The goats were corralled behind his farmhouse, only a few miles from the park. He told me that before eradication campaigns began, Puerto Villamil filled with hundreds of bleating goats when the cargo ship would come every other month. Channeled into the main square, goats were sold to the mainland *en pie*, alive. In those years, he would await with a mix of anticipation and fear the return of his father from a weeklong hunting trip. Appearing smaller than they are, the plains that contour the two large southern volcanoes (Sierra Negra and Cerro Azul) outside Puerto Villamil are in fact immense and labyrinthine, with thick spinose bushes impeding the vista for those who venture onto them. Stories of people never returning still circulate. When Rodrigo grew strong enough, he joined his father in goat hunting. He still hunted when we spoke, his eyes scanning my body as he asked me how I would feel about carrying on my shoulders and neck deskinned quarters of warm goats. Rodrigo lives in the highlands, where subsistence rather than tourism still governs daily chores. "We have few . . . actually, no tourists here!" (*Turistas . . . pocos. En verdad, no hay!*), he told me, oscillating his forearm back and forth longitudinally—the Ecuadorian sign for having a problem. "I keep hunting for as long as God and the park want!" (*¡Sigo con la cacería hasta que Dios y el parque quieran!*).

My friend Gabriela, a farmer, would also mention goats as she reminisced about the Galápagos "before all this [tourist infrastructure] existed." When she was young, activities on the farm, not the regimen of a workweek, marked the rhythms of everyday life. Days were spent planting crops, harvesting, riding horses to the beach, exploring the highlands, and hunting goats. "I don't understand all this rage against goats" (*No entiendo todo este furor contra los chivos*), she once told me, "while *la gente abajo* [people who live in Puerto Ayora and work in tourism] keep smuggling pet dogs onto the island!" Two decades ago, she cofounded a small tourism agency that managed a sailboat. She had always loved exploring the islands and thought that organizing excursions around the islands would allow her to continue her passion. But when tourism picked up, people became competitive and greedy. Her business partner changed too, and their relationship

50 *Chapter One*

deteriorated. Gabriela quit without even claiming her share. Now the travel agency is among the many that benefit from the steady influx of tourism to the islands. Gabriela does not care. Rather, she cares about other things. "There is no awareness that we live in a national park [*Ya no hay conciencia que estamos en un parque*]. Meanwhile, I keep buying *carne de chivo* from hunters, to support them," she told me resolutely.

———

In the wake of Proyecto Isabela, goats' diminished yet defiant presence unravels eradication's goal of neatly dividing endemic and invasive nature. Eradication practices paradoxically produced another instantiation of the ties that bind species together. In Proyecto Isabela, care informed worlding interventions that drew together strands of biology and socialities to recombine them into something new. Knots weaving across the social and natural systems resisted human attempts to untie them. The caring practices that informed Proyecto Isabela added alternative forms of multispecies care between residents and goats. Residents' inscription of goats in their ways of living on and caring for the Galápagos have competed with conservationists' care for tortoises. Counter to its goal, PI created new forms of human-goat sociality under the technoscientific practices of eradication, prompting locals to reaffirm and even create new modes of engagement with goats. Whether from farms or feral, goat meat serves the local market: *seco de chivo* (goat stew) is a delicious dish on the islands. Though there are fewer than before, hunters continue to venture into the highlands to search for goats. Still today, a type of care for goats exists on trails through thorny bushes to the scorched volcanoes and back, drops of goats' blood falling intact on the dry soil.

TWO

∿∿

Unplanned Plan(t)s

On the Galápagos (as elsewhere), public discourse and conservation campaigns often present the issue of invasive species by focusing on the threats of *one* species. On the ground, instead, extricating a single species from the tangle of others can become a futile, even counterproductive exercise. Species interactions are multiple, overlapping, and much like the plants at the heart of this chapter, proliferating. This is especially true in the Galápagos highlands, where both biodiversity and conservation interventions abound. Outside formal models of introduction, invasion, and feedback loops within a SES framework, the interactions between humans (including conservationists) and goats are always plural and contested. Eradication is rarely conservation's end: it certainly was not after the ambitious Proyecto Isabela and was even less so once residents successfully rejected the later proposal for an archipelago-wide goat eradication. Here, I examine the consequences of Proyecto Isabela beyond its effects on humans and goats by looking at the unintended propagation of other invasive species (here, plants) and their interactions among themselves and with native species.

After the elimination of large numbers of goats during Proyecto Isabela, the shrub *Rubus niveus* (hill raspberry) began to grow largely uninhibited in vast swaths of the highlands, especially on one of the islands targeted by PI, Santiago. There, before the choreographed arrival of helicopters, dogs, mules, and hunters, only goats' voracious herbivore diet had kept this plant at bay. Furthermore, as an unintended consequence of the park's measures to eradicate another invasive plant, *Cinchona pubescens*, *Rubus niveus* also reached higher altitudes on Santa Cruz's highlands, in the treeless ecosystems dominated by the endemic shrub *Miconia robinsoniana*. The park's periodic application of herbicides to combat both plants in turn reduced food availability to chicks of the endemic warble finches, decreasing their

52 Chapter Two

chances to survive the parasitic fly *Philornis downsi,* another invasive. For intellectual and practical purposes, electing an individual species as the unit of analysis or target of interventions runs the risks of obscuring the wider reverberations of both the species' presence and conservation measures.

If one were to ask what happened after PI, the abbreviated answer would be more eradication efforts and yet more and tighter unwanted ecological knots. Detailing why, this chapter is the longer answer to the same question. It shifts the focus from mammals to plants, and via conservation failures, it discusses the fraught, incomplete transition from eradication to invasive species control. In conservation, control measures aim to curb the spread of an invasive species, under the assumption that eliminating said species is impossible. Following scientists and conservation practitioners on the ground, I describe conservation's practical departure from the goal of restoring the highlands' ecosystems to their "historical" (i.e., prehuman) baseline. However, attempts to conceptualize such a shift became markedly contentious. For example, the Charles Darwin Foundation's director of terrestrial science, Mark Gardener, proposed to treat the highly ecologically disturbed portions of Santa Cruz's highlands as "novel ecosystems." With this label, he sought to describe sites where anthropogenic change could be mitigated but not reversed. As a result, Gardener recommended that the park increase the area of intervention while targeting only a percentage of *Cinchona*'s adult individuals in the designated area. Sparing some plants would allow coverage, with the same resources, of a wider area. Relieved from the burdensome if not counterproductive goal of complete restoration, Gardener and others argued, a novel ecosystem approach might concentrate on pragmatic ways to deal with invasive species that were there to stay. However, the Charles Darwin Foundation and the Galápagos National Park officially rejected this framework, reinstating the validity of restoration as the unique goal of conservation.

Without leaving the disturbed highlands, this chapter considers the tension between the restoration and novel ecosystem conservation models. The park's official position opposing a novel ecosystem approach and advocating mostly for an exclusive emphasis on restoration, although common among protected areas worldwide, has been increasingly mired in old and new contradictions. Not only has the eradication of targeted species eluded the park's efforts—and in fact led to the introduction of more invasive species—but some of the assumptions about the harm of this category of species have been questioned. Studies of the invasive *Cinchona*, for example, have confirmed how this plant has negatively affected the endemic *Miconia* but not led to its extinction, as previously assumed. And although the general assessment about its impact remains negative, the increased humidity caused by *Cinchona* has also helped some rare endemic ferns. This case of unintended yet beneficial impacts is not isolated: recent studies have shown that invasive plants have improved the diet of even the Galápagos' most iconic species, the endemic tortoises. Together, these findings challenge the understanding that invasive species always harm local ecosystems and species. However, the conservation community has not assimilated these findings about invasive plants as easily as tortoises have consumed the plants. Proponents of the novel ecosystem approach have argued that park officials struggle to conceptualize, let alone operationalize, a vision for conservation that considers invasive species for both their negative *and* positive effects and views their eradication as but one possible intervention.

Local proposals to adopt a novel ecosystem approach for understanding ecosystems and guiding their conservation emerged at a time when the Galápagos National Park was first considering broadening the scope of conservation by including in a single formal framework both protected and human areas, in line with the socio-ecological system framework. Despite different intellectual genealogies and, most of all, opposition by the local conservation community, both approaches promised in fact a shift from maintaining ecosystems' composition and identity to focusing on their functions and services. However, the park showed that, unlike the novel ecosystem approach, integrating social and natural systems under SES did little to unsettle the traditional goals of restoration; ultimately, SES became just a new framework encompassing, rather than challenging, restoration.

However, the following discussion of novel ecosystems is not unequivocal either. On the one hand, this chapter argues that the novel ecosystem approach, although controversial, holds the potential to dial back the in-

54 *Chapter Two*

tensity of restoration measures. Despite calls for persistence, perseverance, and as in Proyecto Isabela, even an explicit eradication ethic, restoration can leave behind a plethora of unintended consequences. Furthermore, the novel ecosystem approach could balance restoration's marginal interest in the ecological complexity unfolding beyond the target species. On the other hand, the novel ecosystem framework seems ill equipped to address who causes harm and who is blamed for ecological change. By focusing on management of invasive species and an analysis of humans only as vectors of introduction for new species, the novel ecosystem discourse continues a rather un-novel approach in ecology that leaves humans as a background and evades political questions. Before setting off to the highlands of the Galápagos, the next section charts some essential coordinates for thinking about species invasion and island extinction.

RESPONDING TO ISLAND BIODIVERSITY LOSS

On the Galápagos, invasive species are an unmistakable problem. With more goods and people moving from the continent, new (or alien, as ecologists put it) species have come to the islands at a higher rate and volume, and a minority have become invasive. Ecologists estimate that invasive species constitute the single most serious threat to the Galápagos' ecosystems (Atkinson et al. 2012). Due to the islands' remoteness, the Galápagos' endemic species have evolved with inadequate defense mechanisms against mainland species. Some alien species have proved superior to endemic species, both physiologically, in matters of nutrition and growth rate, and ecologically, through competition and distribution, and have thrived in their new habitats. For example, the number of introduced vascular plants has long surpassed that of endemic ones: 748 versus ~500 (Tye 2006). These figures reflect worrisome global trends of island biodiversity loss. Islands represent 5 percent of the earth's land mass, but they have been the site of 80 percent of known extinctions since 1500 (Island Conservation 2017). Islands are also expected to be the hardest hit by the current exponential increase in the global extinction rate (Ceballos et al. 2015; Island Conservation 2017). With concepts such as the homogocene, ecologists have decried the increasingly less diverse biota as a sign of the dulling of nature's vibrancy (Olden, Comte, and Giam 2018). At stake there is not just species richness per se. As was the case for all the previous five geological epochs, which all ended with a mass extinction, species that take over—or those that we fail to keep alive, currently at several orders of magnitude higher than this geological epoch's extinction background—add evidence to the dire predictions of a heavily damaged and altered planet (Ceballos et al. 2015).

Whether in conservation circles or in the public arena, discussions about novel ecosystems or invasive species tend to be polarized, as those moved by the urgency of the perceived threat embrace eradication while those seeking value in new ecological configurations advocate for the status quo. Both postures show intransigence and certainty but lack long-term commitment to a site and a willingness to treat these issues as political as much as ecological. Critical social studies, through their anthropocentric lenses, have helped only marginally with this issue. For instance, anthropologists and cultural studies scholars have largely explained away the issue of alien species as projections of xenophobic or nationalistic sentiments (Comaroff and Comaroff 2001; Peretti 1998; Subramaniam 2001). These studies continue to offer an incisive critique of the militaristic, patriotic, and anti-immigrant undertones in present discourse and practices around non-native species (Hernandez 2022; Martin 2022; Ogden 2021; Shinozuka 2022). For far too long, however, this approach has had the unintended consequence of dulling curiosity about changing ecologies, where native and alien species coexist, and interventions that are possible, overall beneficial, and durative—what I call viable.

Drawing on over a decade of research, this chapter follows hill raspberry's intricate reach in the social and ecological fabric of the islands, arguing for the deeper relevance, including on a theoretical level, of such an event. This plant in fact saturated ecosystems as much as conventional thinking about them: *Rubus niveus* on the Galápagos required a change in conservation's old and new interventions against invasive species as much as this plant has enacted a landscape change in the highlands. I take this plant's presence as an invitation to "slow down reasoning," as philosopher

56 *Chapter Two*

Isabelle Stengers (2015) proposes. With this expression, Stengers hopes to promote "a different awareness" from what current forms of knowledge production would grant about concrete situations in which "practitioners" are involved (Stengers 2013, 189; Strathern 2004). Here the thinking that aims to restore original ecosystems by employing aggressive eradication interventions constitutes, to riff on Stengers's lexicon, a normal-paced truth, one that is obvious and unworthy of critical assessment. Similarly, Tsing (2015) proposes an art of noticing that lets go of universal truths and directs our curiosity, and senses, to the always site-specific unfolding of socio-ecological worlds. Walking on the same path but slowly, meandering off, or even getting stuck can foster the noticing of hidden complexities. Curiosity about new species allows us to reconsider conservation's practical measures, especially eradication, along with their ideological foundation. Both aspects are inscribed in Stenger's use of ecology: a concrete, rather than universal, situation along with a practical, rather than a priori, ethos that informs its practitioners. Letting go of general truths about invasive species in favor of ethnographic engagement exposes "ecologies" to forms of vulnerability: to being partial, wrong, or unsure.

Getting embroiled in transformed landscapes and taking stock of stalled conservation measures, this chapter reconsiders the highlands' matters, ecological and otherwise, and our responsibility toward them. In addition to uncertainty, I reflect on another indispensable characteristic of participants in viable ecologies: the awareness of new obligations vis-à-vis species and ecosystems. Obligations here refer to the ways actors think about and maintain their interdependence in the highlands. Eradication and its consequences engendered responses to a situation for which there were no established norms, one that should cause hesitation and slow down thinking about each actor's obligation toward others (Barad 2012; Dave 2014; Haraway 2008; Stengers 2013). Thinking and practicing, if localized and contingent, need not be radically divorced. Rather, they create an "ecology of practice": an assemblage in which the ethos of the participants is derived from the environment and relationships, not universal truths (Stengers 2015).

Plants' stubborn, complicated, and enduring presence in the face of

Unplanned Plan(t)s 57

ineffective conservation plans demands that we consider new scenarios of conservation and human habitation, whereby entanglements ought to be not always severed but rather fostered or attenuated, depending on their effects and ours on them. Obligations emerge from messy ecological intricacies, and these are obligations to what is viable, however tentative, in flux, or compromised.

REMOVING ERADICATION: *RUBUS NIVEUS*, OR, THE INEXTRICABLE PLANT

Let us start with what was supposed to end but did not: goats. Proyecto Isabela's mixed results showed us that eradication is difficult to achieve because invasive species participate in complex ways in human and eco-logical affairs. Even if successful, eradication may result in consequences for other species that ripple out in ways that were not foreseen, let alone desired. Among PI's unwanted, unscheduled results was the one caused by replacing an invasive species, such as goats, with a worse one: *Rubus niveus*. In the early 1970s, a resident of San Cristóbal Island brought a few of these plants from the mainland with the intention of cultivating some blackberry bushes for personal consumption. *Mora* (Spanish for the *Rubus* family (blackberry), on the Galápagos it refers to *Rubus niveus*) looks like the common blackberry plant — hence it is called by the same name. (Ironi-cally, several families on San Cristóbal have the last name *Mora*.) However, *Rubus niveus* bears small, bitter fruit, of little use to humans. The resident had not realized that, although of the same family, the plants were in fact *Rubus niveus* and not *Rubus glaucus*, the common blackberry. The rest is ecological history . . . and present ecological conundrums.

The quote that opens this section is from a friend of mine, a former PI hunter and now farmer. For hunters like Geovanny, the duration of the PI campaign was overwhelming and the amount of killing disturbing. However, park officials and contracted workers drew some satisfaction from accomplishing a tangible goal. By contrast, in later eradication in-terventions that targeted plants, the goal was less clear. At its core, the very act of killing became elusive, even counterproductive. Consider

58 *Chapter Two*

Rubus niveus: the more you uproot and cut it with a machete, the more it springs back. Blackberry coverage increased in spectacular fashion on the goat-eradicated island of Santiago, but it has become an archipelago-wide problem. Overall, *mora* was able to reproduce naturally, without assistance or facilitation from humans, with incredible success under a broad range of abiotic and thropic stressors.

Charles Darwin Foundation biologists have shown the remarkable dormancy of *Rubus niveus* seeds—up to ten years in appropriate soil conditions. This means that even after thoroughly uprooting every blackberry plant in a designated area and excluding seed dispersal by birds, which in fact occurs abundantly, new blackberry plants are likely to sprout back for years in the absence of periodic and thus costly and labor-intensive clearing. Referring to this miraculous growth, farmers would jokingly say to me that blackberry plants "resuscitate." It would be as if the goats that PI targeted, their bodies riddled with bullets and stiffened in death, relaxed their rigor mortis and resumed grazing. But locals witness this sort of miraculous rebirth with hill raspberry: if on the Galápagos goats turned into Judas, *Rubus niveus* became Lazarus.[1] Its incessant resurgence complicated not only PI's objective of definitive eradication but also, more broadly, the underpinning conservation model of a one-off, single-species intervention. While a complex, expensive, and risky search for a pathogen to eradicate it continues (the so-called option of biological control), *mora* is there to stay (Galápagos Conservation Action 2022).

Hill raspberry grows in thick, spiny bushes in the highlands of the five islands where humans live (Santa Cruz, San Cristóbal, Isabela, and Floreana) or once lived (Santiago). Human-introduced, this bush turned invasive on the archipelago only a few years after its introduction. In the Andes, both in Ecuador and neighboring countries, *Rubus niveus* thrives in ruderal ecologies such as along the edges of roads or rail tracks but has never exhibited invasive characteristics. On the Galápagos, by contrast, it has displaced native plant species in an ever-growing area in the highlands. From the ground up, blackberry bushes form dense thickets that top the higher branches of young individuals of *Scalesia*. Emerging from the voluminous but fuzzy bulge of their vines, single blackberry stems shoot

Unplanned Plan(t)s 59

FIGURE 1. *Rubus niveus* and *Scalesia peduncolata*, Santa Cruz highlands, 2014.

up as much as fifteen feet, curved by their own impressive growth. While blocking the view of native vegetation, these lean stems clearly illustrated something else: *mora*'s indomitable will to expand and cover.

The accurate coverage of *Rubus niveus* is unknown, rendering its expansion even more worrisome to the Galápagos National Park and the ecologists who study it. Charles Darwin Foundation (CDF) ecologists have estimated that, largely due to *Rubus niveus*, less than 1 percent of the endemic *Scalesia* forest still exists on Santa Cruz Island. Moving past conservationists' long-held goal of eliminating this species, I discuss below two modes of persistent entanglement with blackberry: the practical one that park rangers experience, literally, on their skins, and the one that results from the failure to find a strategy to eliminate the plants.

During fieldwork, I learned as much as I could about *mora*, accompanying people who study it and those who, like farmers and park rangers, deal with it on the ground. I joined park rangers in their periodic efforts to remove *mora* from designated sites across the highlands. For hours, I

60 *Chapter Two*

would be immersed in the precise movement of their machetes, first cutting through the brambles as if to carve the tangled chaos, then flattened against the stems, swung horizontally at their bases a few inches from the soil, and finally pointed to the ground, with hooks down, to pull the vines out, as if to make hay bales. Even in the face of this art, which despite all my dedication and practice I never mastered, *mora*'s thorns reached everywhere: they lacerated the thick cotton of their long pants and long-sleeve shirts, drawing long, narrow red lines along hands and wrists that hurt long after one was done fighting the plants. For decades, a handful of park rangers had unremittingly worked to eradicate the blackberry. I grew to know them all, as we talked between swings of machetes while I attempted to replicate the swift movements of attack and defense, or over the metallic noise of the sharpener carving their machete blades (*hilo*) during breaks. I also observed how dealing with *mora* had shaped their bodies: their dominant forearm that bulged far more than the other one, the stiffness of their backs, the seemingly permanent scratches on their hands.

More incisively than *mora*'s thorns in their skin, their commitment to fight the plant had informed their lives. In 2014, a CDF biologist proposed a study on the effect of blackberry control on endemic birds. Areas that had been cleared would be left untreated, to compare with others where *mora* control would continue. Before meeting with the park rangers and informing them about her project, the biologist confided to me that she was afraid to hurt their feelings. She was going to share with them the hypothesis of her study, later confirmed, that chemical control used in treating blackberry negatively affects birds, water, and soil. A longtime researcher on the island, she knew that fighting *mora* had justified their work for decades and feared that, paradoxically, their commitment to eradication would impede a viable solution to the problem. We both knew that those park rangers had not climbed any career ladders in the park, instead committing themselves to continuously carving modest islets of soil and light for the young native trees among the proliferating *mora*.

Mora's natural propagation was indeed impressive. Suffocating plant lives and impeding animal passage, *mora* produced a monotonous, dense, almost surreal landscape.

FIGURE 2. Dr. Jäger and assistant conducting a plant species count, Santa Cruz highlands, 2014.

Entering that landscape, as I did following the CDF biologist conducting research there, our bodies strained as we slowed our movements and increased our awareness of the space we occupied. I was reminded of classic movies of bank robberies, in which thieves contort in complicated, sometimes funny, poses to avoid the beams of laser alarms. When a thorn touched our flesh, we would stop and gently guide one arm to the rescue, making sure the movement would not add to the toll of perforated skin.

Mora's dull chromatic variation dominated the human experience of the altered highlands as much as its thorns brought movement to a halt. With the back of the leaves a grayish green, similar to the hue of its stems, and the front pale green, a *mora* forest gently sways and enchants and confounds. The eye loses spatial reference, and one is caught in a plant spell. This monotony projects a different sense of thriving from that of lush, multispecies vegetation, perhaps even the reverse: an abundance that stunts biodiversity, a thriving at a standstill. The maze of its shoots left me

62 *Chapter Two*

wondering, not just thinking, about this at once natural and unnatural growth. In a thick landscape, description rarifies (pace Geertz 1973): plant imbroglios resist the well-rehearsed anthropological drawing together of different elements into a coherent explanation. Not only passage, then, but reasoning too slows down.

Conservation reasoning, specifically, slows down. This is because, unlike goats, eradication attempts proved not just ineffective but also frustratingly counterproductive. Park rangers, far from being surprised or offended by Jäger's assumption that periodic control might be counterproductive, had made the empirical observation that blackberries spread faster in controlled areas than untouched ones. Uprooting blackberries created an ecological disturbance in which opportunistic invasive plants such as *Rubus niveus*, and not native ones, took advantage — and took over. What makes a species invasive is precisely its capacity to grow and reproduce faster and more successfully than native ones. *Mora*'s talent in unassisted propagation, then, was compounded by human actions ironically aimed at the very opposite: eradication. In other words, the natural propagation of an invasive species was accelerated by attempts to halt it. Both in Spanish and English, eradication's etymology refers to "removing roots" (from Latin *radix*, "root"). Yet, for *mora*, uprooting plants did not adversely affect the growth of seeds in the ground; to the contrary, uprooting led to faster propagation. On the Galápagos, *mora* defied eradication, etymologically and ecologically. Unlike goats, "dead" *Rubus niveus* plants not only resuscitated but became more numerous. Theoretically and practically, in the Galápagos highlands *mora* lured, annoyed, and ultimately stayed.

The park continued to clear the plants in relatively small areas, primarily in and around tourist sites. Officially, such clearance of *Rubus niveus* fell under the park's task of ecosystem restoration, which is, in fact, aimed at preserving small portions of the native *Scalesia* woods for tourists, as if this were the only feedback loop the new SES framework added to traditional restoration. The spectacle of native *Scalesia* woods obscured not only the overall dramatic dwindling of such a landscape but also its impermanence without incessant rounds of clearing. *Mora* control, then, become more a tourist intervention and less a conservation practice oriented toward eradication.

INTRODUCING CHANGE: THE *MICONIA-CINCHONA* ECOSYSTEM

To fully appreciate *Rubus niveus*'s entanglement with the Galápagos highlands, I introduce—pun inevitable—another invasive plant species: *Cinchona pubescens*. In the humid highlands of Santa Cruz (above four hundred meters), an invasive tree encroaching on an ecosystem dominated by the endemic shrub *Miconia robinsoniana* has long eluded eradication attempts. While unsuccessful in themselves, these conservation measures have led to other unwanted consequences: the introduction of *Rubus niveus* to higher, treeless areas of the highlands. Just as *mora* profited from goat eradication, as on Santiago Island, conservation interventions against *Cinchona* indirectly helped the blackberry. *Cinchona* constitutes an important knot in this emergent assemblage, which reconfigured the highlands and challenged conservation approaches.

Until fifty years ago, the native shrub *Miconia* (locally known as *cacaotillo*) dominated a land ecosystem otherwise composed of grass, fern, and bog species. This assemblage of plant species has served as breeding site for the dark-rumped petrel (*Pterodroma phaeopygia*) and the Galápagos rail (*Laterallus spilonota*). During the early to mid-twentieth century, livestock grazing and fire introduced some fire-tolerant bracken and gramineous species, but no new species stood out, quite literally, in this treeless landscape. Instead, following the first records of *Cinchona*'s rapid propagation in the 1970s, the park initiated measures to eradicate this plant.

Locally known as *cascarilla*, *Cinchona pubescens* is an evergreen tree of the Rubiaceae family native to the northern region of South America (Jäger, Tye, and Kowarik 2007). *Cinchona pubescens* (the red quinine tree) is the species with the largest natural distribution within its genus. *Cinchona*'s history is as fascinating as it is complex: it branches out and spreads much like the plant itself, which hides and resurfaces, growing from old

64 *Chapter Two*

roots and sprouting from cut stems or fallen branches.[2] For centuries, Indigenous populations of Ecuador, Peru, and Bolivia used this plant as a muscle relaxant in cases of fever, aches, and shivering. Thanks to chemical properties unknown until the 1950s, *Cinchona* was also used for malaria, which manifests similar symptoms. Linnaeus named the genus *Cinchona* after the countess of Chinchón, the wife of the viceroy of Peru. Legend says that an extract from this plant cured her of malaria. Linnaeus's spelling of the countess's name, with the missed h, was not accurate, but *Cinchona*'s antimalaria effects were. The interest in *Cinchona* arose when this property was scientifically confirmed in a compound, quinine, extracted from the plant's bark. Until the chemical synthesis of antimalaria drugs, peasants cultivated *Cinchona* in most regions of the tropics. During World War II, the United States Army listed quinine among seventeen items, including metals and crops, of strategic interest, whose extraction or production were promoted (Cuvi 2011). A few years later, in partnership with local governments, the United States established cultivation of quinine across Central and South American countries, including Ecuador.

In the 1940s, two farmers brought this plant to Santa Cruz, determined to cultivate it to extract quinine for the international market. Like many entrepreneurial projects on the Galápagos, it did not succeed. Chemical synthesis of quinine was invented shortly afterward, and profits from selling natural quinine, which was more expensive, rapidly fell. However, *Cinchona* did not die along with the human ambitions that brought it to the Galápagos. By the 1970s, biologists observed that *Cinchona* was reproducing without assistance (in ecological terms, it had naturalized) and it later began to spread quickly. From covering four thousand hectares in 1987, in 2004 *Cinchona* had taken over more than eleven thousand hectares, half of which was in the Galápagos National Park (Jäger, Tye, and Kowarik 2007).

On the Galápagos, *Cinchona* can reach up to thirty feet—significantly higher than on the continent—with notable impacts on the plant communities and soil of the humid highlands. A tree in an otherwise treeless ecosystem, *Cinchona* on average reduces other plants' exposure to light by 87 percent (Jäger, Alencastro, et al. 2013). Its leaves capture droplets in the air, thereby altering soil humidity. Further, since this plant does not absorb phosphorous from old leaves before shedding them, *Cinchona* increases phosphorus concentration in the soil, facilitating the introduction of alien species (Jäger, Tye, and Kowarik 2007). Because of its profound impact on the landscape, biologists describe *Cinchona* on the Galápagos as an "ecosystem engineer," defined as "a species that directly or indirectly change[s] the availability of resources for other species by causing physical state changes in biotic or abiotic materials" (Jäger, Tye, and Kowarik 2007; see Jones 1994).

For decades, the park had taken aggressive measures to control the spread of *Cinchona*, manually uprooting and spraying pesticides on young plants and poisoning adult ones. The goal had always been restoration of the pre-Cinchona ecosystem.

∽✕∾

In the spring of 2014, I accompanied Heinke Jäger, a Charles Darwin Foundation biologist who is the worldwide expert on *Cinchona,* to her research sites in the Galápagos. With her assistant, we hiked toward the mountain peaks of Santa Cruz, leaving the lower rural highlands behind us. When we reached the plots, the landscape met us with leafless, lifeless, brown *Cinchona* trees, a testament to the recent intense campaigns the park had waged to control this plant. Yet, despite those efforts, the undergrowth was covered with young saplings of *Cinchona*. While some were germinating under the few endemic *Miconia* shrubs, most of them were sprouting from stumps of adult *Cinchona* individuals. With vibrant red stems and green ovate leaves, they were the new layer of a stubborn, unwanted nature.

Walking in this unique landscape of a gently swaying sea of *Cascarilla* leaves affected me strangely. For someone like me whose blood, during previous fieldwork in Senegal, had turned mad as malaria parasites multiplied, swallowed my red cells, and threatened my life, I could not help but note the irony of being surrounded, years later and on another continent, by red quinine trees. As discovered in the 1950s, an alkaline extracted from *Cinchona* could stop the invasion of malaria broods in human blood, which multiply asymptomatically at a vertiginous speed for a couple of weeks. But on the Galápagos and elsewhere, *Cinchona* has created its own invasion, although ecological and not epidemiological. Reproducing sexually, through light airborne seeds, and asexually, through multistemmed growth, *Cinchona* has spread significantly across the Pacific island groups of the Galápagos, Hawaii, and the Society Islands (Kueffer et al. 2010). Currently, the *Cinchona* genus is considered among the hundred worst invader species in the world.[3]

Malaria's invasion has largely been a tropical story, which has affected the health and economy of countries in these latitudes (Middleton 2021; Packard 2007). But malaria also tells the story of Western encounters with the tropics, for commerce, colonial conquest, adventure, religious mission, and as in my case, research (Gunn 2019). Malaria is a marker of an expanded tropical geography that reached Berlin, Brussels, and Paris, in the same way *Cinchona* has expanded across the tropics worldwide to reach China, Indonesia, India, Africa, and Ecuador, initially through cultivation and now through ecological invasion. With my boots disappearing under the leaves of *cascarilla* saplings, I had to dismiss the prism of European colonial medicine, the tropics as the laboratory of the Western world, the collective deliria of colonialism, and the personal delirium that my malaria-infested blood had once triggered. The mat of young red quinine trees, so densely packed as to look like cultivated tea, ceased to be medicinal. That understory spoke of ecological and axiological dislocation: of a tree invading highland ecosystems and of a plant that was once lifesaving but now an ecological nuisance, a weed. From being the cure, *Cinchona* had become the problem.

Control methods had long combined manual felling and uprooting of trees with various chemical methods, such as "hack and squirt, basal bark, cut stump, girdle and squirt, branch filling, tree injections, and foliar spraying" (Jäger and Kowarik 2010). If this array of means seems impressive, the results, unfortunately, were not. "Most of these methods were ineffective in the long run," a research article concluded (Jäger, Alencastro, et al. 2013). The soft rustle that my guide and I heard as we strode through dense packs of *Cinchona* saplings confirmed the finding. Following the first study, the

Galápagos National Park employed a revisited combination of methods, recommended by the author, over an area of 110 hectares, barely 1 percent of *Cinchona*'s coverage on the Galápagos. In general, Jäger recommended this approach to "small populations of *Cinchona*" elsewhere (Jäger 2015). "Small" is crucial: eradication of *Cinchona* works when the invasion is small, or, one might say, an invasion is not yet an invasion.

With the goal of restoration progressively receding, approaches that are more limited in scope began to present themselves. The shift was tactical or, in Stengers's term, "ecological," addressing conservation's obligations to other species. It turned out that *Cinchona* was decreasing the abundance of the Galápagos rail and, in conjunction with black rats (*Rattus rattus*, introduced by the US military during the Second World War), adversely affecting nesting of the dark-rumped petrel. Aiming to preserve these two species, the park concentrated control of *Cinchona* and black rats in targeted areas during the nesting period. Through this approach, the park successfully controlled — relative to the goal of increasing the population of these two avian species — *Cinchona* and black rats in, respectively, five hundred hectares and fifty hectares of the highlands. This "success," however, stood on precarious ground. *Cinchona* control had introduced *Rubus niveus* in the highest areas of the highlands: Jäger found a positive correlation between the intensity of *Cinchona* control and the abundance of *Rubus niveus*. Uprooting and cutting created a disturbance that proved fertile terrain, literally, for the advancement of hill raspberry. The results were, once again, more *mora*.

As in the aftermath of Proyecto Isabela, the new invasive species was more worrisome than the previous one, given that hill raspberry demonstrated a far greater potential for altering ecosystems than *Cinchona*. As a result, Dr. Jäger recommended implementing intervention again *Cinchona* only in conjunction with control of *Rubus niveus*. The promise of eradication complicated as the target species doubled, with one ready to take over if eradication succeeded with the other species. With the time frame necessarily extended, availability of resources became a crucial factor. Absent substantial resources for periodically removing the new harvest of hill raspberries, Dr. Jäger (2018) recommended that the "quinine population

68 *Chapter Two*

should be left untouched"—a statement that captured an eradication ethic slowing to a stall.

INTRODUCING NOVEL ECOSYSTEMS

To Mark Gardener, then CDF director of terrestrial ecosystem, the unwanted outcomes of restoration projects in the humid highlands of Santa Cruz exemplified the need to manage such heavily altered sites as novel ecosystems. The novel ecosystem is a young and controversial concept in ecology aimed at guiding the management of young and controversial ecosystems (Hallett et al. 2013; Hobbs et al. 2014; Hobbs, Higgs, and Harris 2009). The latter are the result of profound anthropogenic alterations that have pushed an ecosystem markedly beyond its historical range of variability. Ecologists often concur on assessing ecological change; decisions about how to respond, however, diverge. Proponents of novel ecosystems all agree on the benefits of eradication and contend that eradication should be adopted when feasible. Differences arise once eradication methods have failed. Then some ecologists submit that management should abandon eradication and shift from restoration to mitigation (Hobbs, Higgs, and Harris 2009).

Eradication can prove not only ineffective or counterproductive (by accelerating the plant's propagation) but also harmful, when chemical herbicides poison species that feed on the targeted plants and cause large-scale contamination by leeching into the soil and water. In short, unscheduled ecological reverberations, like the invasive species that triggered them, cover ever more ground and species, while eradication (effectiveness) lags behind. The concept of a novel ecosystem offers a framework for conservation that, its proponents argue, is useful when eradication projects end, disillusion settles in, and perhaps some acknowledgment of the unfeasibility of restoration dawns. Conceptually, *novel ecosystem* designates an ecological state in which restoration is "prevented by the presence of potentially irreversible thresholds" (Groffman et al. 2006). In ecology, thresholds refer to either ecological or social limits to possible change in the current organization ("state") of an ecological community. Irreversible thresholds mark the limit of the system's capacity for recovery; their crossing thus means that restoration is no longer possible.[4] The novelty of the novel ecosystem approach lies not in the identification of transgressed thresholds resulting in "altered" or "disturbed" ecosystems but in recognizing that these changes are not reversible.

Gardener (2013) argued that, on the ground, management of *Cinchona* had already shifted from eradication to control: over the decades the goal had moved from complete landscape restoration to preservation of targeted species. The rebound in the petrel and Galápagos rail populations rewarded these efforts, which Gardener saw as an incipient novel ecosystem approach. Yet problems continued despite these changes. Subsequent research found that the herbicide used against *Rubus niveus,* which was present even in the less humid highlands due to *Cinchona* control, affects the diet of warbler finches, leaving their chicks more vulnerable to the *P. downsi* parasite and ultimately decreasing their survival rate. Alien species and measures to control them no longer looked to be occupying neatly distinct value camps. A full-fledged novel ecosystem approach, Gardener proposed, would increase the area of intervention but reduce its intensity. It would control the species' population over a larger area but spare some adult individuals to minimize disturbance.

Generally, conservation practitioners and researchers responded to the novel ecosystem approach more sympathetically than did environmental organizations. Awareness of an ecosystem's actual state of invasion and the limitations to restoring it was more acute among conservationists than environmentalists. Although avoiding any explicit repudiation of restoration, the park's framing of the Galápagos Islands as integrated socio-natural systems allowed for a new emphasis on pragmatic measures to control, but not erase, permanent anthropogenic change. However, the park and the CDF showed themselves unwilling to officially abandon restoration as the chief goal. Following Gardner's proposal to consider novel ecosystems, ecologist and CDF board member Dennis Geist affirmed that "embracement of invasive organisms have no place in the nearly pristine ecosystems of the Galápagos" (Vince 2011). This posture reduced the goal of SES integration of protected and human areas to measurement of the effects of the latter

70 *Chapter Two*

on the former. A longtime mecca for the natural sciences, the Galápagos appeared to be hostile terrain for the theory of novel ecosystems as much as its fragile ecosystems had unfortunately been receptive to becoming one.

THE OLD TRAPS OF NOVEL ECOSYSTEMS

Santa Cruz's humid highlands offer an important illustration of the positive outcomes of novel ecosystems in conservation. This approach sets more pragmatic goals than restoration does. First, a focus on what is achievable, rather than attempting to recover the "historical ecosystem," allows for interventions that are less ambitious but stand a higher chance of success (Hobbs and Harris 2001). Second, once the historical baseline no longer exclusively guides conservation, the latter becomes open to a higher degree of nuance and complexity, since adjusting conservation to an ecosystem's key properties and functions, as well as how they might change over time, proves more difficult than committing to reconstitute an "original" ecological community. These moves toward pragmatism and uncertainty can lessen the unintended consequences of traditional conservation—which range from the introduction of other invasives to water and land contamination and poisoning of native species—while increasing our awareness of these consequences. The novel ecosystem approach can slow down the fast-paced, hubristic posture in conservation, allowing more time to recognize conservation's unintended effects.

Novel ecosystems, Gardener claimed, would shift the conservation approach from the (invasive) species to the (novel) ecosystem level. In so doing, conservation would be able "to clearly see the wood in its entirety instead of just the tree" (Gardener 2013, 188). A broader and less intense approach could also allow for a better understanding of the interactions of invasive species with their environments. *Cinchona*, for example, spreads quickly and with consequences that are largely negative. However, despite early predictions, this species has not caused any plant extinctions (Jäger, Kowarik, and Tye 2009). *Cinchona*, in fact, doesn't saturate the vegetation: it rarely exceeds 20 percent of the plant count (Jäger, Alencastro, et al. 2013). Some rare endemic plant species, such as native epiphytic ferns, have even benefited from the increased humidity produced by air droplets captured by the *Cinchona* leaves. Lastly, a novel ecosystem approach would not only extend conservation's spatial scale (from one species to larger webs), but also its temporal scale. Adaptive management such as the novel ecosystem approach can cope with an extended temporal framework better than, say, a conservation approach that invests in expensive eradication campaigns tasked with fixing the problem once and for all. In addition, a longer commitment makes it possible to notice changes that challenge the status quo of altered ecosystems as much as our thinking of them. For example, the *Cinchona* population in the humid highlands, thriving undefeated despite many eradication campaigns, later unexpectedly plummeted, both in sites that had been treated and elsewhere. It was then discovered that, due to the exceptional density of *Cinchona* (a result of conservation's failure), the root fungus *Phytophthora cinnamoni* had been able to reproduce exponentially and ultimately cause a significant die-off of the *Cinchona* population.

INTEGRATED ANTI-POLITICS

The novel ecosystem approach can introduce a dose of antidogmatism and measurably improve conservation's well-rehearsed reactions to alien disturbance. However, this approach hardly delivers the systemic change that could meet current challenges to ecology and conservation. Conceptually, the approach frames a dichotomous choice between restoration's denial of irreversibly altered ecosystems and technical management. However, regardless of how systemic the novel ecosystem approach claims to be (focusing on the forest of a full ecosystem instead of the tree of an invasive species), this framework continues to evade political questions about who benefits from this management of nature and who is blamed for ecological deterioration. This approach in fact runs the risk of strengthening dominant neoliberal strands in conservation that, under the guise of pragmatism, celebrate the status quo rather than interrogating it critically (Büscher and Fletcher 2019).

With a foothold in both academia and large environmental non-gov-

72 *Chapter Two*

ernmental organizations (ENGOs), these neoliberal strands touting green growth, resilience, and the marketization of nature celebrate pockets of emergent ecological flourishing while forgetting the current planetary conditions of a sixth mass extinction, climate change, and gaping socio-ecological inequality.[5] Although not always overt or even unanimous, the inclination to focus solely on managing existing altered sites, while not questioning the inevitability of such harm or at least in finding the responsible actors, is often not too deep under the surface. One of the main proponents of novel ecosystems, for instance, coauthored an article on the beneficial ecological consequences of decommissioned offshore oil and gas platforms. The article, funded by an oil company, endlessly reiterates the few benefits of such infrastructures to aquatic life without once touching on the crucial role of oil in causing climate change or of oil companies in deliberately burying scientific truth for decades (van Elden et al. 2019; Le Billon 2021; Dembicki 2022).

While perhaps extreme, this study is not an isolated case. While looking for causes for optimism or opportunities, novel ecosystem theorists often overlook the planetary emergency and its nameable culprits in the name of resilience and adaptation to the status quo. Small technical adjustments are sometimes preferable to hubristic interventions, as this chapter has shown. However, the managerial approach of novel ecosystems, geared to tactical wins only, avoids probing for political responsibility, arguably even more than traditional restoration. At the same time, it continues old tendencies of including humans only as a cause of ecological disturbance. On the Galápagos, such analysis would reveal the crucial role of tourism as a driver of biodiversity loss, since it is the biggest contributor to the increasing human footprint and anthropogenic change. Current conservation measures instead factor in tourism as a goal, as clearance of *Rubus niveus* in touristic sites of the highlands demonstrates. While management of invasive species needs to be dialed back in intensity, as the novel ecosystem approach rightfully suggests, there is also a need for more profound rethinking of how to live on the islands.

∾ᕬᕬ

Whether explicitly adopting the novel ecosystem paradigm or not, biologists and ecologists have increasingly acknowledged that nonnative species may have positive effects (Schlaepfer, Sax, and Olden 2011; Simberloff et al. 2013). Scientists are discovering that native species may feed on invasive ones or take advantage of modified soil or microclimatic conditions, such as growing under the shade of invasives. Or, contrary to prediction, organisms may not go extinct despite the invasion (Jäger, Kowarik, and Tye 2009). In 2015, herpetologist Stephen Blake published the results of his research on the Galápagos tortoises' diet. His study is symptomatic of a shift in natural sciences research on the Galápagos Islands. Blake showed that endemic tortoises on Santa Cruz feed on invasive plants, some of which were targets of unsuccessful eradication (Blake et al. 2015). The correlation between the new diet and tortoise health is positive: body weight, an accurate index of chelonian wellness, increases with the amount of invasive plants found in their diet. Blake recognizes that invasive species on islands tend to have negative and even catastrophic consequences on endemic species. Yet "there are nuggets in this story that make it a little more complicated" (Blake et al. 2015). Sifting through tortoises' feces to find such nuggets in plant seeds, Blake demonstrated this point. Yet, much like its response to Gardener's opening to novel ecosystems, the Galápagos National Park promptly issued a statement reaffirming the unequivocally negative role of invasive species, without addressing Blake's surprising findings and their far-reaching implications.

More important than what different people think of these species, however, is the question of what to do with them. Puzzling scientific studies and stalled conservation measures suggest a shift to a zone of uncertainty that few are willing to admit, let alone engage. In the highlands of the Galápagos, changes in altered ecosystems might be irreversible but not irredeemable. Discussions about novel ecosystems in the Galápagos test the park's new understanding of the archipelago as a complex, integrated socio-ecological system and expose the lack of integration with traditional restoration interventions. Shouldn't the latter be studied dispassionately and analytically in all of their consequences, much like any other feedback loop?

INTERMEZZO I

✿

Encountering Illegality

One afternoon in the highlands, I couldn't find the small plot of land belonging to a farmer I had met at the Saturday market in town. I resolved instead to visit Lucia and Joel, who later became some of my closest friends on the islands. At that time, however, I felt uneasy walking down the dirt road that leads to the farm where they work and live—though they don't own it. For months I had tried to break past our polite yet fixed set of interactions, whether at farmers' meetings or while visiting their farm with the state agronomists. I sensed there was something more to their lives worth learning, but it remained inaccessible. Lucia and Joel were temporary residents, or so I thought. Temporary residents have to renew their visas every year to legally reside on the islands. I knew about their unclear participation in a farmers' association, given its requirement of permanent residency. What I didn't know was how to broach their residency status and their feelings about it. I feared that, as a white foreigner, to their eyes I belonged more to the people in power, who live in the city on the coast, than to those *del campo* (from the farms). I had experienced a similar reaction from most of the farmers during our initial meetings. To many of them, I looked like a an *ingeniero agrónomo*, a state agronomist, someone who mostly works in an office and not outside like them, *gente de poncho*, as they would sometime describe themselves self-deprecatingly.[1]

During my first months of research, I mostly accompanied MAGAP agronomists on their visits to farms. The logistics involved in reaching isolated farmers in the vast area of the highlands, with no public transportation and minimal directions, seemed daunting. I had opted to follow along with the state agronomists and learn about their interactions with local farmers. While convenient and instructive in its own way, my choice was preventing me from understanding their condition beyond what they let emerge during interactions with state officials. More importantly, the officials' presence only confirmed farmers' first impression about me. In my meetings with Lucia and Joel at the weekly farmers' market in the city, our relationship had stagnated on a plateau of courteous yet evasive conversation. On that afternoon, as I walked down the road to their house, my willingness to meet their unleashed, furiously barking dogs sunk to the bare minimum, but I continued nonetheless.

I finally found Lucia inside their impromptu greenhouse. I had to walk half a mile past their house, past the dogs, and down to the flat portion of the farm, where tall *pasto elefante* (*Pennisetum purpureumis*), invasive but used as pasture for cows, covered all but the sparse crowns of trees at a distance. Her older son ushered me past the dogs. Children of temporary residents were lawful on the islands only until they reached eighteen, the threshold for adulthood. He was then twenty years old and was thus beyond legal residence. Cognizant of his new legal status, he mostly helped his parents on the farm and tried to avoid going to Puerto Ayora except for Sunday Mass. Police controls in Puerto Ayora were infrequent but possible. Along the only road that connects the coast to the highlands, by contrast, checks were probable, since police know that many undocumented residents live and hide in the highlands but commute to the city to work.[2] The last exception to Lucia's son's self-imposed confinement was when he went to the transportation office to legalize his motorbike, only to hear that the first requisite was to present his permanent residency card (*tarjeta de residencia permanente*). He returned home more frustrated and humiliated than before, his mother later confided to me.

Inside the greenhouse, the dried compost Lucia was piling up raised dust in the hot humid air. The particles held for a moment the rays of sunlight coming through the plastic roof, emanating an unexpected radiance in an otherwise barren place. That year, Lucia and her husband could not save enough to grow anything inside. It was the beginning of the dry season. Without money to buy water, they could only cultivate outdoors and use the greenhouse for storage. Embarrassed to be receiving me while working, she plunged the shovel into the mound, rested her elbow on its round top, and listened to me, with small pearls of sweat slowly descending her cheeks. I again explained to her my research and the reasons I was there.

Descriptions of my projects changed depending on the ideas I was wrestling with at the time, the people I was speaking to, and the time or attention they made available to me. On that occasion the combination worked, and I was offered the chance to enter their lives. My interest in temporary residents had consolidated enough to make it into a credible proposal to know more about how their legal status affected their livelihoods and life. Finally, for the first time, Lucia spoke to me openly, like an unobstructed river. Halfway through, however, she stopped abruptly and asked, "But I have a question for you, Paolo. Will you use all this information to help us or to kick us out of the islands?" (*Pero una preguntita Pablito: ¿todas las informaciones que vas a sacar de las entrevistas las vas a usar para ayudarnos o botarnos afuera de la isla?*) A tentative smile soon covered her face: it was a rhetorical question. She had a residue of fear over disclosing her legal status, given how much it determined the possibilities and dangers in their lives. Rather than voice her skepticism, she wanted to make explicit the heavy implications of speaking up. By asking, she had already given me her trust, and her last bit of diffidence resolved before I could answer. After months of attempts to understand more about their lives, I had finally asked Lucia the right question. Almost a year into my fieldwork, I could talk to farmers about the implications of their migratory status. I smiled back, and we continued to talk.

THREE

Uncertain *Vivir*

When Ecuadorian president Rafael Correa arrived in Santa Cruz in June 2013, a conspicuous number of cyclists blocked his car at the entrance to Puerto Ayora, on his way from the airport. These residents were urging the president to support sustainable mobility on the islands. Although visibly upset at first, he soon accepted the invitation to join the crew and bike downtown, thus sending a message about the importance of using bicycles, polluting less, and conserving the Galápagos. The objective of the protest aligned well with the popular image of the Galápagos as the Ecuadorian province whose environment the government had a clear mandate to protect. The means of the protest, too, fit neatly with Correa's widely publicized persona, at least by his own telling during the hours-long weekly live radio and TV show called *Enlace Ciudadano* (popularly known as the *Sabatinas*). Among the ever-growing list of facts about his private life—including being a singer, soccer analyst, economist, and protector of Ecuadorian mores, while also a revolutionary—Correa described his passion for cycling in more than one *Sabatina*, a detail protesters made sure to remind him of. Lastly, the spectacle of a parade of Ecuadorians with their president at their helm resonated nicely with Correa's description of his revolution as a *marcha*, a march toward a better future for the nation.

However, at the entrance of the building where Correa was going to hold a cabinet meeting prior to his *Sabatina*, a more discordant issue awaited him. There, Lucia and other farmers on a temporary residency permit, which had expired for some, were holding signs asking Correa's help in legalizing their precarious or undocumented status on the islands. Lucia was even prepared to beg him for a resolution for her family. The populist vein of Correa's politics infused her with a sense of desperate possibility that entailed both skepticism and determination. Lucia and the other farmers risked showing themselves in public, but only in the tumult of the presidential visit, because they saw the president as their last chance to change the situation by overriding local politics. Correa's reaction was not what they expected: he didn't react. Surrounded by his entourage after dismounting from the bicycle, he walked straight to the entrance waving and smiling, as bodyguards parted the crowd and walled off his path, impeding any contact with locals. Lucia and the others decided to wait until the end of the *Sabatina* hours later, when he would exit the building. Yet the initial disappointment only simmered and grew under the burning sun, as Correa left the meeting in the same impenetrable fashion. Lucia and her *compañeros* handed a sheet of paper explaining their plea to the president's staff, but the farmers' morale was low.

Inside the doors, one of the items on the agenda for the presidential cabinet was, ironically, agriculture on the Galápagos. Moving up the governmental hierarchy, the Ministry of Agriculture (MAGAP) minister had received a slide show the provincial director had created with one of the state agronomists. On that day the MAGAP minister was going to present it to President Correa. The presentation charted a road map toward the newly coined "*buen vivir insular*." At that time, buen vivir informed all government politics and had become an obligatory referent of all provincial and even local policies. The MAGAP director had added the adjective *insular* to buen vivir, tying together the national call for human and nonhuman "good life" with the local goal of protecting the Galápagos' delicate ecosystems.

Officially titled the Plan for Organic Agriculture on the Galápagos (Plan de Bioagricultura para Galápagos), the 2013 Plan for the Buen Vivir Insular articulated ambitious goals for farmers, farms, and the islands' ecology. Like the Plan Piloto discussed in the introduction, it was the result of an agreement between the provincial MAGAP and the Ministry of Environment (MAE). And like the Plan Piloto, it clearly linked the social and environmental benefits to be derived from this project. A more productive and environmentally friendly agriculture, asserted the plan, would benefit the whole archipelago by manually controlling the invasive species that covered large swaths of the highlands and had eluded eradication. Second, the veritable agricultural revolution that was part of the island buen vivir would reduce food imports and thus the risk of introducing new harmful pathogens and species (Guzmán and Poma 2013).

The plan also promised, through agro-ecological practices, a more productive agriculture, to the benefit of farmers and the local community. Local and environmentally friendly agricultural production spoke to buen vivir's national plan to shift agriculture from an overreliance on agribusiness and international markets toward food sovereignty and national well-being (Giunta 2018). In order to optimize rural land use in line with that new goal, the plan provided a wide range of financial, technical, and political tools. MAGAP had just created an agreement with the Inter-American Development Bank (BID-FOMIN) to offer subsidized loans for farmers and fishers. The provincial director of MAGAP, the presentation added, also planned to recruit some of the new resources of the Citizens' Revolution, such as the agronomists he had received two years prior to initiate revolutionary agricultural schools (ERA) on the islands and the provincial office for the Popular and Solidarity Economy (IESP), tasked with supporting productive associations.

The presentation on that June day began with an overview of land distribution on the archipelago. Based on the 2000 census (INEC 2000), the first slide analyzed the concentration of farms of different sizes: up to one hectare (ha), between one and twenty, between twenty and fifty, and larger than fifty. This assessment of land distribution, however, showed that farmers owning very small or small plots added up to much more land than what the numbers in the same graph determined was possible.[1] The discrepancy of the two estimates was great, as was its relevance. Falsely showing that 16 percent of the rural land belonged to very small owners suggested a somewhat balanced picture of land distribution in the Galápagos. Furthermore, according to the same graph, very small (<1 ha) and small (1–20 ha) farms constituted over half of the farmland in the province. Reassuring, but not true. This overview eliminated any evidence of the glaring imbalance in actual land ownership, in which a third of the farm owners controlled well over two-thirds of the rural land in the province. While the ensuing plan for the buen vivir insular articulated progressive goals of organic agriculture, agroforestry, and food security, its overview neglected to treat land redistribution as a necessary piece of any plan for local agriculture. The missing component of land redistribution was hidden not only in an erroneous chart but also behind the room's thick curtains, where Lucia and other farmers were asking the state to grant them full citizenship and a chance to own land on the islands.

The plan contemplated funding for water-saving infrastructure, invasive species control, and organic composting to the benefit of the environment and, by increasing productivity and strengthening food security, of farmers too. It also specified that buen vivir in the highlands would not require any additional workers. Indeed, as the presentation on buen vivir insular falsely claimed, the number of small farmers capable of working their land without additional workers, as opposed to larger estates, was adequate. On the other hand, the plan enlisted certain farmers as recipients and dutiful agents of the *revolución agraria*. By encouraging them to form *asociaciones*, attend farming schools, and apply for new state financing, the planners ensured that farmers would engage with buen vivir's bureaucracy and thus fulfill one of the most immediate goals of any ideology: to become real.

Months later, I talked to the agronomist who had worked on this presentation along with the provincial director. He shared my concern about the erroneous numbers and, especially, the implications of the skewed representation of land distribution. I also talked privately to the director, who denied any responsibility for producing those numbers and asked me to remove his name from my report and presentation to MAGAP about buen vivir insular. The problem with the plan, however, went farther than neglect. A stricter codification of farmers' citizenship, farm use, and MAGAP's work resulted in excluding the farmers who did not comply with buen vivir and its prescriptions for an agrarian revolution. While missing the issues of land tenure and undocumented farmers, buen vivir insular engendered further marginalization and unwanted changes in the highlands at the very moment it claimed to ameliorate the conditions of both farmers and farms. Like earlier discussions of animal and plant control, the outcomes of state interventions aimed at improving both rural and protected highlands proved less obvious than the motivations that justified them.

Uncertain Vivir 83

TEMPORARY AND UNDOCUMENTED
FARMERS UNDER *BUEN VIVIR*

Facing mounting concern about anthropogenic threats on the islands, Ecuador passed a law in 1998 restricting immigration to the Galápagos. Sanctioned by the 1998 Constitution, the Ley Especial para Galápagos (LOREG) created three legal categories of people on the islands: permanent residents, temporary residents (a work visa for twelve months, renewable), and tourists (Congreso Nacional 1998). LOREG, however, was hardly enforced for almost a decade after its promulgation. Mainland Ecuadorians who traveled to the Galápagos as tourists and overstayed faced few, uneven consequences. If the legal status of applicants in the tourism industry (hotels, restaurants, and cruise ships) was the most scrutinized, in the highlands it was the least. Thus, aside from construction workers in the coastal cities, who often stayed on the islands for limited periods, most of the undocumented Ecuadorians were farmers.

In 2007, the government declared the islands in crisis a few months before UNESCO listed the Galápagos among its "at-risk" World Heritage Sites (UNESCO 2007; El Confidencial 2007). Both reports denounced widespread political mismanagement by local institutions regarding fishery, immigration, and biosecurity. Nationally, these declarations took place at a time when a new president of the republic, Rafael Correa, was building alliances with trade unions and Indigenous and *campesino* movements and, in collaboration with progressive intellectuals, was coining the new political rubric of buen vivir. Following the at-risk declarations during Correa's first full mandate, enforcement of LOREG became significantly more stringent. The first *batidas*—police checkpoints on the road connecting the highlands to the coastal towns—and raids at the Saturday farmers' market began then, as did the first deportations. For undocumented farmers, the promise of an improved citizenship, which the government publicized profusely on TV and radio, and in street ads, added to the bitter irony of being excluded from full citizenship on the islands.

Correa's populist emphasis on citizens resulted in a renewed presence of the state at odds with the informality regarding residency and work permits in the rural highlands. In this new era, state agronomists needed to produce a report for each visit signed by farmers, de facto excluding those ineligible to receive state assistance. As a result, farmers without a valid residency permit could no longer buy land, participate in labor associations, or receive assistance from the Ministry of Agriculture. These farmers included not only the undocumented, but also temporary workers who, for many months of the year, had to wait for the Immigration Office to approve their visa. In addition to being time consuming, a temporary visa is expensive and requires sponsorship from a permanent resident, who often weighs the advantages of avoiding legal repercussions if they legalize their workers against the value of having more control if the workers remain undocumented.

∽✗∾

Joel arrived in Santa Cruz fifteen years ago, soon after the immigration law had passed. His brother had already been there for more than a decade and invited Joel once he found a job for him. A member of one of the richest families of the island offered Joel work on a large (80 ha) farm. With a job offer in hand, Joel was able to receive a temporary residence card and join his brother on the island. Every year after the approval, he had to apply for renewal of his temporary status. Whereas migration is usually a responsibility of national government, the Galápagos, granted the status of a special province by the Constitution, directly control local residency. Restrictions on immigration apply to all mainland Ecuadorians and foreigners who are not permanent residents. The province's Consejo de Gobierno (Governing Council) has a branch that regulates immigration: officially called the Dirección de Población y Control de Residencia, everyone on the islands simply calls it Migración.

Every year, Joel presented the same official documentation (*papeles*) that *Migración* asks of those applying for the first time, compiling all the documents and then submitting the heavy folder to Migración. Unforeseen complications and costly delays always abounded. To start, the required form of identification was not one but three (*cedula*, *votación*, and *resi-*

Uncertain Vivir 85

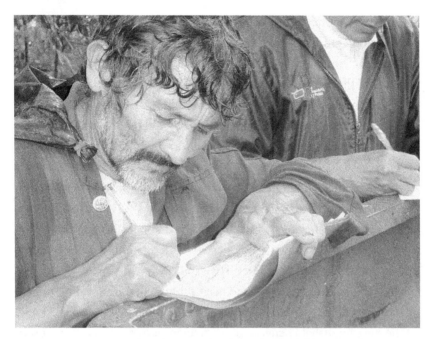

FIGURE 3. Farmer signing his name in MAGAP's new log for field visits, Bellavista, 2013.

dencia). Whereas in most contexts, including elsewhere on the islands, an identity card was sufficient to identify someone, three cards had to be presented to Migración. One year Joel complied with such requirements yet was asked to correct his application because he had made one photocopy of the three cards when he should have made three photocopies, one for each card.

Aside from the identification cards, every year Joel had to include a photocopy of his birth certificate, as if his birth on the continent was a fact of his biography so beneficial to his application that it demanded iterative scrutiny on the part of Migración, and not the reason he had to apply for temporary residency in the first place. Even if being born on the continent were advantageous for residence on the Galápagos, why ask for the same birth document every year? "They still don't know where I was born?" Joel commented. "They should have a stack of copies of it!" Once he added, "After all, the birthplace is not something you change many times in your life." Aside from the birth certificate, the list of documents was long: all

86 *Chapter Three*

changes in residency from past years, tax files, work contracts, firefighters' certification of the safety of the workplace (if indoor), identification cards and bank account number of the sponsor, social security cards of the applicant and the sponsor, and so on. All documents had to be notarized. In 2014, the notary official in Santa Cruz usually signed each sheet, without reading it, for $5. Once I accompanied Joel there, but the notary had just left for the lunch break. After a few elusive words and a clear exchange of looks with Joel, the secretary ventured into her boss's office, swiftly stamped the sheets, and forged his signature. Joel gave her a $10 bill, which immediately disappeared in her purse, for four sheets. Half price. But such luck comes only once in a while, Joel told me under his breath as we left the office and looked down at our feet to let our eyes adjust to the blinding midday sun—but also to hide a furtive smile.

Once the *carpeta*, or folder, had been submitted, the effort put into the meticulous analysis of its individual documents would be surpassed only by the inextinguishable energy of Migración personnel in finding problems and, once the applicant resolves those, adding new ones. Requests to resubmit may have stemmed from the assigned date of the new yearly contract, which should predate the expiration date of the previous year of residency, or, as Joel was once told rather perfunctorily, begin after it. Or, it may have been the type of photocopy, signaling Migración's dissatisfaction with the dull chromatics of a cheaper black and white photocopy. Once the petition is submitted, if possible, the applicant goes to Migración to periodically inquire with a permanent resident of a certain power on the islands, to neutralize the power imbalance. A farmer's wife, for example, worked as janitor for the Biosecurity Agency of the Galápagos (ABG). As she worked in the evenings, she barely interacted with anyone there. However, she would always tell me with pride that she personally knew Dr. Cruz, then director of the agency. In the face of insurmountable challenges in her renewal, Dr. Cruz decided to go to Migración to personally inquire about her employee's *carpeta*. The latter, which had long been declared missing, was immediately found and the renewal approved within weeks.

Joel and many farmers, however, never benefited from such help. While they might work for well-established figures on the islands, it was rare that the latter cared enough about the legal condition of his or her workers to endure any legal hurdles. Unlike, say, a director of public institutions like the Biosecurity Agency, their workers lived on farms, away from public scrutiny. Given the uncertainty of the process and his lack of social clout, Joel had to start months in advance, navigating the bureaucratic idiosyncrasies at the Ministry of Work, the municipality, provincial government offices, banks, and so on to gather the required documents. His residency expired at the end of January; he usually started working on the renewal in October.

If the renewal was accepted, it could take months before receiving a temporary residency card. This was because, once he was notified of the acceptance of the renewal, Joel needed to request issuance of a new temporary residency card (*tarjeta de residencia temporal*), without which farmers could be deported. The last process could take anywhere between a few days and several months. To cover those days, weeks, or months, applicants like Joel needed to ask for another document to attest that they were in the process of obtaining a residency card and thus (temporarily, at least) lawful residents of the islands. Slowness of the bureaucratic process of issuing a temporary residency card bred one more form in the procedure: the request for a temporary (thirty-day) document that certifies that the applicant was waiting for an only less temporary residency card (indeed, called the temporary resident card, which lasts for one year). Over months of daily conversation about this subject, farmers seldom challenged redundancy and complication. No one did—me included, eventually.[2] But the absurdity of it all, especially in the context of a new emphasis on all citizens, was not lost on them. "This is buen vivir," Lucia dryly told me once, ending yet another conversation about the deterioration of their citizenship on the Galápagos over the years.

The struggle, however, did not end there. The paper attesting that one's renewal was being processed could take anywhere between a couple of hours and several days, but it only lasted one month. Since proof of residency was required to buy an airline ticket with the subsidized price for residents, the thirty-day validity prevented buying tickets back to the mainland (often in hopes of better health care) in advance, when they are

88 *Chapter Three*

cheaper, or staying on the mainland for more than a month. The ability to afford the renewal was indeed key. For instance, a crucial step of the process of acquiring temporary residency was paying a deposit, allegedly used to cover the cost of airfare in case of deportation. In fact, police used the military airplane that services the islands and not the private airlines whose prices for a one-way ticket were used to set the deposit (in 2014, it amounted to $214). Many farmers could not afford to set aside that sum of money for a year for each member of the family—some, not even a tenth of that amount. Certainly they could not afford *not* to recuperate it at the end of the year. In 2006, at the end of a good season and with optimism for the future, Joel and Lucia paid the residency deposit for themselves and their three children. But the following year the agency did not refund their deposits. Corruption was rampant, and they were not just poor farmers, as many books about campesinos in Ecuador have lyrically portrayed, but also citizens fighting to avoid becoming undocumented in their own country. What were they going to do if they didn't get the money back? Nothing.

Over the next days and weeks, Joel shared with me more stories of rejections and requests for more documents. I accompanied him several times during my stay. I witnessed his applications (*peticiones*) going nowhere and Joel returning home empty-handed. For most years, Joel and Lucia resolved to have only Joel legal. Just the price to issue his card, Lucia once remarked, was, at the time of my fieldwork in 2014, $43. Joel and Lucia, who had three children, could not afford the money for the card, let alone for the whole process that precedes it (notarization, fees, and lost days of work). His sponsor had been considerate enough to legalize him and thus grant him, among many benefits, nationalized health coverage, but many other landowners did not extend the same courtesy to their farmworkers.[3]

The situation of a temporary resident produced a form of vulnerability that was more than economic. From when Joel started working on his renewal to when he received it, four to six months could lapse. Half of the total time he would be legal (twelve months) was consumed in the process of petitioning (six months), as my own experience confirmed. Those were the months in which he felt most acutely the risk incurred had he raised his voice against state institutions and the people who work there. No matter what complaint he had, what abuse to report or injustice to fight against, he needed to keep it quiet: the process was lengthy and local families extended, leaving little room for risking a disagreement with anyone. Because of the renewal, Joel and other temporary residents lived according to a new seasonality. It overrode other rhythms to which they were more accustomed: rainy and dry seasons and the monthly cycle of the moon, which set the cadence of their farmwork and told them when to plow, harrow, and till; when to seed the hotbeds and when to sow; and when to fertilize, prune, harvest, and clear the land. Over the years, however, this new cycle had resolved into a stable condition of guarded circumspection and fear. Temporary residents lived a diminished citizenship all year long, as a new renewal is always on the horizon.

Under buen vivir, the state enforcement of new legal categories created illegality. This happened not simply on a formal level—that is, when enforcement of the residency law logically made illegals of those who didn't meet the requirements. Instead, even people who (tried to) belong in the categories of legal residents, whether temporary or permanent, experienced marginalization, and those with fewer means often slid into illegality, as happened to Lucia and Joel's family.

CONVENIO

In 2012 an agreement (*convenio*) between MAGAP and the state-run Development Bank (Banco del Fomento) established low-interest loans for entrepreneurs falling within the scope of MAGAP (fishers, farmers, ranchers, and so on). In Galápagos, this initiative started the usual way: by holding a meeting between the authorities and other interested parties. The provincial director of MAGAP, various personnel from the national headquarters of MAGAP in Quito, local officials of the Banco del Fomento, and leaders of farmers', ranchers', and fishers' associations walked to the stage of the municipal town hall and sat on chairs, importantly or uneasily, behind a long table facing the audience. I recognized some of these officials from the mainland in the highlands during the following weeks, wearing the same formal attire they had on that night. In his speech, the MAGAP di-

90 *Chapter Three*

rector stressed the advantageous interest rates but quickly pivoted to the goals of buen vivir in the highlands and the islands as a whole. "We all need to assume our responsibilities for a better future," he admonished. "For farmers, this means to produce more and better (*una producción de quantidad y qualidad*), which in turns means achieving food security and each doing our part for conservation." "This [the subsidized loans] will help," he concluded. "It is not a present but it surely is an opportunity of a lifetime that you should not pass up."

With such a grand opening, many farmers began to seriously consider the offer. The borrowing rate was undoubtedly better than any loan with a private bank. Instead, farmers remained skeptical about the reality of the offer. Would the bank really give *them* money? The offer came from public institutions with which locals had dealt their entire lives, and regarding which many had learned to harbor sentiments of diffidence if not open mistrust. Memories of the 1999 national bankruptcy (*feriado bancario*) were still fresh, the confidence in state institutions low. The offer, unsurprisingly, required an extended list of documents to file and conditions to meet. This perhaps granted the offer more credibility in a system where verbosity and elaborateness bestowed gravitas. Expectedly, there were heated discussions and endless inquiries following the presentation. The audience eventually divided among farmers, ranchers, and fishers. All participants could directly address their concerns to the experts from MAGAP headquarters in Quito, whom I later saw posing for pictures by the night attractions of Puerto Ayora.

The *convenio* rekindled a modicum of interest in a population diffident of but also to a certain extent used to expecting new promises from the state. These promises signaled both the insufficiency of structural policies and a paternalistic state. Farmers' reactions reflected both sides: skepticism but also willingness to hear about the newest program. To many, gaining better access to credit seemed to be key for having farmland that was productive once again, and they agreed to try again. Months later a farmer told me that, soon after the meeting, he had incurred debts with a private bank, certain that he would secure the subsidized loan and soon extinguish the less advantageous private one. As part of the agreement, MAGAP promised assistance in gathering the documentation and preparing the application. MAGAP also offered logistic support to the bank officials for the financial assessment of loan applicants, as they ventured outside their windowless offices to the farms in the highlands.

∾∞∾

Lidia and Ramiro received just such a visit from a bank official when I was with them. Lidia and Ramiro had arrived on the island more than twenty years earlier. Since then, they had lived in the biggest rural village of the archipelago, El Cascajo, on Santa Cruz Island. Through hard work, they had managed to purchase a small piece of land and build greenhouses where they grew tomatoes, peppers, and cucumbers year round. They relied on large volumes and chemical additives to have consistent production. The loan would have allowed them to install a new irrigation system, since the old one broke long ago. Greenhouse agriculture requires higher volumes of water as the indoor temperature in the summer can be very high (above 100°F), and farmers like Lidia and Ramiro thus had to water twice a day. A new irrigation system, they thought, would save water and labor, both very scarce on the islands.

After a few uncertain steps in the greenhouse, the bank official proceeded to ask the questions on the evaluation form. For every product she asked the median profit it generated per month. Lidia and Ramiro struggled to estimate volume and revenue for their harvest, which follows a seasonal and not a weekly or monthly logic. Tomato plants, they suggested, are productive thirteen to fifteen weeks after they germinate, and they produce for three months or more, yet not with the same volume. The cucumbers, they continued, had been doing just fine until they could not water them for a few days and a type of bug attacked them. The watermelons outside, well suited to the summer drought, used to be a good business but do not produce for more than a month and half. Unwavering, the bank representative pressed for numbers, unconcerned that the latter might be rough approximations and, in fact, more a request for help than final estimates. Without looking at them, the bank official filled out the form as Lidia and Ramiro talked. She then inquired about their costs

FIGURE 4. Lidia discussing the new loan program with a MAGAP agronomist outside her greenhouse, El Cascajo, 2014.

(seeds, products, transportation, and workers) and subtracted them from their profit. Her endeavor was hampered by a shaky knowledge of basic mathematics and fake nails, which complicated the use of the calculator application on her phone. Lidia, without makeup and wearing unadorned cloths, and Ramiro, in a frayed pair of pants and shirt, and both wearing flip-flops showing muddy feet, stood still, in silence. They finished the evaluation tired and mute, embarrassed for making public their poverty and not even in convincing terms. The bank official was noncommittal. "We will put everything in the folder and then let you know," she told them with an open smile but inscrutable intentions.

∽∞∾

Extended fieldwork allows for cultivating relationships and gaining trust. On a more basic level, it affords a memory that institutions rarely possess or their reports show. In the months that followed, I caught up with Lidia

Uncertain Vivir 93

and Ramiro periodically. Their folder at the bank was never complete. For every missing document turned in, the bank asked for another. Bank officials asked for documentation the bank should have archived from previous loans. They asked for notified copies of Lidia's and Ramiro's national identity cards, their birth certificates, the property act of the land, their financial and credit status, notarized copies of their three children's birth certificates, and more. All at different times and more than once. The list of requisites was expandable, uncertain, its logic inscrutable, and its completeness frustratingly unachievable. The experience, I learned, was anything but an anomaly.

At the time of my fieldwork, the two political officials who represented the rural districts of the island in fact lived in town. Indeed, politics, tourism, money, restaurants, hotels, and noise all dwelled in the towns. To go to Puerto Ayora, Lidia, Ramiro, and other farmers I knew would put on their best clothes, as if going to church. They would comb their hair at length, struggling to make out their reflected images in small or cracked mirrors that hung outside their houses. They would make sure there was no mud on their shoes. They would shout at their dogs to keep them quiet when the taxi arrived at their farm, or say goodbye to them if they walked to the main road and waited for a car there. I could recognize farmers in town even when I didn't know them personally, based on their careful yet distinctive attire. The dresses, the combed hair, the perfumes first perused in paper magazines, discussed at the Saturday market or in the penumbra of their modest houses, then bought by mail and applied parsimoniously on their necks and wrists in front of cracked mirrors—I became familiar with those intimate routines as Lidia, Ramiro, and other farmers tried to get their petitions approved. The journeys from fresh woody farms to the sun-stricken downtown and the freezing, air-conditioned bank continued over months, to no avail. Such trips were time consuming, costly, humiliating. Four months down the line, they gave up. Everyone did, both fishers and farmers. Instead of a formal rejection, the bank procrastinated and complicated the process to the point of reaching its impossibility and the applicants' exhaustion.

One year later, MAGAP and the Banco del Fomento reviewed the proj-

94 *Chapter Three*

ect and shared their conclusions. A report about the "experience" was produced, its results "internally shared" but never made public. The MAGAP director alluded to this initiative in his yearly public accounting (*rendición de cuenta*), mentioning again the goals of farmers' and the highlands' well-being but skipping the results. I later discovered that the majority of farmers who had applied were temporary residents, others undocumented. Although perhaps surprising, these farmers had seen in the *convenio* an opportunity to improve not only their finances but also their social standing. No temporary resident, let alone undocumented farmer, was granted a loan, and only one small farmer out of the fifty who applied was successful. The subsidy instead went predominantly to large landowners who, despite their estates in the highlands, were mostly involved in tourism on the coast. Given their limited investment in their farms, these landowners preferred to abandon farming in favor of raising livestock and to leave large swaths of their property fallow, which became a breeding ground for invasive plants.

THE NEW RURAL CITIZEN

Although a few measures were directly designed for individuals, the bulk of the plan's incentives was intended for workers' associations. The plan for the island buen vivir deliberately articulated one of the major ideological axes of the national government's political economy: collective economy (*asociacionismo*). In the "new nation," in Correa's double declination (borrowing from Fidel Castro) of "*patria grande*" (Latin America) and "*patria chica*" (Ecuador), associations would steer the economy away from neoliberal precepts of growth and competition and instead organize it around cooperation, solidarity, and collective well-being. The 2011 Law of Popular and Solidarity Economy (Economía Popular y Solidaria) positioned workers' associations as the fulcrum of the future economy by tying future financial assistance to workers' collectives rather than individuals. On the Galápagos, the Ministry of Agriculture began to tout forming associations as a key element for the success of agriculture on the islands.

Under this law, all cooperatives had to register under the regulatory

Uncertain Vivir 95

agency (Superintendencia de Economía Popular y Solidaria, SEPS). This new requirement forced a profound reorganization in the way cooperatives operated within and were recognized by the state. Whereas farmers' cooperatives had previously fallen under MAGAP's jurisdiction, the new law transferred oversight to the Institute of the Popular Economy (Instituto de Economía Popular y Solidaria; IEPS). Existing cooperatives had to be recognized by this new institution, with new requirements and new procedures. IEPS had given cooperatives a year to comply with the new requirements. MAGAP soon after signed an agreement to offer help in this transition, adding its support to the goal of building a better future for farmers and the highlands alike under the aegis of buen vivir.

"The associations will be the key," Cecilia, a state agronomist on the islands, stated resolutely. We were driving to the uplands to conduct a focus group on the results of a local agricultural school and its potential to become an association. In 2010 the government had launched the Schools of the Agrarian Revolution program (Escuelas de la Revolucion Agraria; ERA) to educate farmers about a mix of ancestral and experimental farming knowledge.[4] On the Galápagos, the local MAGAP office received funds to hire more agronomists to run the schools, which offered weekly meetings in the parishes' communal centers. Aside from monthly oral presentations, each school—composed of a group of farmers led by a state agronomist—used a small lot to practice techniques to accomplish such tasks as producing organic compost and natural pesticides. The MAGAP provincial director had described to me his plan to leverage ERAs to form dynamic and motivated farmers' collectives. With an emphasis on solidarity and cooperatives, it was the project of forging a new rural citizen (*nuevo ciudadano rural*) that might succeed in curbing pests and what he viewed as other unwanted presences, such as illegal immigrants, trash, and fallow land, that slowed down agriculture on the islands.

"We have received a clear message that, to fight against harsh [soil and climatic] conditions and a small market, farmers need to pool resources together," Cecilia offered. "With the ERA, we have been working on a green agriculture [*agricultura limpia*] with less pesticide, while the new policies to boost cooperation and increase productivity [*la reactivación del campo*]

96 *Chapter Three*

will result in reducing imports of food and pests [from the continent]. Ultimately, farmers' buen vivir will mean the islands' buen vivir."

When we arrived at the parish communal house, Cecilia got out of the pickup carrying a thick folder with printed instructions for each member on how to register their association with IEPS. However, only one person greeted us. Without any other members, the goal of evaluating an association soon faded away, and we went back outside. The afternoon in the highlands was warm and pleasant. Walking behind the communal house, we arrived at the school. The only member present complained about other members' lack of commitment to the group and lamented the state of the abandoned land. That small piece of land was supposed to be the site for experimenting with the revolution's distinctive blend of old and new agricultural techniques and knowledges. Instead, members could not agree on how to manage the lot as a collective. Initially, some members had accused others of not doing their part or of stealing vegetables. Over time, they had divided the lot into micro-lots, one for each member. We walked past minuscule rectangular plots, some cultivated with one crop, such as corn, others with a mix of vegetables, and others fallow, silently noting the manifest lack of unity among the farmers.

Rather than hold the focus group, in the following days Cecilia resolved to talk individually to the members, so that MAGAP's planning for the island's buen vivir could continue. However, the most significant finding that afternoon—farmers' disinterest in associations—was carefully ignored. Reasons for their lack of engagement, I discovered later, were several. Farmers complained that the agronomists were not as knowledgeable and useful as they purported to be. ERA agronomists came from the mainland, with limited knowledge about the social and ecological aspects of farming on the Galápagos. Tenacious weeds, water scarcity, a unique climate, little mechanization, and few workers had shaped agriculture differently from the mainland, which provided the point of reference for MAGAP's agricultural policies and agronomists' educational endeavors alike. Second, ERA had attracted some farmers but mostly residents working in other jobs that were more profitable or offered them some free time, such as taxi drivers or state employees. Some of these residents participated in ERAs because of their interest in cultivating land they had inherited but left fallow to pursue their careers in the coastal towns. These residents, who enjoy full citizenship (as permanent residents) and often higher status, joined ERA because they could, and they perceived no harm in seeing if they could benefit from this new project. On the other hand, full-time farmers and farmworkers largely avoided ERA's evening meetings, as those offered no answer to the most pressing problems of a limited workforce for large landowners or poor state support and precarious status among the temporary or undocumented workers.

By then, many temporary residents did not feel comfortable renewing their membership in farmers' associations under IEPS knowing that legally they should have never joined the associations in the first place. Previously, MAGAP agronomists had been responsible for farmers' associations but with little control. Instead, becoming a cooperative member under the new law required signing documents to be reviewed by a new state institution in Quito, with little knowledge of what it would do with this registry. Until then, the assumption of a certain degree of insularity among the Galápagos' provincial services had often permitted some leeway for farmers who are not permanent residents. As a result, undocumented farmers could participate in cooperatives and, to a varying degree, receive some forms of social welfare (social security, health care, and education) since the registry for immigration did not superimpose on the national ones of other public institutions. Aware of their uncertain status as temporary residents or undocumented on the Galápagos, farmers had counted on the disconnect across public institutions' practices to circumvent state requirements while still participating, albeit partially, in their programs. A new institution (IEPS) and a new superintendency (SEPS) raised concerns about the chances of maintaining the delicate balance between legality and informality, exposure and anonymity.

I attended the meeting when a farming association in Santa Cruz approved the new statute under IEPS's requirement. I knew all the members, as I had visited their farms and conversed with them individually for some months by then. The meeting was at a member's house on the outskirts of *El Cascajo* in the highlands. José, the association president and a taxi

98 *Chapter Three*

driver, picked me up in Puerto Ayora on our way to the highlands. We then stopped at the farms of other members, discussed the latest news, then slowly made our way to the meeting, many of us in the back of the president's pickup. The occasion was solemn: the rechristening of the association under the aegis of IEPS. After taking attendance and discussing the agenda, José proceeded to read aloud the new statute in its lengthy entirety.

> Currently operating in legal and proper form, [the association] adapts its bylaws, submitting its activity and operation to the Organic Law of the Popular and Solidarity Economy and the Popular and Solidarity Financial Sector, in compliance with the First Transitory Provision of the Organic Law of the Popular and Solidarity Economy and the Popular and Solidarity Financial Sector, and in accordance with the regulation issued for such purposes.

> *Actualmente funcionando en legal y debida forma, [la asociación] adecua su estatuto social, sometiendo su actividad y operación a la Ley Orgánica de la Economía Popular y Solidaria y del Sector Financiero Popular y Solidario, en cumplimiento de lo establecido en la Disposicion Transitoria Primera de la Ley Orgánica de la Economía Popular y Solidaria y del Sector Financiero Popular y Solidario, y de conformidad con la regulación dictada para el efecto.*

The contrast between the formality of the text and the circumstances where the meeting was taking place, as we sat outdoors on plastic chairs with children and chickens roaming among us, was striking. Struggling through more than ten pages of impervious legal language, José stood for a long time while the other members maintained a courteous but increasingly alienated silence. The bureaucratic stiffness of the language clashed with the practicalities of reading aloud or trying to follow along while listening in silence. The statute was composed of different sections; at the end of each section, members would look up at José, hoping he had finished. But soon after, the page turned, José's uncertain voice would rise again, and the gaze of the other members, along with their morale, would drop. Time and again José had to retrace his steps and reread the

Uncertain Vivir 99

beginning of a sentence because, once at the end of it, he realized he had misread. At last, he finished reading the statute, which the association, exhausted, approved.

Lucia and other temporary residents decided, however, not to sign. Doing so would have further exposed their unlawful participation in the cooperative. The stilted and verbose language of the new statute, painfully evident to everyone at the meeting, convinced them even more of their choice. Following ratification, these farmers continued to participate in the cooperative's meetings and activities, but not officially. A few months later, MAGAP launched a new initiative whereby they selected a farmer from each island to visit farms on the mainland and learn about best practices in agro-ecology. Although Lucia was one of the most skilled and committed farmers of her old cooperative, she could not go. Instead, another member, a permanent resident and the friend of a MAGAP agronomist, became the candidate from Santa Cruz. She owned land but did not farm—unlike Lucia. Instead, she worked in a vegetable shop in the city, selling mostly imported produce.

∾✕∾

Despite recognition of cooperatives' vital role, failure to comply with new forms of accreditation pushed many cooperatives on the continent to informality and even dissolution (Guerra et al. 2016; Peñafiel and López 2017). At once, the 2011 Ley Orgánica de Economía Popular y Solidaria y del Sector Financiero Popular y Solidario promoted the concept of co-operatives while making many of them de facto unlawful. While this was true at a national scale (Novo 2014; Martínez Novo 2018; P. Clark 2017) , restriction to citizenship on the Galápagos made it so that cooperatives, along with ERAs and all other tools of the island buen vivir, exacerbated, rather than resolved, the problems of informal labor on small farms and of semi-abandonment of large farms.

The Plan of Bio-agriculture presented to Correa expounded on the crucial role of agriculture in achieving societal and ecological well-being in the province. It clearly set a progressive political agenda for both politics and conservation in the highlands, with the goals of ensuring food sover-

100 *Chapter Three*

eignty and establishing ways of protecting the islands that involved locals. At the same time, the plan avoided long-standing issues of land ownership and insecurity among farm workers. These policies recruited, while in fact producing, a *nuevo ciudadano rural*, always enthusiastic about the revolution (agrarian and otherwise) unfolding in Ecuador and willing to do their part. But this process excluded the farmers that were most committed. The buen vivir policies not only missed them but further marginalized them.

INTERMEZZO II

∽∾

Cultivating Belonging

Marco talked to me as we looked at the crops in front of us, lined up in imperfect rows in the rocky terrain. We were standing on his farm in a remote corner of the low highlands of Santa Cruz. I had struck up a conversation with him the week before at the Saturday farmers' market in Puerto Ayora. He had laid out a few lines of produce on the sidewalk outside the indoor market, which was occupied by the large and colorful stands of more established sellers, many of them not farmers but vendors of imported produce. My questions convinced him of my genuine interest in farming, and he agreed to meet the following week. He described the lot's location, relying on a mix of natural and social landmarks ("Two kilometers after Don Navarrete's farm . . . to the right after the dense cane stand on your left") along the nameless roads of the uplands. The fact that I followed through on my promise, and that I found him, surprised him. "Why should I lie to you?" Marco said, fifteen minutes or so into our conversation. "I am undocumented [*soy ilegal*]. My wife is too." "We came here without documents," he continued, "but this small lot is ours—we bought it thanks to our pastor." He was referring to the practice of undocumented farmers buying farmland with the help of a permanent resident, the only category of residents who can own property on the islands. Marco's pastor, the minister of an evangelical church in town, did it for them. I had known this minister for years but never heard of his underground, illegal aid to—by their own definition—*los ilegales* (the undocumented).

Marco's lot was small, only one thousand square meters. The topsoil was thin, as the farm bordered the transitional plains that separate the higher, humid highlands from the dry coastal and littoral climatic zones. Marco and his wife, Helena, could not afford a greenhouse, although it

102 *Intermezzo II*

would have helped in that environment. They only grew vegetables in the open field (*a campo abierto*), which limits the types of vegetables they can grow but is cheaper. In fact, they barely had money for seeds, let alone the infrastructure for growing the plants. Instead of plastic frames, they used young *porotillo* trees (*Erythrina herbacea*, an introduced species of leguminous tree) to prop up their tomato plants. Residents had traditionally used *porotillo* as a natural fence for their farms, since cut branches grow into trees when planted. In their lot, instead, crops grew alongside the *porotillo*. "All plants help me," Marco told me, gesturing to vegetables, *porotillo*, and the fruit trees along the borders.

Toward the end of our chat, Marco excused himself to take a phone call: an agronomist on the mainland was returning his call. This is how Marco sought help when his plants were sick. Being undocumented, Marco and his wife could not ask the local office of the Ministry of Agriculture for assistance. Instead, he relayed the symptoms to a private agronomist, noting the sudden discoloration of the stem, the tardy maturation of the fruit, and the type of puncturing on the bottom leaves. On the other end of the line, one thousand kilometers to the east, the expert offered his paid advice.

As Marco stood in the semiarid land, intently speaking on the phone to an agronomist an ocean away, I took a picture of him against an odd landscape of tropical trees in the distance and tentatively cultivated denuded land up close. He had climbed to the top of a small mound, perhaps unconsciously to get better reception, his right arm gesturing as if to help him better describe the type of insect he had seen crawling under the leaves. Themselves illegal, illegally owning a minuscule lot at the margin of the marginalized area of the islands, the rural highlands, Marco and Helena had not given up. Quite the opposite: gathering help wherever they could find it, whether from an agronomist in mainland Guayaquil or through branches turned into agricultural infrastructure, Marco and Helena had found ways to farm. "This small piece of land [*esta tierrita*] is a blessing," he later reflected. He was not referring to the way he had acquired it—through a pastor—although I jokingly suggested that to him. We laughed, at last, after a difficult conversation. Rather, he was thinking

Intermezzo II 103

about the modicum of hope that their lot, against all odds, allowed him to cultivate. When he and his wife arrived there, with all the difficulties of farming on rocky soil and the constant threat of expulsion, Marco did not think they could make it.

But there they were, with no intention of leaving.

FOUR

Minor Thriving

Vicente had arrived before the 1998 immigration law and thus enjoyed legal residency on the islands. He owned a small lot in the highlands that served as a farm, with a carpentry workshop that supplemented the meager revenue from farming. His farm, however, looked perhaps more like his carpentry workshop than any other farm on the islands. He called the farm "my lab" (*mi laboratorio*), where he experimented with a method that was unique on the islands: hydroponic farming. He had first heard about this method during a church trip to Chile, then started to read and watch videos on the internet. Vicente used a minimal amount of soil mixed with the gravel available in his farm. The real nutrients for his plants consisted instead of a careful blend of mineral supplements that filled long halves of pvc pipes lined with plastic sheeting and mounted at a modest incline to collect drain water, all choreographed in a rigorous mess: a laboratory.

His crops (lettuce, kale, cilantro, parsley, and celery) were planted at regular but close intervals. This technique drastically reduced the water and soil needed for agriculture, which are the main physical limitations to growing food in the thin soil and rocky terrain of volcanic islands such as the Galápagos. The minerals he used (nitrogen, potassium, calcium, magnesium, and iron) in lieu of soil were too expensive on the islands. Instead, Vicente bought them on the continent. Because of the restrictions on importing agricultural products to the Galápagos, he smuggled them in plastic soda bottles tucked away in his luggage.

The yield was impressive, and Vicente was proudly aware that the credit was his alone. At every visit, Vicente would show me his latest experiments, playfully bragging about the results: the two hundred-gallon plastic storage bins he had gotten for free from a cruise ship owner, in which he had cut small holes on the sides, out of which thriving parsley plants shot out. Or the rows of lush eight-foot-high tomato plants, sitting on the ground in minuscule plastic bags filled with gravel and minerals.

Vicente had long been a regular attendee at the training sessions (*capacitaciones*) offered by the state agronomists. However, the agronomists always repeated conventional techniques: the ones they had learned at universities on the continent, which applied to land, climatic, and labor conditions on the continent. In recent years, however, a local MAGAP branch had seized on Vicente's success in innovative, environmentally friendly farming. After all, increasing production while saving water, soil, and labor had always been the agency's proclaimed goals. Since then, Vicente regularly figured in countless reports as an example of MAGAP's commitment (*compromiso*) to promoting agriculture. Though the agency had contributed nothing to his success, MAGAP's countless official visits to his farm tended to take a lot of his time—time he would rather spend with his plants.

Vicente's charisma and energy were perhaps unique, but many farmers possessed similar inventiveness in the face of social and ecological variables—both more in flux than ever. Over the span of a couple of decades, climate change had not only extended the dry season but also worsened the periodic yearlong droughts of the ENSO cycle, forcing farmers to seek alternative ways to help plants survive. Sometimes their resourcefulness manifested itself in generating new solutions to vexing problems. For example, during a severe drought that lasted seven months, a farmer cut wild plantain trees at the base of the trunks and placed them next to dying orange trees. Rich in minerals and water, these trunks helped her orange trees survive. Other times farmers' inventiveness spurred them to recover near-forgotten strategies from the past. When the pasture dried out during another harsh dry season, a farmer turned to his grandfather's solution: cutting and crushing banana leaves to feed cows deprived of pasture for a few months. Other times farmers repurposed farming techniques to suit new needs. For instance, scions of the *porotillo* tree, which grow without help if planted on the ground, had long been used to delimit farms. Now

FIGURE 5. MAGAP personnel taking pictures of Vicente's plants, Santa Cruz highlands, 2014.

farmers with exiguous capital, often undocumented as in the case of Helena and Marco, used them in their lots to prop up plants with heavy fruits, such as tomatoes and green calabash, as a cheaper alternative to wires and stakes.

All farmers faced archipelago-wide issues of costly seeds, fertilizer, and machinery, lack of public transportation, and a difficult soil and climate. Most of them struggled to sell their products as shops were inundated with imported produce sold at competitive prices because of the lower cost of labor, easier farming conditions, and greater production on the continent. Imported food fed the local community and tourists in cruise ships year round, as tourist agencies perceived it to be a more reliable source than local producers. These disadvantageous circumstances for local farmers were the result of longer processes of discursive and practical marginalization of agriculture on the Galápagos, which conservation had long considered a threat to the ecosystem and rarely a resource for conservation or a benefit to the islands as a whole. In addition, undocumented farmers needed

108 *Chapter Four*

to worry about police road checkpoints (*batidas*), prohibitions against buying land, and lack of access to state financial and technical support. Since well-paid jobs in the touristic coastal towns require proof of legal residency, a sizable portion of the mainland Ecuadorians who arrived after the 1998 immigration law without authorization live and work on farms in the highlands. There police presence is minimal, but so is economic opportunity. Under these conditions, farmers' illegality had far-reaching consequences for their economic, political, and civic life. Vulnerable to blackmail at the hands of private and state actors, their ability to invest in the future was limited.

However, through other means, undocumented farmers managed to acquire land, receive assistance, and sell their products. Undocumented farmers counted on limited political interest in agriculture, and thus limited state presence, to protect them in the highlands. While buen vivir and SES-inspired conservation policies did little to ameliorate their marginalization, these farmers found unexpected affordances within this political scheme, no matter how tenuous. Coming from a landscape of legality and continental ecologies, they learned to read a new environment and social conditions. Through persistent practice, undocumented farmers accrued a site-based, experiential knowledge of dynamic, complex ecosystems. In areas that ecologists describe as the most degraded ecosystems on the Galápagos, these farmers distinguished the species and natural elements that benefited them, their crops, and their farms from those that harmed them. Through experimentation and mutual help, such as that coming unexpectedly from people like Marco's pastor, undocumented farmers survived, endured, and to some extent even thrived.

Thriving here refers not only to their livelihood, but to incipient webs of life. Cultivated land curbs the spread of particularly aggressive invasive plants that have defeated eradication campaigns, such as hill raspberry (*Rubus niveus*), *sauco macho* (*Citharexylum gentry*), and guava (*Psidium guajava*) (Atkinson et al. 2012). Surrounded by invasive weeds and toiling on impoverished land, some farmers began to reactivate the soil and the connections among plants, crops, and animals. Admittedly, their participation in the landscape did not result in the radical improvement promised by conservation campaigns, aimed at fully reestablishing the ecosystems of native species, nor did it reflect the park's recent emphasis on ecosystem services or MAGAP's emphasis on agricultural productivity. These farmers instead enacted alternative modes of being on the islands in contrast to the dominant paradigm of tourism and conservation. Reclaiming scattered dots in a landscape that old settlers had abandoned and invasive species transformed, undocumented farmers cultivated ecological conditions to sustain themselves, other species, and their environment over time. While carving out alternative futures, these farmers also uncovered marginalized, past forms of living on the islands. Although the economic fulcrum had long moved away from the highlands, farmers kept alive landowners' affective attachments to the highlands when, for the first century and a half of the islands' colonization, agriculture almost exclusively guaranteed settlers' survival. To be sure, some of the characteristics I describe below also apply to small farmers with residency permits. They too weaved together social and ecological strands to form viable ecologies. However, undocumented farmers best illustrate the mutual imbrication between socio-ecological vulnerability and efforts to keep the highlands viable.

THE CONCEPT OF MINOR THRIVING

The concept of *minor thriving* seeks to analyze the unresolved tensions between the constraints of undocumented farmers' status and the vitality that, with endurance and empirical learning sustained through multispecies alliances, they nonetheless possess. I take inspiration from Gilles Deleuze and Félix Guattari's conceptualization of "the minor," a mode of writing that proliferates in spite and at the margins of the dominant canon (Deleuze and Guattari 2004; Deleuze 1986). Drawing on feminist science and technology studies, the minor helps us attune to forms of collaboration while acknowledging ongoing processes of marginalization and degradation (Tsing 2015; Lyons 2018). Here, "the minor" accounts for farmers' tenacity and unruly generativity under conditions of undesirability.

In their analysis of language, Deleuze and Guattari identified two independent modes of its articulation: the major, which proclaims and enforces rules, and the minor (Deleuze 1986). The second mode (*puissance*) lacks power (*pouvoir*) but produces itself in constant variations that threaten to unmake the major rule. While the major affirms constants, the minor breeds "generalized chromatism" (Deleuze and Guattari 1987, 97). Deleuze and Guattari's analysis, although a theory of signs, holds relevance for understanding the uneven distribution of power and agency in society writ large. In the Galápagos, conservation and tourism have been the *major* articulation of politics—producing the Galápagos as an exclusive site of tourism and science. This convergence of scientific and touristic imaginaries has sustained a politics of nature shaping the understanding of, as well as access to, society and nature over the past sixty years (Ospina 2006; Bocci 2019; Quiroga 2009). The minor, Deleuze and Guattari contend, is not what the major excludes but what populates the margins. What form of thriving could this mode afford? In language, the minor presents itself in a form of transgression and simplification ("a shedding of rules") coupled with a "strange proliferation" (Deleuze and Guattari 2004, 104).

Farmers' minor thriving articulates an alternative to the dominant politics of conservation and tourism on the islands. This politics is predicated on forms of separation of people (residents, tourists, and scientists) from the islands. Instead, farmers' ecology furthers entanglements that, far from being a singular event, require constant attention and, to borrow Whyte's (2023) term, coordination. The nexus of conservation and tourism professes a logic of scarcity; farmers envision one of possible abundance. Off the grid of legality and yet difficult to get rid of, undocumented farmers constitute a form of unwantedness and thus, for the logic of the major, a strange proliferation. Uncovering marginalized actors' minor thriving moves our analysis past recognition of their subordination to dominant forms of the economy and political time. Deleuze and Guattari recognized that the power of the minor rests in its ubiquity and proliferation. "It is obvious that 'man' [the major rule] . . . is less numerous than mosquitoes, children, women, blacks, peasants, homosexuals, etc." (Deleuze and Guattari 1987, 105). Discursively and practically marginalized, they possess a collective, cumulative force: "The minority is the becoming of everybody"

(Deleuze and Guattari 1987, 105). While Deleuze and Guattari emphasize its potential to be otherwise in the future, I treat the minor as a lens for the present unfolding of new socio-natures.

Rather than an exception in either space or time, the politics of nature on the Galápagos draws on a long history of colonial use of nature and aligns with contemporary technoscientific, market-based approaches to conservation worldwide (Collard, Dempsey, and Sundberg 2015; Turnhout et al. 2012). Globally, these approaches have done little to dislodge the epistemic, classist, and colonial thrusts underpinning conservation (Hughes 2010; Mulligan 2002; Jacoby 2014). What lies outside this powerful paradigm — invasive species, undocumented farmers, and unwanted heterogeneous knots between them and protected nature — might sow the seeds not of a better variation of the paradigm but of a new one. Or, in Deleuze and Guattari's words, a strange proliferation and endless variation that saturate and exceed the normalized discourse and practices. Disrupting dominant logics as well as material arrangements, forms of minor thriving help us appreciate recuperative forms of making contested landscapes viable not as a potentiality but in the present.

RESILIENCE, RESISTANCE, AND THRIVING

Minor thriving invites us to move past rigid frameworks of peasant resilience (in ecology) and resistance (in social sciences) to reflect on practices and sensibilities that produce, however tentatively, alternative life worlds. While seldom in dialogue, the analytics of resilience and resistance have informed scholarly debates of socio-ecological change in rural settings and beyond. Arguing for systemic characteristics such as novelty, surprise, and complexity, resilience has challenged equilibrium-based theories in ecology and anthropology. Resilience — the ability to absorb disturbance — now occupies an important place not just in conservation but also in resource management, finance, security, and climate change response (Walker and Cooper 2011; González, Montes, and Rodríguez 2008; Berkes, Folke, and Colding 2000; Cons 2018). Yet, counter to claims of flexibility, resilience

112 Chapter Four

has continued a dualistic understanding of human and nature, whereby humans can only respond to a crisis or, in the best case, better prepare for the next one. Couched in the government's rhetoric of buen vivir and the Citizens' Revolution, the understanding of the Galápagos as a resilient socio-ecological system prevents recognition of how undocumented farms could adapt to, let alone value and recover, disturbed ecosystems (González, Montes, and Rodríguez 2008).

A crucial concept in critical agrarian studies and political economy, resistance has informed the scholarly understanding of "politics from below" that has contested old and new forms of land tenure and use (Borras and Franco 2013). Confronting contemporary forms of economic and conservation enclosure, today resistance no longer depicts peasants as always passive and united, but reveals how they create counternarratives and participate in dominant economic forms (Hall et al. 2015). Yet the ability to generate alternative ways of life, whether or not they are legible politically, often remains unexplored. The focus on resistance over generativity aligns with the contemporary understanding of social marginalization more broadly, which often points to a condition of indefinite stasis (Baldwin and Allison 2015; O'Neill 2017). At the margins, individual and collective agency is reduced to endurance: that which "maintains the otherwise that stares back at us without being able to speak" (Povinelli 2011; see also Alexandrakis 2016). In these analyses, the configuration of alternative economics, identity, and landscape is alive only in potential. Instead, the farmers' tenacity not only constitutes a mode of resistance or resilience but also enables forms of world-making.

This chapter focuses on a form of temporality that I call the *dense present*, which enables farmers to thrive despite their exclusion from economic and affective investments in the future. I thus challenge a linear model of political time, not only for its forward orientation but also for its singularity. Renewed attention to present, unscheduled assemblages, I argue, complicates linear narratives of conservation's technological fixes to the planetary ecological unraveling.

ECOLOGICAL HISTORY

"Those who own cruise ships made the law" (*los que tienen los barcos hicieron la ley*), Rosa, a farmer, uttered under her breath as she shook her head in resignation. We were talking about the 1998 immigration law for the Galápagos Islands (LOREG). Demagogic by neither character nor possibility—she is undocumented on the island—Rosa meant it literally: powerful cruise ship owners had leveraged their connections to draft a law suited to their interests. This law was the result of years of debate both on the islands and in the national government over the rise of tourism and its effects on the local population in the archipelago. In 1997, the Galápagos provincial government instituted roundtables (*mesas participativas*) to discuss and propose new policies regarding a variety of topics, including fishing, agriculture, tourism, and residency. Despite its veneer of horizontality and equal access, influential local figures often chaired the groups (Heylings and Felipe 1998). The results reflected this skewed representation. Confronted with an unbridled increase in tourism and immigration, the proposals focused only on immigration, while tourism remained unregulated, as it remains today. As the flux of tourists continued to rise, so did the number of mainland Ecuadorians who moved to the islands to escape unemployment and poverty. Some became legal residents, others not.

Undocumented immigration became a contested issue soon after the promulgation of the Law. In local public discourse, the topic crystallized around young Indigenous males from the Ecuadorian Andes or the Amazon who work in construction in the islands' sprawling coastal towns. They were the most visible group of undocumented workers, the one most talked about and in fact assumed to be the whole. However, they did not constitute the entire population of undocumented on the islands. Among the estimated four thousand *ilegales*, there was a visible and an invisible part (INEC 2017b). Undocumented farmers constituted the invisible part: unable to find work in the coastal towns, they served as day laborers on large farms and ranches in the vast, scarcely populated highlands.[1] Like Rosa and her husband, they often resided on the farms where they worked. Contrary to the image of undocumented who had just arrived, with no

114 *Chapter Four*

roots and little understanding of the islands' fragile ecosystems, some had been there for decades.

LOREG affirmed political and economic interests that reproduced the image of the Galápagos as an (almost) people-free tourist destination and scientific laboratory, itself the result of a layered socio-natural history of the islands (Bocci 2019; Hennessy 2018). This political and geographical arrangement, which the imagery of the Galápagos as a laboratory has motivated and sustained, establishes the norm in contrast to which farmers, and even more so the undocumented, appear an aberration. However, the supposedly uninhabited islands have attracted more tourists every year, thus driving immigration (Epler 2007; Grenier 2007). As a result of the progressive shift from agriculture to tourism, and from the uplands to the coastal towns, farm abandonment has rapidly accelerated the propagation of invasive plants. Infesting hill raspberry (*Rubus niveus*), *sauco macho* (*Citharexylum gentry*), and guava (*Psidium guajava*) have covered large swaths of the uplands, both in the farm and the park areas. Although they were hired to clear cropland and pastures of invasive plants, undocumented farmers were perceived as similar to invasive species. In the eyes of the public, saturated by conservation discourse, invasive species and undocumented farmers alike threatened the Galápagos. Attempts to resolve the issue of undocumented farmers were caught in a crossfire. On the one hand, the local government was wary of taking extreme measures such as mass expulsion that threatened to alienate the rest of the population, which often relied on undocumented workers. On the other, environmental organizations showed little interest in challenging anti-immigration rhetoric, as much as they avoided discussing tourism as one of the main threats to the islands.

While the politics was at a standstill, novel assemblages of unwanted presences such as undocumented farmers, crops, and other introduced and native species began to form in the highlands. These formations have been pressing at the edges, geographical as much as conceptual, of conservation. Through the biographies of three pairs of farmers and their farms, I analyze below distinct aspects of both motivations and practices of viable modes of living on the islands, showing that farmers' participation in the highlands not only contests conservation but also offers resources for rethinking it.

GROWING TOGETHER

I first met Juan at the Saturday market in town through another farmer who vouched for my good intentions. After the introduction by our mutual friend, Juan knew that, although I expressed interest in his life on the islands, I was not there to report him to Migración and seek his expulsion. Shy but polite, he gave me his phone number, and we agreed to meet the following week. A few days later, I walked a good mile to find his place, after my taxi driver refused to continue the search in the maze of nameless dirt roads in the low-central highlands of Santa Cruz. At last, Juan alerted me of his presence with a quick, unobtrusive whistle, which I registered only seconds after it had receded among the sounds of birds and wind. He met me on the road after standing up from his spot next to a stone wall. We walked back to his farm but sat just outside, on unused asbestos pipes by the dirt road. He lived alone in a small shack made of odd wood boards and leftovers from construction work, with several metal sheets as a roof. His house's tight quarters were perhaps the reason we were balancing on broken, toxic pipes outside.

Juan raised a few pigs and some chickens and had short rows of vegetables amid the otherwise dry vegetation on his three hectares of flat, rocky terrain. We were courteous, but our interaction was awkward at first. During the silences we looked up at his house, of whose modesty he was perhaps not openly embarrassed but also not proud. He was undocumented, he finally told me, abandoning his reticence. Juan had lived on Santa Cruz for over ten years. The owner of the farm, ironically also named Juan, had never shown any interest in legalizing him. For Juan the owner, the time and money involved in completing a petition for temporary residency for his worker made this option unappealing, especially since the negative consequences of not legalizing his worker were not his to face.

Juan thus owned and did not own the farm. The Juan I spoke with lived

116 *Chapter Four*

on the farm but did not own it, and vice versa for Juan the landowner. This confusion — a coincidence of name and divergence of destiny — was symptomatic of the hidden role of some of the key actors in the highlands. The Juan who officially owned the farm, as a matter of fact, did not even live on the island, let alone in the highlands. From time to time (*de vez en cuando*), Juan would fly to the Galápagos to check on the farm, Juan the worker told me, raising the pitch of his voice as his right hand drew backward circular motions, both to remark the rareness of the event. The real business for Juan the owner was downtown, where he owned a restaurant. Otherwise, most of the time he lived in Quito. As a permanent resident of the Galápagos Islands, he could move on and off the islands as he pleased. For him and the many other well-to-do residents of the Galápagos, their permanent resident status seemed inversely proportional to their actual permanency on the islands. The permanent card, in other words, mainly served as a passport to get in and out of the islands, not a document to stay. The Juan I met, by contrast, had lived for years in the impermanent shack made of multicolored, patched-together construction materials.

Over the previous three years, police had caught Juan twice. He had received the two notifications that the authorities sometimes issue to undocumented residents before, on the third arrest, deporting the person. Juan had already played his only two cards, as it were. "I'm done" (*Ya estoy hecho*), he told me tersely, gazing down at his shoes. After the second notification, Juan kept an even lower profile, with shorter and fewer visits to the city. And yet he continued to work every day on the farm, determined to stay and tend to his plants. He had to adjust his everyday activities to avoid further exposure: for example, he sold his pigs directly to the few restaurants in the highlands but not to butchers in Puerto Ayora. Also, he still went to the Saturday town market (*feria*) every week, although with only a few boxes of produce, which allowed for a quick retreat in case of police raids. These adjustments did not, however, diminish his motivation to live on the islands and farm. "Being done" in fact gave him a sense of calm defiance that heightened, rather than lessened, his pride in being a farmer. "I am not afraid anymore, I have no fear," he said in matter-of-factly. "I go down [to Puerto Ayora] to feed the people [*dar a comer a la gente*]. If

FIGURE 6. Juan's house, Santa Cruz highlands, 2013.

the police stop me again [on my way to the market], I will show them what I have: broccoli, carrots, herbs [*hiervita*], tomatoes.... These are to serve my community! I'm here to serve them [*para servir a la gente*]. I have an honest job [*un trabajo honesto*]. I work every single day. My plants and I are here to feed the people."

Aside from his modest farming and pig raising, he worked on large estates whenever they needed help planting new banana trees, clearing invasive plants from pastures, or harvesting tomatoes. For transportation, he flagged collective taxis that passed by, since they were more discrete than using a motorbike. More often, Juan simply walked, sometimes for hours. "I like it," he told me at the end of our talk, as we walked to Bellavista. "I check on other farms, the animals, the pasture, the trees.... The landscape is beautiful. There will always be a need for people like me to keep it alive [*con vida*] and clean [*limpio*], so that it doesn't undo [*deshacer*] itself."

Months later, I met with Juan the owner at his restaurant in town. He was pleased to hear about my interest in agriculture. For him as for many

118 *Chapter Four*

other residents, his farm represented a past he was not ready to relinquish. His parents had moved to the Galápagos in the 1960s. At that time, the only tourism consisted of a few millionaires circling the islands on their private yachts, with marginal impact on locals' livelihood. His parents bought eighty hectares of land, where they planted large swaths of pasture for cows and short rows of *camote* (sweet potatoes), yucca, and corn for personal consumption. Thirty years later, the family moved to Puerto Ayora, where, he told me, bursting out with laughter at the thought of it, clean clothes could finally dry in the coastal climate, and his parents could stay more updated on new personal and home products from the mainland (*las novidades continentales*).

To buy a restaurant, Juan the owner later sold a large portion of the farm but not all of it. For multigenerational settler families like his, farms are a repository of the time when the highlands were the center of family and social life. The long treks on foot and, when possible, by horse down to the Puerto Ayora for trade or perhaps leisure were rare, always requiring long preparation and generating endless discussions afterward. Although the majority of residents had moved to the islands' coastal towns, their transition was incomplete. These residents imagined their farms as sites of a future business: a hotel, a rental house, or maybe a restaurant. Islanders' investments in tangible assets, especially hotels and apartments, were ubiquitous. Many houses had no roof; instead they were topped by the unfinished floor of a hoped-for second floor that would make their house bigger and their social status higher. In the coastal towns, construction iron bars, which locals call "the beams of hope" (*las vigas de la esperanza*), sprouted invariably from the last floor of almost every house. These curved, denuded bars dotted the urban landscape by the hundreds, like the antennae of animals sensing the constant flow of tourist money pouring into the islands. Sometimes these landowners justified an economic investment in their family farm because of their affective attachment; other times they hid their attachment under the more impersonal goal of making an economic investment.

Either way, farmworkers, often undocumented, kept these farms alive and made landowners' dreams of going back to the upland still possible.

Like Juan the farmer, most farmworkers were confronted with the impossibility of becoming permanent residents as they progressively strengthened their ties to the islands. At the same time, these farmers sustained landowners' unresolved relationships with their land, bridging their remembered past and aspirational future engagements with the highlands. Thus the temporality of illegal farmers and landowners is complementary: the landowners split between past and future, the farmers concentrated in the present and its interstitial affordances. Like other undocumented workers, Juan found ways to adjust to the ambiguities and restrictions of his status. The changes in his lifestyle since his last arrest had offered him more time to appreciate his life on the Galápagos. As we continued walking, we talked more and more freely.

> Before the Galápagos I was in the Oriente [the Ecuadorian Amazon]. Land was cheap, but it was too violent. I like it here instead. Since I moved here I mind my business and have a honest job [*un trabajo honorable*]. There is always work to do: [harvesting] coffee, tomatoes, clearing invasive plants. . . . [As an undocumented immigrant] I need to be careful but I am accustomed to that. I have been here for almost fifteen years. I am a Galapagueño more than anything else . . . and have been for longer than many other people! Farm animals and plants help me. . . . We do everything together. I want to continue to stay here, I've learned how.

SUBTERRANEAN LEARNING: HOW TO GROW HEALTHY FOOD IN HEALTHY SOIL, IN THE SHADOWS

Julio came to Santa Cruz less than a year after the 1998 immigration law was passed. A landowner, Don Patricio, informally hired Julio to clear four hectares of forest and plant *Cedrela odorata*, an introduced tree with beautiful wood used for furniture. Julio's wife, Rosa, and their son quickly joined him. They had lived on the Galápagos ever since. Together, they looked after Don Patricio's cattle and a small banana orchard. The owner's economic interest in these activities was limited. In the dry season, which

120 *Chapter Four*

begins in January and ends in May, Julio had to remind him multiple times to request a MAGAP water tank for his animals. As for the fruit (bananas, avocados, and guava) that Julio and Rosa harvested for him, some weeks Don Patricio did not even pick it up. He lived in Puerto Ayora and owned a successful hotel and restaurant. His thirty-hectare farm was his share of a larger farm owned by his parents. They had arrived on the islands in the 1960s and successfully grew coffee and raised cattle. But when tourism took over in the 1990s, their children moved to Puerto Ayora.

In recent decades, Don Patricio's farm had played a marginal role in his life and that of his children. His latest idea of harvesting timber failed: the *Cedrela* trees thrived, but competition among farmers kept prices low. *Cedrela* is invasive, after all: it grows and multiplies without human assistance, making it common on the island. Since he abandoned the plan, a dense forest of cedar trees had grown, all of the same height. Don Patricio was not doing anything with it — or, truthfully, with anything on the farm. He just wanted to keep the farm alive because it had belonged to his parents. He paid Julio and Rosa a small salary and provided some staples (rice, meat, legumes, and vegetable oil). Some years he agreed to sponsor Julio's temporary residency and that of his family. Other times, he evaded their requests until the year has passed.

Julio complemented his meager salary by growing vegetables and working on other farms, where he got the idea of setting up a greenhouse for his vegetables. On the Galápagos, greenhouses allow continuous production of short-cycle crops such as tomatoes, cucumbers, and peppers, which are among the most requested produce at the market. Julio thought that a small greenhouse could boost their production of vegetables, which were growing in the open field. When, years earlier, Julio and Rosa had begun to farm and sell their vegetables at the market, Don Patricio did not mind, nor did he ask for a percentage of the profits. But he saw building a greenhouse as a different affair altogether. Julio proposed that Don Patricio pay for the greenhouse and, in exchange, receive a percentage of the profits. Don Patricio rejected the plan. Why go through so much trouble if his hotel and restaurant were doing well? They were free, Don Patricio told Julio and Rosa, to do whatever they wanted, just not with his money.

Yet the materials alone—the tubes, wires, and plastic sheeting—cost several thousand dollars, to which they would have had to add assembly costs. By then, Julio and Rosa had three children, and the fixed salary they received for maintaining the farm was barely sufficient to cover their expenses. And they were, depending on the year, temporary residents or undocumented. Either way, they held no certainty whatsoever that they would still be on the island the next year, or even the next week. Why invest in a farm they did not own if the very variable that would permit them to reap the benefits, *time*, was so uncertain? The landowner did not invest because he did not care; Julio and Rosa could not invest even though they did care.

Their solution was a form of minor thriving: a small investment with limited yet measurable results. Despite the lack of support, dearth of means, and uncertain time frame, Julio and Rosa decided to build the greenhouse. Instead of light, sturdy, but expensive steel bars, they used large dried logs from the trees strewn around the farm. Instead of the roof's full arch motif that repeats exactly every couple of meters, Julio used an intricate assemblage of PVC pipes covered by plastic sheets, flat and overlapping. During storms, rainwater leaked down the logs into large buckets that Julio and Rosa used to collect water for the plants. Messy, but it worked. New to this type of cultivation, they had to learn about soil and pest management in greenhouses by trial and error. Despite bugs, constant repairs, and a lack of state assistance, Julio and Rosa regularly sold fruits and vegetables from the greenhouse. An infinite string of ad hoc measures kept the greenhouse structure from undoing itself and their production from halting. Minor but thriving.

Their thriving pertained also to the type of agriculture they practiced. Working on other farms, Julio had often applied synthetic pesticides and herbicides, which, he had concluded, caused him intense stomach aches, joint pain, and severe fatigue, once severe enough to keep him in bed for several weeks. Since his illness, Julio and Rosa decided to utilize natural pesticides and uproot weeds by hand. After repeated attempts, they determined that a combination of garlic and jalapeno peppers, fermented in vinegar for over a week, worked well as a pesticide on all their plants, in the

122   *Chapter Four*

greenhouse or the open air. Their viable ecology, however, ran deeper—literally—than applying natural pesticides; it related to the health of the soil too. Rosa and Julio had long struggled with tomato plants: high humidity most of the year is conducive to parasites. Natural pesticides, they discovered, helped only partially. And although their son, studying in Colombia, had learned about permaculture techniques for soil recovery, Julio and Rosa could not afford any of the equipment their son recommended. Instead, they activated a burnt log by immersing it in urine for a day to improve air circulation and retention of water and nutrients. An old gasoline tank became the home for thousands of worms, which Rosa fed chopped coconut leaves mixed with good soil and a sprinkling of chicken manure. Other tanks were just filled with soil and left for weeks under the sun, so that it would be free of parasites before planting.

Julio was especially enthusiastic about the results of composting: plants were healthier and could fend off parasites more effectively. "They [the plants] are like human beings: if you are healthy [i.e., strong] you never get sick. . . . The same happened to me: since I've stopped with the chemicals [in the garden] I don't get sick anymore. . . . Eating well has made us both stronger!" Years later, the local high school asked Julio for a sample of his compost for a national competition aimed at promoting organic farming. Julio's compost, he related with pride, won first prize! There was no money associated with the award nor did he receive much recognition, aside from the respect he elicits every time he tells the story. The jury notified the students on the Galápagos, and they notified Julio, but no journalist interviewed him. Small enough not to threaten his anonymity as an illegal, yet sizable enough to make him proud, this indirect recognition encouraged him to continue to grow organically.

Because of their need for anonymity, Julio and Rosa did not promote their products as organic at the local market. Although they grew organic for their own health, they knew that it would add value and increase their profits if clients knew. Julio and Rosa could simply write it on a small banner in front of their stand, as I naively proposed at first, but they responded that customers would not care. Their answer, as I saw over time in similar cases, deflected attention from them to something else, in this case, their

FIGURE 7. Rosa at the farmers' market, Puerto Ayora, 2018.

customers. That locals would not be interested in paying more for an organic product was a partial truth but certainly not the reason Julio and Rosa did not put up a banner publicizing their organic products. Rather, Julio and Rosa did not want to draw attention to their stand—and jealousy from other farmers. The real reason—the calculus of exposure—was expressed in the form of their answer, negative and elusive, rather than its content. Being undocumented, they aimed to blend into the crowd rather than stand out: the opposite of any marketing strategy. Their thriving had to be kept in a minor key.

THE RURAL HIGHLANDS NEED US!

Ernesto came to the Galápagos in 2000, a few years after his brother Jorge. Because he arrived after the promulgation of the immigration law, he could

124 *Chapter Four*

not become a permanent resident, unlike Jorge. Both brothers worked on a cattle ranch — one legally, the other not. I first met Ernesto at a meeting of a farmers' cooperative, of which he was a proud member. Not being a permanent resident, he could not officially participate, but he was in fact among the founding members of the association. Both brothers joined the nascent farmers' cooperative to receive state incentives for agriculture, in a time of bombastic government rhetoric about a post-neoliberal, collective economy (Acosta 2015; Guzmán and Poma 2013). But Ernesto was also worried about his tenuous legal status and hoped that joining the cooperative would provide paperwork attesting to his ties to the islands. As the promises never materialized, he became less optimistic about any help the association could offer on his illegal status. However, his passion for his job, the animals, and the land continued — and perhaps even increased.

At 6:00 a.m. every day, the brothers would go to the ranch, where for the rest of the day they cleaned the stables, fed the cows, and milked them. An important task was to keep the pasture lush and free of invasive grasses and plants. As was common in both the protected and rural areas of the highlands, clearing was done by machete and manual uprooting. Although taxing, this proved the best method to get rid of invasive plants while leaving grass intact. Also, with a machete, farmers could reach plants in irregular terrain. Using a machete (*dar de machete*) demands strength and stamina but also precision. Properly used, the machete often hits rocks below the soil with a swing ample enough to cut the plant but controlled enough not to break the *hilo*, the blade's sharp edge. The sound of machetes on rocks produces a distinct pastoral soundscape. It did not bother them, they told me, and it did not bother me either: it was a sign of work well done. Both brothers shared a passion for their work, but for Ernesto farming demonstrated his commitment to the Galápagos. With me, his brother Jorge mainly lamented the state's neglect of the rural highlands. But for Ernesto, being a farmer constituted his chance to live a respectable life despite his undocumented status. Surprisingly, he was more positive about their work than his brother was. "I like my job," Ernesto told me one evening. We were talking outside his house before dusk, after the workday had ended.

Minor Thriving 125

We know about plants [*nosotros sabemos de las plantas*]. You need to take care of the pasture, otherwise it withers. . . . When the hill raspberry grows dense in thickets it's too late, you know, cows can't go through, not even us Christians [humans]! Only the pigs, with their heads pointing to the ground, can go there. The *sauco* also kills cows. She [the cow] looks weaker and weaker for a couple of days and then can't even stand up. She dies after moaning for hours. . . . It's horrible. If you don't care for [*si no cuidas*] the land or abandon it . . . everything falls apart [*todo se descuida*]. Other plants are good, but you have to know them. The *musgo* on the guava trees [an epithetic fern on the branches] helps the soil stay humid. . . . There are good and bad plants. You need to know, it's not that everything is the same. You need to know how to do things [*Hay que saber las cosas*].

We sat on plastic chairs on their porch as the evening began to fall and mosquitos encircled us. We watched the quick, vertical equatorial sunset through the tangle of thorny vines on the property in front of us, which had grown tall after the neighbor cleared the land.

That man [the owner of the neighboring property] lives *abajo* [down], in Puerto Ayora. He is legal [permanent resident]. . . . He has a restaurant and a house there but also owns twenty hectares of terrain here that he leaves fallow. Years ago he cleared one hectare right here in front of us—he wanted to build a house. He cut everything, *lechoso, matazarno, mayagua, palo santo, caco.*[2] But at the end he didn't build anything, he ran out of money, or he didn't care anymore. There were beautiful *mayagua* trees, how old must they have been? Even if he did build the house, he could have spared the rarest and most valuable trees. People say they are Gualapaguenos, but in truth they don't care about nature.

From the bush in front sprang young *guayabillo* and *maracuya* trees; earlier I had recognized the latter from their flowers with delicate white petals and bright yellow and mauve pistils. The park listed both species as invasive: they outcompete slow-growing endemic trees such as the *matazarno* and *caco*, whose conspicuous absence was on display before our eyes. "There used to be tens of *matazarno* right in front of us.... They are all gone," Ernesto continued. "Instead, [in my property] I only cut the dead trees and used them for my house!"

Earlier his wife, Belgica, had showed me the small plot of land behind the house, where watermelon and pineapple plants spread across the dry soil, and some tomato plants were tied with string to frames of dry bamboo sticks. Because of the little rain and too many rocks, these were the only crops Ernesto and Belgica could grow. They lived in the western part of Santa Cruz's low highlands, where land is flat but rocky and precipitation scarce. Due to poor soil, farming was limited and land cheap. It was the only type of land they could afford to buy. They wished they could buy more land and have a proper farm but could not, because they were not permanent residents. Meanwhile, the owner of the land next to theirs left it fallow. As I listened to Ernesto and Belgica, their situation grew as clear in my eyes as sitting there became intolerable for my body. Well past dusk, we were surrounded by hundreds of mosquitoes, their buzzing barely audible but their bites clearly felt. However, my interlocutors seemed unconcerned, finally enjoying the cool air and immersing themselves in the rich texture of the evening's sounds.

At last, the night closed in on us. There were no neighbors nearby nor lights in the distance. "We like living in the highlands," Ernesto and Belgica explained, calmly but continuously waving their hands around their necks, foreheads, arms, legs, and feet to shoo away mosquitoes. "We are not cut out for the city." I jotted down these words, my right wrist pressed against the notebook on my leg as my pen scribbled, while my left arm blindly attempted to disturb the mosquitoes before they could bite. "We wouldn't be able to live crammed together [in the coastal towns], away from the farmland. And here [the rural highlands], too, what would happen here? After all, you need to take care of the land [*hay que cuidar la tierra*]. If not, look what happens!" His chin lifted imperceptibly, pointing at the darkness that enveloped the abandoned land in front of us. "If peasants like us don't work the land, who does?"

Helena and Marco, Juan, Julio and Rosa, and Ernesto and Belgica articulate overlapping forms of minor thriving. Helena and Marco cultivated not only crops but also introduced plants such as *porotillo* as allies that allowed them to farm. Juan's commitment to feed residents infused his work with purpose, which rendered his solitude and fear of deportation bearable. Julio and Rosa's pesticide-free agriculture benefited the land, themselves, and unknowingly, their customers. Ernesto's work gave rise to a vernacular moral ecology, which mapped constellations of plants to care for and others to find and uproot. Their minor thriving resides in their ability to make calculations about their livelihood against the odds and to foster connections amid limiting and shifting conditions—with all the uncertainty these involve.

Uncertainties about their future had not prevented them from cultivating, literally and otherwise, ties to the Galápagos. On the contrary, their marginality had heightened their purpose: to sell healthy food, care for the land, and provide for the local population. Their commitment was not to a resilient ecosystem—in its distinct specification of what subjects ought to participate in and for what goals—but rather to a viable highlands. Similarly, the insistence on rural exclusion and, consequently, resistance, which draws on a long and rarely questioned tradition in peasant studies (Sherwood, Arce, and Paredes 2018), misses the opportunities that farmers not only seize but create.

There were, of course, clear limitations to the yield of their present actions and the likelihood of their future hopes becoming reality. Rather than anticipate a dramatic rupture in the present, undocumented farmers lived in its fissures. Resolution toward a more stable condition—legal or economic—was constantly deferred. Instead, putting aside long-term planning and investments, undocumented farmers devised ways to procure a livelihood that, although neither incremental nor certain, was enduring. In the face of these limitations, they exemplified generative persistence. Their exclusion from the future tense, by not being able to access loans or invest in farming equipment or plants with delayed yield, did not lead to an impasse. Rather, they fostered tentative ecologies but viable ones nonetheless, which mixed endemic with introduced species, the work of microorganisms with that of improvised infrastructures. This socio-ecological system of sorts, much less neat but also richer than the interactions in a socio-ecological system framework, multiplied what was available to farmers in the present. Such webs heightened, dilated, and expanded a parceled present that is reproducible but not cumulative. Making connections across species becomes a technology to augment an uncertain resource: time.

In the face of coupled social and environmental unraveling, scholars have suggested slowing down as a tactic for gathering new intellectual resources and political allies. For others, this tactic runs the risk of implicitly putting off into the future the possibility of political change, while committing to slowing the pace of reactive forces (Sodikoff 2012; Ripple et al. 2017). Here, instead, the forward linear temporality assumed in both instances refracts in the simultaneous, entangled life cycles of organisms. Rather than relying on a hopeful anticipatory future (Mankekar and Gupta 2017) or orienting their actions toward it (Graeter 2017; Lyons 2016), undocumented farmers widen what is available to them in the present. Rather than a line, the tempo of illegal farming enlarges into an area: the dense knotting and juxtaposition of other species' traces, life cycles, and effects on each other. Farmers' cultivated time was never a line but an ecology.

FIVE

~∞~

Native Farming

Heading to the outskirts of the sprawling town of Puerto Ayora to a denuded area soon to become a new neighborhood, Celia was, in fact, going to work. "I'm going to farm" (*Voy al campo*), she had told me, half laughing, minutes earlier, after we had discussed her coming of age in a farming Kichwa community on the continent. She had referred to her current work as farming in a musing way, although it contained a grain of truth: she was, after all, going to harvest plants. The municipality of Puerto Ayora had recently swapped land with the bordering national park, ceding rocky coastal terrains in exchange for an area north of the city's current limit. Her goal was to save endemic plants from inevitable death when the digging of foundations, the erection of houses, the installation of electric and water grids, and the paving of roads commenced. Later, she would use those plants to create endemic gardens outside hotels or public offices.

I accompanied Celia on the back of a motorcycle that she drove confidently along the new dirt roads, finding almost a rhythm in her repeated swerves to anticipate bumps and avoid potholes. The landscape looked desolate. Large lots had been cleared, and piles of earth had accumulated at the intersections of gravel roads. In the process, construction workers had leveled much of the vegetation, including rare plant species. The same fate awaited the remaining vegetation. Although depressing, for Celia it was not surprising. She had lived on the Galápagos Islands for three decades and had witnessed the dramatic increase in urbanization and its ecological effects compounding over time. In the late 1980s, the Galápagos began to attract more tourists and, in turn, mainland Ecuadorians seeking work. Celia and her family were among those migrants. The expansion of Puerto Ayora, which we had just left, was a prominent sign of the growth in tourism and the human population. With traffic and construction noise roaring in the background, the city looked like a sea whose edge was swelling, preparing to propel forward another wave of construction in the future neighborhood north of the bay, where we were standing.

There, according to the municipal plan, nature would turn into city. Yet the inexorable reclamation of the territory from spiny bushes, arid terrain, and solitary trees to allow an imbroglio of streets and buildings would take place gradually. Despite plans for massive construction, with multistory houses and incredibly narrow streets similar to the previous new neighborhood of La Cascada, we could see only the most superficial outline of future interventions. Dirt roads met at squared intersections; orange-tipped posts tentatively delimited future lots and properties. Though not yet human-dominated, the bulldozed land and cleared vegetation of the area was not the humanless landscape of the Galápagos National Park's lowlands either. Before our eyes, the new neighborhood of El Mirador presented itself as a strange interregnum: a new, ever-expanding membrane between the city and the larger geography of the bay and the rising hills behind it, mostly protected areas belonging to the park. In addition, it provided a transition between two temporal domains: from a peopleless past to its human-inhabited future. That day, however, did not belong to either. Celia was taking advantage of the time lag between the design of the new neighborhood and its implementation to offer preemptive remediation to a sample of the endemic plants that would be obliterated. We walked undisturbed among rocks and plants, in the fleeting moment before their irreversible reconfiguration.

In line with the park's goals, Celia worked to keep alive plant species that had preceded human arrival on the islands, many of which are unique to the archipelago. Unlike official conservation, however, this motivation did not lead to restoration, at least not as conceived by the park. With her new business, Celia collected native plants, protected in the park from residents and mercilessly bulldozed in the human areas, and brought them inside the city, installing them on streets, in houses' gardens, or in front yards of public and private buildings. The idea of repurposing native plants in urban settings was original and entirely Celia's. I had first met her at the Galápagos National Park's headquarters months earlier, as she prepared

Native Farming 131

to justify once again the lawfulness of her business. The native plants that she rescued, grew, and eventually sold, she told me then, came from urban areas and thus fell outside the park's jurisdiction. However, whether vested with legal authority or not, park representatives—and some influential members of the local community—repeatedly objected to her business and even tried to shut it down several times.

While resisting bureaucratic and political hostility, the challenges of her work were also of a more practical nature, as she uprooted spiny plants from hardened, dry soil. Like her business plan, the method of harvesting such plants had to be original. On that day, juvenile endemic cacti (*Opuntia galapageia*) were few and far between. She and her assistant Luisa carved a little circle around the plant, carefully avoiding severing its roots. Then, using small squares of cardboard, Celia and Luisa slowly pulled each small cactus to uproot it and place it in one of the boxes hanging on the sides of their motorcycles. To test my confidence as I prepared to help, Celia suggested with a sardonic smile that, once past the initial discomfort, the cacti's spines would stop hurting me and even start talking to me. Luisa, perhaps not new to the joke, simply glanced at her punctured and seemingly permanently swollen hands and began to work.

For Celia, finding cacti triggered many joys: of being able to later install them in her gardens and of having found them alive in a time of rapid ecological change, after the spread of invasive species and before the new wave of urbanization. The cacti we found were survivors of present and past, and of human and nonhuman ecological deterioration. For Celia, however, the joy of salvaging endangered plants had, above all, a religious significance. In a syncretic blend of Kichwa and Christian (Jehovah's Witnesses) beliefs, Celia believed that the coming paradise would establish multispecies abundance on earth. The promise of terrestrial restoration by divine intervention animated Celia to "plant the seeds" of that plentiful future. While Celia registered environmental degradation as a sign of the impending end of the world, her work was a form of, in her words, "acting toward" the terrestrial restoration that would be realized in the coming paradise. As she stood and dusted off her pants, she looked at the small cactus she had just uprooted and was carefully holding like an unfledged

132 *Chapter Five*

bird. Sotto voce, her breath blending with the wind, Celia muttered, "We already know that, by doing this, we head to paradise."

With her charisma and hope, Celia had convinced other Jehovah's Witnesses to do similar work. They gave Celia endangered plants found in pasture on their farms or joined her in her shop after work, as I did that day. Celia's commitment was contagious, and it touched my thinking too, leading me to reflect on the role of religious environmentalism extending beyond Celia and the Galápagos. The secular world has long dismissed religious preoccupation with the end of the world as an issue of marginal significance (Waddell 2014). Today, however, the current planetary ecological crisis has renewed similar millenarian sentiments (Masco 2016). What would it mean for activists, anthropologists, ecologists, and religious scholars to take seriously Celia's future-oriented action in thinking about this crisis? Although not reflecting official Jehovah's Witnesses doctrine or the stance of most of the congregants on the archipelago, the religiosity of Celia and her friends evokes this question.

THE ANTHROPOCENE BLUE

As the scope and the urgency of the current environmental crisis increase, hope is rare in environmentalism — on the Galápagos or elsewhere. To be sure, pessimism has accompanied scientific modeling of our planet's future since its inception in the 1970s, and it later defined crisis disciplines such as conservation biology, invasion ecology, and recently, attribution science (Lockwood, Hoopes, and Marchetti 2013; Meadows 1972; Soulé 1985; Stott et al. 2016). Today, growing evidence in climatology, geology, biology, and archeology suggests that humans have ushered earth into a new era, the Anthropocene, the first to be defined by the human footprint (Ceballos et al. 2015; Head 2014; Waters et al. 2016). Interpretations of its beginning vary widely as they relate to different markers of anthropogenic alteration, spanning from the human mastery of fire four hundred thousand years ago to the Holocene ten thousand years ago, to the spike of CO_2 concentration during the Industrial Revolution or the explosion of nuclear bombs in Hiroshima and Nagasaki at the end of the Second World War. Contrary to the uncertainty about the Anthropocene's inception, the dramatic J-shaped spike in resource extraction and anthropogenic environmental degradation over the last fifty years—what scholars call the Great Acceleration—has caused widespread trepidation about the future of the earth and humanity (Steffen et al. 2015).

Calls for establishing a form of human planetary stewardship to redress this catastrophic course have made a forceful appearance among natural scientists (Richardson et al. 2023; Steffen, Crutzen, and McNeill 2007). While it gained wide popularity, the Anthropocene debate has also promoted generalized blame of the human species that has obscured, rather than illuminated, the individual responsibility, to different degrees and intentionality, of financial and oil corporations, the ultrarich, and the world's affluent societies (Rammelt et al. 2023; Otto et al. 2019; Dembicki 2022; Malm 2016). This framework has also engendered equally vague calls for "meeting the challenge" and leveraging human ingenuity and technological progress, again deflecting attention from the culprits of planetary unraveling. Stuck in a rarified abstraction of humanity, invocations of hope for the future often appear to stem more from desperation than conviction. Such invocations are currently ubiquitous in nearly all speeches on the current global environmental crisis, as presenters pivot from the current crisis and its predicted worsening to what looks like a groundless leap of faith ("We can still change the course *if...*"). On the Galápagos, the messages of NGOs and scientists to the public trace a similar narrative arc ("There is still time to save the Galápagos *if...*").

Some conservation biologists, too, have remarked on the need for hope in their discipline to combat "apathy, inaction, and despair" (Hobbs 2013; Swaisgood and Sheppard 2011; Robbins and Moore 2013; Webb 2005). Discussions of the dangers of "conservation despair" map onto well-established critiques that millenarian denominations, well before the advent of the Anthropocene, have produced resignation and indifference toward the present (Johns 2016; Maier 2010). In his analysis of the Jehovah's Witnesses, sociologist Andrew Holden contends that "the belief in the imminence of the end of time as we know it prevents [the Jehovah's Witnesses] from making advanced plans for the future" (Holden 2002, 98).

134 Chapter Five

FIGURE 8. Painting outside the Galápagos National Park office, Puerto Ayora, 2013.

Thus, pessimism about the present state of affairs precludes believers from either fully participating in the present or planning for a secular, near-term future, maintaining instead their focus on the post-apocalyptic domain. "The Witnesses," continues Holden, "are prevented by their own doctrine from romanticizing the past and the present, but they do romanticize the future" (36). However, for Jehovah's Witnesses such as Celia, the end of time in fact blends into the vision of a restored future that calls for action, participation, and responsibility in the present. To her, revelation signifies not an end in absolute terms but a threshold that marks the end of time as a finite domain. These "romanticized" visions of the future inform today's awareness of, and actions within, a changing environment.

Celia suggests a type of incipient environmental care that questions the pervasive scholarly understanding that today's environmental crisis justifies, or even engenders, cynicism about the fate of the earth. Through Celia's story, I contend that, on the Galápagos, local Jehovah's Witnesses' religiosity has inspired a vibrant form of environmentalism that responds to ecological unraveling rather than eschewing it. Specifically, this vision of the ultimate future informs action rather than despair. In contrast to the Anthropocene's generalized blame and desperate optimism, this chapter investigates the possibilities for giving substance to hope. Some voices in Christian feminism and eco-theology have expressed interest in reclaiming eschatology, the theological doctrine about the ultimate end, for its imaginative valence. Yet, unlike invocations for hope with little consideration for their viability, my ethnographic approach contributes a view of the practical reverberations of eschatology. If Christian theology has long drawn on the end of the world to cast dark futures, and if feminist and eco-theology have argued instead for eschatological hope (for nonetheless unspecified future scenarios), I show eschatology for its present affordances and capacities.

While discussions about reconciling eschatology and environmentalism continue, there is often a tendency, sometimes even deliberate strategy, to couch this conversation in anthropocentric terms by centering nature's worth around human values and needs. In contrast, the long temporality and earth-centric vision of Celia's religious environmentalism affirms a decidedly biocentric sensibility—the longing for and action toward a restored earth, where humans are but one participant. Further, to recognize nonsecular, non-Western actors means to argue for a redistribution of agency—also over who produces theology—between the First World and the Global South, thus recalibrating the decidedly Western understanding of the Anthropocene. Reasons for this move are both practical and theoretical. There is growing evidence that the most vulnerable suffer the most from climate change and will continue to do so as the environmental crisis escalates. In the Anthropocene's optics, concerns about a dystopian ecological future are increasingly pervasive and justified. And yet, such concerns have often reinforced conservation approaches based on expert-driven knowledge that excludes the involvement of local populations (Crist 2013). Excluding residents and alternative interpretations of the ecological crisis informed by their religious views deprives conservation of a potent ally. Additionally, if scholars rely on the concept of the Anthropocene to ultimately dismantle the human-nature divide (Chakrabarty 2016), part of this project must also challenge the sacred-secular dichotomy, which confines

136   *Chapter Five*

the sacred to the subaltern pole (Bubandt 2018). If, as many have noted, the crisis of the Anthropocene is narrative (Rossing 2017, 328; see also Ghosh 2016), then we need resources and stories to address it.

In the Galápagos, the ecological care that local Jehovah's Witnesses have enacted offers an alternative to the conservationists' approach to ecological degradation. To be sure, Celia's story does not reflect the Jehovah's Witnesses' official doctrine nor the sensibility of all members of her denomination on the islands, let alone globally. However, it speaks to a form of environmentalism present among Jehovah's Witnesses because of their religious convictions. By presenting subjects that, practically and intellectually, are usually absent from the discourse of the Anthropocene, this chapter demonstrates that responses to ecological crises do not lead univocally to apolitical, large-scale scientific models of a worrisome future and increased reliance on technological solutions. Instead, some Jehovah's Witnesses are responding to ecological change with actions that are gendered, collective, and committed to the well-being of other species; these actions renew, rather than relinquish, ethical commitments and practical responses vis-à-vis troubled ecological times.

MULTIPLE EXCLUSIONS

Celia's care for endemic plants diverged significantly from the official conservation approach to these species, although she had certainly not planned for that outcome. Years before, she had joined the Charles Darwin Foundation to work on an educational project about endemic plants. The project, Siémbrame en Tu Jardín, produced an engaging booklet that helped readers recognize native plants and discover their potential uses in a garden. While instructive, targeting individual residents' actions and not, for example, the municipality for its disregard of native plants in the city was a source of frustration for Celia. The project's neglect of ecologies outside the park spoke to an unnecessarily narrow approach to conservation. A decade earlier, the city had relocated its compost facility away from the arid climate of the city to the more humid transitional zone of the low highlands. "Why locate such a facility in the only climatic zone of the archipelago where invasive seeds could germinate?" she asked me. Although she was grateful for the formal training and field experience on local flora that she had received at the foundation, she aspired to effect change rather than just, in her own words, "lecture everyone on everything" while leaving policies intact and letting consequences worsen.

Life conditions in the city, not just in Celia's eyes, had long been on a downward trend. Puerto Ayora had become more and more crowded, its population growing at an average 8 percent a year over the previous two decades and with little room to expand. By then, Santa Cruz, which had long been the most populated island, hosted over 60 percent of the archipelago's population. While 88 percent of the island belongs to the park, the city only covers a fraction (4 square kilometers) of the remaining, mostly rural land (115 square kilometers). Aside from issues of poor housing, mobility, and sanitation, residents' ability to experience a semblance of the Galápagos as tourists know them was almost nonexistent. There was no simple access to the sea, for starters. The Charles Darwin Foundation and the Galápagos National Park headquarters, private hotels, the port, an Ecuadorian navy base, and a bank lined the bay, separating the city from the sea. Furthermore, although locals have long proposed a scenic walkway (*paseo*) along the coast from the southern tip of the bay to a public beach several miles from the city, this proposal had been repeatedly denied. As I was told in 2008, and it still holds true today, it is cheaper for residents to fly to the continent than see their archipelago on a cruise—the only means to visit it. Frustration, like population, had long been on the rise.

Of this *encierre*—enclosure of residents in a crammed city with limited access to its surroundings (Grenier 2007)—Celia lamented the resulting lack of connection with local nature. In the CDF project Siémbrame en Tu Jardín, Celia learned the names and characteristics of many native plants, especially those of the littoral and arid zones. But at the end of the project, she found herself dissatisfied with its conservation approach, which left little room for involvement of locals beyond planting their own gardens—for the few who had a garden. Learning about plants gave her an appreciation of the local ecosystems and motivation to respond directly to their profound changes, especially the ones unfolding before

138 *Chapter Five*

her eyes. She quit and started a business creating endemic gardens. Private owners and government building managers who requested her services wanted to show their support for the park's goal of protecting the islands' fragile ecosystems, although Celia's approach did not quite align with the park's conservation policies. "The truth is," she told me once with a smile expressing genuine happiness but also a hint of defiance, "I am happy to finally see the [native] plants among us [residents], and not just tourists."

I visited Celia regularly during my years on the Galápagos. I would usually find her watering her plants in the midafternoon at the Charles Darwin Foundation headquarters. The CDF had initially let her use a small plot for her plants even after she quit her job there. One day, however, at a time when she was challenging the park's refusal to grant her a business permit, she was told she had to leave. I later joined her on several trips to El Mirador and her new shop, sharing her concern about the progressive development of the neighborhood but also her satisfaction in rescuing more plants. In the same months, the park implemented the new overarching SES framework for conservation, with its emphasis on interactions between populated and protected areas. Moving away from focusing only on the protected areas made sense to her because, if anything, the increasing number of tourists and residents on the islands, producing an inevitable mounting pressure on the local ecosystems, was hard to ignore. Yet the traditional separation of human and natural domains continued; in fact, it consolidated even more. Swapping land between the municipality and the park, while serving a practical purpose of giving the city almost 40 percent more space to grow, also more neatly separated the town from the park. Bulldozing native plants in the urban area combined with the little support for, if not open hostility toward, the one person who was trying to salvage them were other important signs of the limitations of this "integrated" conservation approach.

Celia was among the many urban residents with whom I regularly spoke who felt that local conservation leaders not only limited their access to nature but also showed little interest in listening to their ideas and contributions to the well-being of the islands. Specifically, SES conservation included residents in a twofold manner: with campaigns educating them about how to care for the Galápagos and with studies on their impact on the islands. The interactions that SES formalizes—and that schematics in the SES literature never failed to represent—seemed to restrict connections between residents and valued nature rather than fostering such connections. These residents reclaimed their environmental agency, whether against an uncertain future due to residency and access to the land or a worsening one because of exclusionary conservation, urban sprawl, and—as Celia showed me that day—invasive species.

SENSES OF PLACE

"Look at this plant," she said that day in El Mirador. Talkative and outgoing, Celia was teaching me about shrubs and flowers, native and invasive, that we encountered in the semiarid terrain. I quickly learned that the causes of ecological degradation went beyond urbanization. While we walked, Celia showed me plant species that had come from the mainland and spread without human help, some suffocating endemic species. Because of the largely arid climate and biogeographical isolation, the Galápagos' tally of land species—what ecologists call biodiversity richness—is drastically lower than in lush continental ecosystems such as the Amazon. Yet these and other features have allowed for the unfolding of distinct evolutionary lines on the archipelago. What is remarkable about the Galápagos' biodiversity, then, is its uniqueness rather than its abundance. In this context of distilled ecological scarcity, each species counts. And conversely, the threat of extinction to each species also matters a great deal.

With increased flows of people and food between the islands and the outside, Celia had noticed the dramatic consequences of invasive species to the local ecosystems (Atkinson et al. 2012; Graham and Cruz 2007). Celia identified each plant species by noting the color of a flower, running her finger over the serrated indentation of a leaf, or pointing to the pattern of encroachment of a new invasive bush. Little by little, the site would reconfigure itself into a complex herbarium of plants, some in danger and others taking over. With patience, she invited me into an understanding of the composite plant assemblages that came alive through all senses: the

140　*Chapter Five*

hues of flowers, the olfactory quality of pistils, the rustle of wind through thickets and bushes, the dust rising from newly exposed soil that tickled our throats. As we examined plants and, through them, the profound changes on the islands, joys and worries were suspended in focused moments of synesthetic encounter.

"Look at this plant," she told me, as she cupped a crown of small white flowers surrounding bright yellow pistils. From the Verbenaceae family, *Lantana camara* is an ornamental species; it is also, due to its extraordinary adaptability to a wide range of altitudes, sunlight exposure, and soil conditions, a weed. The first experiment ever attempted at deploying an insect to eradicate a weed (called biological control) took place at the turn of the twentieth century and targeted *Lantana camara* (Zalucki, Day, and Playford 2007). Yet that attempt, as well as those that ensued, failed. *Lantana camara* has continued to expand across tropical and subtropical regions in the Americas, reaching the Galápagos in 1986 (Rentería B. and Ellison 2004). As we stood at the edge of a lot, Celia pointed to horizontal stems of *Lantana* already moving into an area newly cleared of vegetation.

Lantana camara seeds had taken advantage of urbanization to establish new sites in the archipelago and, from there, move to even more sites. While a consequence of human pressure on the Galápagos' ecosystems, invasive species such as *Lantana* also amplify anthropogenic change: they reduce the abundance of endemic plants and adversely affect the nesting habits of endangered avian species endemic to the Galápagos, such as the dark-rumped petrel (Rentería B. and Ellison 2004). In El Mirador, the newly denuded terrain was accelerating the propagation of *Lantana*. But with or without the help of urbanization, *Lantana*'s expansion was impossible to stop. Celia saw this as a sign of the accelerating degeneration of the human and natural fabric of the earth — or, as her religion helped her understand it, the end of the world.

Celia had become a Jehovah's Witness a few years earlier. She had certainly not planned it, nor did she think such religion had anything to offer her as an Indigenous woman from the Andes living on the Galápagos Islands. One day, however, a couple of Jehovah's Witnesses knocked at her door, not for the first time to be sure, and greeted her with an intriguing question: "Do you know there is hope in the Bible?" Celia had cared little about any religious doctrine, but she had started to be bothered by the environmental worsening of the islands. "Perhaps because it is so small here [compared to the Ecuadorian Andes]," she confided to me once, "but each year there is something new." She was certainly aware of the more frequent crises the islands were facing, whether the recurrent threats of tsunamis or oil spills, or the worsening of the ENSO cycle. But in response to their question that day, she began to imagine ways to meet with hope the incremental but inexorable changes in the vegetation that she had noticed on her island.

Although fully aware that she could not reverse the course of events, she had since then busied herself collecting imperiled endemic plants for the time *after* the end of the world. This idea of terrestrial restoration resonated with her, she once reflected, because of her upbringing in a Kichwa community, which left her with an underlying belief in nature's abundance. Beyond the ongoing crises, Celia believed that the earth had resources capable of sustaining it despite the current visible injustices. Origin stories took center stage in her Kichwa religiosity, much like the story of Genesis in a Christian denomination like the Jehovah's Witnesses. Kichwa oral narratives about the *kallari uras* (beginning times) often described a primordial imbalance and a consequent tear in the tightly woven abiotic and biotic (including human) fabric (Reddekop 2022). To mend these fractures, she had learned, humans must develop skills that she would describe to me as deep—cross-species—listening or feeling. Unlike the clear hierarchy of beings articulated by the Jehovah's Witnesses, her Kichwa traditions offered her an understanding of nature as involving a plethora of beings of equal worth, divided by different languages and purposes (Kohn 2013). Despite the noticeable differences in doctrine, Celia accepted the Christian mandate to assume the responsibility of nature stewardship, while she saw the Kichwa injunction to strive to understand other species as the means of being a good steward.

Celia rarely articulated these beliefs to others, but her resulting certainty and optimism proved contagious, as other women from the Jehovah's Witnesses community decided to lend her a hand when they could, not just out of friendship but also as a spiritual practice. "There are only so many times you can knock at the same people," Celia told me once laughing, in reference to the Jehovah's Witnesses' periodic visits in the community but also to deflect attention. "It is time to pay some visits to plants now," she added. By uprooting cacti, Celia and her friends were determined to give these endemic plants a second chance in a new, perhaps permanent, home elsewhere: "When the paradise comes, these plants will be already there." Her vision of a terrestrial paradise colored her hopeful anticipation of the future and governed her actions in the present. As much as she could, she salvaged plants that the advent of paradise would glorify through its ecological restitution. Though not paralyzed by ecological decline, Celia was not waiting for the ultimate restoration either. "You need to work toward paradise," she told me once with conviction as we walked across a field behind the last houses of the city. The future had to be built—or planted, I thought, as she paused. As if she had read my thought, she smiled and reflected, "I'm planting the seeds of the future" (*Estoy sembrando las semillas del futuro*).

The future she intimated and, eyes gazing intently beyond the horizon, invited me to see, was the one after Judgment Day. Then, for the Jehovah's Witnesses, there would be neither hell nor a celestial paradise but rather a restored earth.[1] Until then, Celia and her fellow Witnesses expect a worsening of human and natural conditions. Continuing to walk and look for cacti, she admonished, "Jehovah will destroy those who destroy the earth; you know this [*ya sabes*]." She was referencing to a passage in Revelation (11:18, KJV) that we had read days before at her house: "And the nations were angry, and thy wrath is come, and . . . that thou shouldest give reward unto thy servants the prophets . . . and shouldest destroy them which destroy the earth."

Religious scholars have often interpreted millenarian beliefs such as the Jehovah's Witnesses' as leading to disinterest in the mundane aspects of life. Crucial in this widespread interpretation of Christian millenarian eschatology is its marked pessimism (Johns 2016). In the case of Jehovah's Witnesses like Celia, however, their reading of current human and natural affairs, although negative, did not lead to pessimism; rather, it confirmed

FIGURE 9. Celia's endemic harvest, Puerto Ayora, 2013.

that their religious understanding was correct. Further, the conventional theory misses the crucial role of the belief in a terrestrial paradise as a catalyst for present intervention. Not simply deflecting pessimism, Celia and other Jehovah's Witnesses cultivated modes of religious ecological hope. As she continued working, Celia went on with our conversation: "Remember Psalms 37, that we will inherit the earth forever.[2] "Everything will return back to its original place, humans and animals," she continued. "And the introduced species?" I asked. She replied calmly, "Everything will return to its natural state, as Isaiah says."[3]

FUTURE IN ACTION

A more positive and earth-centered vision of the future is not the exclusive prerogative of the Jehovah's Witnesses on the Galápagos. Christian feminist and eco-theologians have articulated eschatological interpretations aimed to "correct [the] tendency to discount this life on Earth in favor of an afterlife" (Keller 2007, 13; see also Mercer 2017). Seeking concrete responses to urgent issues such as gender, Indigenous, and nature's rights abuses, these theological currents have refused a reading of the end of time as damning or as justifying detachment. Barbara Rossing notably expands on the usual translation of *eschathos* ("end") to signify "brink" or "edge" and asserts that the Anthropocene constitutes an instantiation of *eschatos*, or edge, for humanity and the earth. With this premise, Rossing (2017, 328) resists what she calls "escapist eschatological thinking," which focuses only on the afterlife. Instead, she argues that eschatology matters because it "gives people a sense of hope for the future." Similarly, Joyce Mercer (2017, 288) reflects on the etymology of witnessing (*martyria*) as "both accompaniment and acknowledgment," a practice that "can produce the possibility of change," 288). Lastly, Catherine Keller (2015, 11) aims to reclaim eschatological hope from the strictures of "a nature-transcending and patriarchal God" and insists on the not-yet-known possibilities that arise from relating with others, which she calls "apophatic entanglement" (Keller 2014, 7; see also Bauman 2015).

Yet this longing for the future, optimistic though it may be, is often confined to the realm of possibility and can thus lead to a sense of detachment from the present. For Celia, rather, the promise of a restored earth in the future reverberates back to the present. Theological proposals for an optimistic eschatology often fall short of articulating the possibility for action in the here and now; instead, the future for Celia operates as responsibility as well as a template for action. Feminist theology reclaims experience as a theologically relevant way to challenge intellectualist approaches that absolve religiosity from taking responsibility in the present (Mercer 2017; Radford 2017; Jenkins 2013; Ruether 1996). Here I let ethnographic sensibility inform my understanding of Celia's practice as a form of world- and faith-making: she participates in the urban landscape as well as in the Jehovah's Witnesses theology.

For Celia, endemicity was an argument for inclusion, not education. And environmental realism was a reason to practice (optimism), not to stall (and be pessimistic). Without dismissing the native/invasive divide, Celia situated it within the context of what is achievable and beneficial to a heterogeneous, multispecies community. Conservation excluded not just land or people, but also resources valuable to its very mission, such as local forms of environmental knowledge, attunements, and purposes. These forms emerged outside the practices and spaces of tourism and scientific research, both offering little to no opportunity for involvement of residents. Celia's search for viable ecologies—through arrangements among species that are mutually beneficial rather than destructive, extractive, and non-reciprocal—was experimental but also tangible, in the present. With her business, Celia valued those plants beyond their worth in the Galápagos' tourist economy. Plants were a crucial aspect not only of future abundance and restoration but of today's possibility for integrated coexistence on the islands. In Celia's vision and practice, rescuing and cultivating endemic plants allowed for people's emplacement: the experience and coproduction of a complex site. This renewed, different sense of place in turn created conservation practices different from the official ones. Viable ecologies are only possible with the support of voices and actions outside official conservation.

∾∞∾

Back at her shop, we carefully removed the cacti and placed them in small plastic bags with fresh soil. We then arranged them among other endemic plants that Celia and Luisa had previously collected: *Scalesia affinis*, *Lecocarpus de Darwin*, and *Lantana peduncularis*. For both of us, the thoughts that our discussion about paradise had incited still lingered. "Sometimes," she finally said, breaking that full, absorbed silence, "I think about Santa Cruz, how it will be then [during the terrestrial paradise]. I imagine rivers flowing, the vegetation abundant and lush, the mangroves covering all the shores." Over the last three decades, her city, Puerto Ayora, had used up all the sand and gravel along the bay. The small beach and the mangroves had vanished as a result. Instead, the shoreline was covered with hotels and restaurants. While occluding the vista, those buildings clearly indicated something else: to Celia and other Jehovah's Witnesses, they confirmed the entwinement of human and ecological degradation. With the terrestrial paradise, the mangroves and the rich habitats they sustain would return and flourish again—I had no difficulty understanding that. Her mention of rivers flowing, however, was more puzzling to me. Santa Cruz does not have permanent streams or creeks, so how could there be rivers flowing? Celia later explained her vision: over time, the rainwater would build reservoirs in the uplands and stream downhill. Assumed in the detail of river formation was the notion that, much like the water carving new courses, time would continue to flow as paradise announced itself by establishing a terrestrial restoration. The possibility of the end of secular time is in fact a critical edge (Rossing 2017), which invites response rather than despair.

Conclusion

Vicente rolled out a long sheet of paper on a long workbench on his farm after brushing dirt off the surface with the back of his hand. The excitement of sharing his project with me had finally surpassed his coyness. On the paper, a series of hand-drawn nested squares took up most of the space, leaving a brown area at the center. Each square, he explained to me with precision, represented a raised garden bed at a specific height, with each inner bed slightly lower, so that it could collect the water from the outward one. The brown area in the middle would serve as a reversed stage: although at the center, visitors would converge there and admire the spectacle of the agricultural infrastructures surrounding them. His plan, in fact, was to show residents of the Galápagos Islands methods of cultivating food that harnessed the few climatic and geographical advantages of the islands and worked around the many limitations.

To counter soil and water shortage, Vicente enlisted hydroponic farming. To avoid fungal diseases during the long, wet summer months, Vicente planned for greenhouses. Against the droughts of the other season, he envisioned a capacious water reservoir nearby. Vicente also included a poultry farm, whose manure would become organic fertilizer for the crops. Given the high air humidity for most of the year, a vast area of lush pasture next to the entrance would feed cows. The drawing also detailed a parking area for cars as well as bicycles, a roofed area for visitors to put on rubber boots, and wheelchair-accessible trails all around the farm. At the top of the map sat his future house (where I would always be his honored guest, he assured me), next to small residence for volunteers and workers. Beyond the individual farming techniques that he planned to share with volunteers and visitors alike, Vicente aimed for all residents to learn, or rediscover, a way to live in a place long understood as a touristic or scientific

148 *Conclusion*

site. Vicente had found a landowner interested in selling a suitable area in the higher area of the uplands, and he insisted on taking me there one day. They talked about this transaction periodically, though both knew that at present Vicente could not afford it, regardless of the outcome of their negotiation. Still, Vincente continued to refine and revisit his project, as he prepared to ask the city for help with financing. Although that too, even by his own admission, seemed very unlikely.

While ambitious for him and all the other parties involved, Vicente's plan was minuscule in comparison to the massive conservation pledges and projects that the Galápagos has attracted, some of which I have described in this book. As late as in 2021, Re:wild, a new environmental organization created by Leonardo DiCaprio, pledged $43 million to support efforts by the Galápagos National Park and Island Conservation to save endangered endemic species on the Galápagos, such as the pink iguana and the Floreana mockingbird (Murphy 2022). These projects not only mobilize considerable sums of money, but they also require strong political support at the local, national, and international levels.

These famed conservation projects, while valuable, often focus on more of the same: enlarging a protected area or attempting to save a species. However, they rarely confront the underlying causes that have endangered these areas or species. The claims of defending nature are loud and bombastic, their likelihood of changing the economic systems that profit from, while irreversibly damaging, nature, nearly nonexistent. In fact, as in the case of the latest bold initiative by the Ecuadorian government and Credit Suisse to enact a debt swap for conservation on the Galápagos, goals and areas of intervention are identical to those in past initiatives: "Achieving effective management, upgrading fisheries, promoting sustainable tourism, and fostering the 'blue' economy," with no mention of local agriculture (Villamil 2023).

It is unsurprising that, in 2021, the newly elected right-wing president Guillermo Lasso, supported by banks and big industry, also espoused this type of conservation. During the first year of the Lasso presidency, Ecuador increased protected areas to 62,000 hectares from 18,000 in 2020. With funds from Norway ($34 million), Ecuador launched a few projects

Conclusion 149

to combat illegal deforestation. It fought animal trafficking and even performed 2,897 wild animal rescues (Ministerio Ambiente 2022). Ecuador was also among the countries that organized the Marine Litter and Plastic Pollution Conference in Geneva.

Perhaps the most spectacular national proclamation came in November 2021, at the UN Climate Change Conference of the Parties (COP26) in Glasgow. There, President Lasso announced Ecuador's decision to finally pay heed to young people's demand that world leaders, in his own words, "stop talking about climate change, and move to decisive action" (*dejar de hablar de cambio climático, y dar paso a la acción de forma decidida*). How? With much solemnity and poise, President Lasso announced an executive decree that would add "nothing less" than 60,000 square kilometers to the 133,000 square kilometers of the Galápagos Marine Reserve (El Universo 2021). In so doing, the Galápagos will serve "as the living laboratory to develop more scientific investigations that so much contribute to the world's progress" (*come laboratorio viviente para el desarollo de las investigaciones científicas que tanto contribuyen al progreso del mundo*).[1]

In a climate change conference where the largest delegation was the fossil fuel industry, Lasso said little about how his decision to expand agribusiness, especially palm oil; to double oil extraction; and to increase mining by 74 percent in one year fit into his pledge to "move to decisive action" against climate change (Global Witness 2021). Eschewing any political consideration, he relied instead on the nearly undisputed conflation of scientific research with conservation, which assumes that more research is needed to realize conservation goals, and hence what is missing to solve local or global issues such as climate change is data.[2]

A little over a month later, the assassination of Víctor Joel Guaillas Gutama, a farmer organizing to block the Rio Blanco mining project south of Cuenca, ended a year of violent state repression of environmental activism (Astrid 2021). Lasso used the Galápagos as a place where focused intervention and extraordinary care could serve as a counterbalance to and a distraction from his politics on the mainland. The Galápagos, again, as an exception: a laboratory that can safeguard the nature that worsens and degrades anywhere but within its protected walls.

150 *Conclusion*

FIGURE 10. "Let's hope they won't find oil in Galápagos." This graffiti appeared in late August 2013, soon after President Correa abandoned the Yasuní ITT initiative and allowed for oil drilling in the protected area, Puerto Ayora.

Viable Ecologies has unveiled efforts, such as Vicente's, to resist this paradigm and build instead a thriving territory. These efforts took place at a time of profound rethinking by the state about conservation, the economy, and the well-being of citizens in Ecuador. Although progressive and at times revolutionary, state plans became mired in ecological, technical, and ethical difficulties. More importantly, as residents listened to new state promises and offered suggestions and more ways to engage, these policies revealed their limit in challenging well-established practices and ways of thinking—as the latest conservation promises illustrate. Conservation frameworks such as the socio-ecological system (SES), officially adopted by the park, and the novel ecosystem model, put forward by some Charles Darwin Foundation ecologists, proposed a systematic interpretative framework for interactions between the protected and human areas, the so-called feedback loops. However, they failed to dislodge the focus on certain forms of anthropogenic change, mostly farmers or poor residents, while ignor-

Conclusion 151

ing the damage wrought by unchecked tourism and even conservation. Similarly, government promises to achieve the harmonious well-being of socio-natural communities articulated plans for an agricultural revolution and collective, solidarity-based forms of participation. But they did little to address crucial determinants for their own success, such as access to land, legal status, and a dearth of state incentives supporting local agriculture. By partially engaging with or leveraging the unintended effects of these state plans, farmers experimented with alternative ways to make a living and care for the highlands. Poor and often undocumented farmers who cultivated small lots relied less on chemical additives and were more productive than large farms. The latter were often left fallow—and thus filled with invasive plants—since their owners were busy in the much more lucrative tourism industry. Unable to benefit from, or unsatisfied with, state agronomists' assistance, small farmers created new alliances and configurations with crops, farm animals, and native and introduced species. In contrast to tourism's practices of quick visits, high consumption, and a focus on the spectacular, farmers established ties with the islands that are reciprocal and long term, based on perhaps mundane but continuous observation. These farmers, I argue, not only contribute to food security and the well-being of the highlands, as buen vivir and other progressive state policies tried to capture, but also offer an alternative mode of living on the islands in contrast to the dominant one, based on tourism and exclusionary conservation. Perhaps minuscule or, as in the case of Vicente's plan, even impractical, these residents' efforts create unexpected spaces of proximity between locals and endemic species, draw on a more expansive pool of motivations for conservation, and convey the need for a different paradigm of human coexistence with a biodiverse nature.

This focus on an alternative environmentalism enjoys good company. It builds on the robust theorization of communities and territories in the Americas and on recent elaborations of such varied knowledges in the social and natural science and beyond, some by members of such communities (Moola and Roth 2019; Diver et al. 2019; Lele et al. 2013; Whyte 2017; Walsh 2022; Liboiron 2021b). This work rightfully insists on the continuous harm that land occupation, resource control, and epistemic oppression

152 *Conclusion*

causes to Indigenous peoples and territories, as well as the impossibility of a commitment to conservation devoid of efforts to decolonize it (Ferdinand 2021; Mulligan 2002; Ybarra 2018; Mabele, Krauss, and Kiwango 2022; McCullagh et al. 2021). On the Galápagos, humans' later arrival on the islands precludes drawing on knowledge and practices indigenous to the islands. However, this book has heeded the political significance of marginalized voices and their similar attempts at composite well-being. Both Indigenous and marginalized voices point at abundance, care, mutual obligations, and site-specific reparations (Collard, Dempsey, and Sundberg 2015; Whyte 2023). On the Galápagos, too, attuning to emergent practices can foster new inspiration for co-living.

∽∞∾

I saw Vicente on the street on my last day on the Galápagos in 2018, as I left the house for the airport. In an unusual circumstance, he lamented his poor judgment. A few months before, he had planted crops that he later harvested and sold all at once a few weeks earlier. Excited by a new crop of salad, he had used all his space for it and forgot to diversify. Consequently, he had to wait at least two months for the new plants to grow, with little income until then. It was difficult seeing him feeling low and almost embarrassed, in contrast to his habitual upbeat, playfully bragging tone. He returned to that cheerfulness almost at the end of our conversation, when he assured me that when he eventually harvested and sold the new salad at a premium price, "I'll have money *hasta a reír*"—so much money that he would laugh. Until then, however, he was looking for work as a carpenter while preparing to get by for weeks with almost no cash.

On that day, his project of an educational farm looked more distant than ever, maybe even utopian. Still, the significance of his plan was bigger than its feasibility, illustrating the tenacity sustaining Vicente's and other farmers' daily practices of farming, their strategies to procure a livelihood, and the forms of care in the farms and the highlands at large. This creativity emerged not only despite the many limitations on farming but also outside the strictures of these very limitations. His farming, let alone his future plans, always exposed Vicente to risks, given that state agronomists lacked the technical knowledge or the political mandate to support innovation in farming practices. His loose affiliation with MAGAP, on the other hand, allowed him to pursue new opportunities, such as hydroponic farming, with little interference. Marginalization, then, had carved out a space of autonomy.

Perhaps without the scale and impact of his planned farm, Vicente and other farmers nevertheless enacted modes of island living that diverged from official conservation. By cultivating relationships with other species and the pride that derived from enabling this thriving, these farmers attempted to root themselves in the islands and for the islands. They thought about the islands' future as an embodied responsibility, as a space they would inhabit. In a place that continues to be presented as timeless and prehuman, there might be something utopian yet worth considering about attempting to create conditions for everyday co-living.

Notes

INTRODUCTION

1   In 2023, the Consejo de Gobierno, the highest regional government body, adopted SES in its draft of a ten-year plan for local sustainable development.

2   Because of the term's ambiguity and proximity to the government, activists in Ecuador have largely preferred to explain their intervention as against "extractivism" and not for "buen vivir" (Riofrancos 2020).

3   In this spirit, then, my choice of "viable" is a nod to Joao Biehl's (2013) decade-long work with an HIV patient in Brazil and his theorization on how life/vita/ *vida* finds ways to persist, and even celebrate itself, amid unabated challenges.

4   As in the concept of MVP (Minimum Viable Population) (Flather et al. 2011; Traill, Bradshaw, and Brook 2007).

5   As used by Dempsey and Suarez (2016) and Büscher et al. (2012), mainstream conservation is broad concept that highlights common traits of most conservation projects globally. See Holmes 2012; Hill, Byrne, and Pegas 2016. For a more recent yet concordant analysis of general trends in conservation, see Fletcher 2023.

6   As late as 2019, the obstacles to realizing biodiversity offset programs to mining, as reviewed by the World Bank, were predominantly caused by local activities, from charcoal production to small-scale hunting and farming (Maddox et al. 2019).

7   The number of environmental activists murdered, almost exclusively in the Global South, rises each year (Global Witness 2019).

ONE | ESCAPE GOATS

1   Urbino was one of the prime centers of fifteenth-century European humanism and home of the Duke of Montefeltro, the influential promoter of artists such as Raphael, after whom Benelli named one of its signature guns. Arguably, PI's use of Benelli's arms repurposed the late Renaissance aesthetics of

156 *Notes*

natura morta (still life; literally, dead nature). On the Galápagos, though, stillness resulted from lethal technology rather than artistic sublimation.

2 A Spanish church contacted the park to protest the use of biblical names. On Judas goats, see Taylor and Katahira 1988.

3 Etymologically, chimera means "goat" (*Xi´maira, himera*). In Greek mythology, Chimera was a monstrous animal that, with a lion's head and a caprine trunk, terrorized a province in south Turkey. The hero Bellerophon, who finally killed it, was aided by Pegasus, a winged horse—perhaps a precursor of PI's helicopters. For other chimeric uses of animals in contemporary technoscientific practices, see Etches 2014.

4 Buen vivir ensures the establishment of a good life and dignified death, the ability to love and being loved, and the healthy flourishment of everyone in harmony with nature (*El Buen vivir asegura la consecución de una calidad de vida y muerte digna, el amar y ser amado, y el florecimiento saludable de todos y todas, en paz y armonía con la naturaleza*; SENPLADES 2009, 6).

5 "We are rather like a collective Noah, deciding with a biblical coldness which life forms will be able to accompany us on our new journey in the Ark" (Lavoie et al. 2007, 9).

TWO | UNPLANNED PLAN(T)S

1 Not to be confused with the actual Lazarus taxa, originally used in paleontology, which has come to refer to species that are thought to be extinct, only to be found later (Fara 2001).

2 In addition, there are more than one hundred synonyms recorded for this genus and five common names only in English. To confound matters even more, *Cinchona pubescens*'s taxonomy has been often imprecise due to its frequent hybridization.

3 Given *Cinchona*'s ability to expand across stories, names, taxonomies, and geographies, it may come as a surprise that currently it is considered rare and endangered in many countries of its natural distribution, such as the cloud forests of mainland Ecuador. Yet *Cinchona* is but one case of an endangered plant (for instance, see *Cedrela odorata*) that is also invasive on an isolated archipelago such as the Galápagos, which illustrates some of the specific challenges of island ecology and conservation.

4 Ecological barriers can be global phenomena, such as climate change, or local ones, such as "changes in salinity or local nutrients, . . . the local extinction

Notes 157

of a key-stone species, plant invasion, or a combination of these" (Groffman et al. 2006).

5 Apolitical celebrations of multispecies life unfortunately fit quite well in this narrative (Bond 2022; Hornborg 2017).

INTERMEZZO I

1 The poncho, the traditional wool coat of people from the Andes, here symbolizes the poverty and powerlessness of farmers that characterized Ecuador's modern history.

2 Drivers of the small buses used for public transportation, called goats (*las chivas*), knew they had to slow down significantly before the checkpoints to allow those without residency, as they explained to me, to run in the fields "like goats" and evade the police.

THREE | UNCERTAIN *VIVIR*

1 Ninety-five farms (Unidad de Produccion Agropecuaria, UPA) composed the first category, which was shown as covering 16 percent, or 3,685 ha, of the total farmland, 23,426 ha. However, the largest possible cumulative area in this category of farmer (owning farms smaller or up to 1 ha) is 95 ha, and not 3,685 ha. A similar mistake was made for the second category, in which farmers with 1–20 ha of land supposedly covered the staggering area of 9,386 ha, well above the maximum possible coverage of 484 ha, given the total number of farmers owning 1–20 ha. The census number of UPAs is a much more certain variable than land coverage estimation.

2 Although for research and not for work, for two years I applied for temporary residency as Joel and many farmers did. My experience allowed me to understand more about the process, while it also offered a shared experience that drew us close. In my case, my renewal reached a climax in which I was asked to leave the islands within a couple of days and provide evidence of my departure. I had to resort to pleading for exceptional help, move between islands, and mobilize an improvised, desperate, and unconventional architecture of support through the most disparate connections, wasting weeks of research and money. I had started to work on the renewal six months prior to the expiration. Yet it served no purpose during those days, as I confronted the very tangible prospect of having to leave the islands for an undetermined

period until Migración could issue a new temporal residency card. Though I managed to avoid this scenario, the resources I spent on this endeavor initiated me into the frustrations of being a temporary resident. Interestingly, problems continued even after I left the Galápagos. For more than a month they followed me while I was in Europe and the United States, though I had duly mailed a hard copy of my outbound ticket to my local sponsor institution, which sent it to Migración. It ostensibly served as proof of my departure, despite my passport being scanned by the very officials of Migración at the airport on the Galápagos as I left. Yet for weeks afterward I was asked to also mail the temporary residency card, as a third proof I had left in addition to the passport scan and the mailed air ticket. (Weeks earlier, I had asked the director of Migración about the triple redundancy of such policy. She told me that it is because some data may be lost). All things considered, the renewal of my residency, legally valid for one year, lasted for a total of eleven months. My own navigation of the local bureaucracy involved in renewing my visa provided me with a glimpse of what permanently living as temporary involves. However, how bureaucracy affects farmers is dramatically different from my experience. My income and life did not depend as closely on the Galápagos as, for instance, Joel's did. I didn't have a family to provide for or that I could not afford to leave alone on the islands if I were deported. And I had other places where I could go and hope to prosper, or at least get by. My misadventures with Migración became a favorite topic of discussion with many of the farmers I knew well. Invariably, halfway through the story, they would start laughing with gusto, hitting their hands on their legs and looking at each other in a delightful mix of surprise ("Does this happens to *colorados* [white people/foreigners] too?"), validation of their own experience, and amusement. I didn't take offense: unsaid but assumed was the awareness of both parties, those who laugh and those who are laughed at, that sooner or later the roles will switch.

3   However, Joel had to contribute part of his health care insurance (*seguro social*), which was around $50 per month—a considerable sum for him. Furthermore, it covered only him: health insurance for the whole family would be too expensive.

4   Funded with an initial investment of $175 million, the ERAs addressed topics such as productivity, innovation, soil fertility, and hotbeds. MAGAP hired 350 *facilitadores* (facilitators) with the goal of promoting farmers as agents of empowerment and development.

FOUR | MINOR THRIVING

1 In 2017, 750 farmers identified themselves as mestizos, white, or other, while only 3 farmers identified themselves as *afrodescendientes* and 8 as Indigenous (INEC 2017a).

2 *Scalesia cordata, Piscidia carthagenensis, Hibiscus tiliaceus, Palo santo, Erythrina velutina* (endemic trees of the arid and transitional zones).

FIVE | NATIVE FARMING

1 Jehovah's Witnesses doctrine establishes that, aside from a fixed number of people who will ascend to the sky (which is already full), the remaining members will live in the eternal paradise on earth. This doctrine is an exception among Christian millenarian denominations, although it is consistent with early Christian eschatology (Wright 2008).

2 "The righteous shall inherit the land, and dwell therein forever" (Psalms 37:29).

3 "The wolf and the lamb shall feed together, and the lion shall eat straw like the bullock: and dust shall be the serpent's meat. They shall not hurt nor destroy in all my holy mountain" (Isaiah 65:25).

CONCLUSION

1 On January 14, 2022, President Lasso signed the decree onboard a GNP vessel, together with Colombian president Iván Duque, Costa Rican national authorities, and Ecuador's minister of the environment, water, and ecological transition Gustavo Manrique. The new reserve, called Hermanedad (Brotherhood), "will considerably benefit the Galápagos Islands, Ecuador, and the world" (*generará importantes beneficios para las Islas Galápagos, el Ecuador y el mundo*). Witnessing the event was a cast of celebrities including actress Bo Derek, former US president Bill Clinton, and marine biologist Silvia Earl.

2 The fetishization of data underpins techno-optimism and justifies complete detachment from the politics at play (Archer 2024). It follows that, to save corals, more data about "fish and shrimp noises" amounts to no less than preserving the coral reefs, as Kate Brandt, chief sustainability officer at Google, proclaims: "I'm actively participating in the preservation of coral reefs

from my desk. How? With Google Arts & Culture's new interactive experiment, that allows you to participate in this research by listening to coral reef audio recordings and giving feedback that helps marine biologists monitor ecosystem health. It's pretty fun listening to fish and shrimp noises too" (Brandt 2023).

References

Acosta, Alberto. 2015. "El retorno del estado: Primero pasos postneoliberales, mas no postcapitalista." *Contextualizaciones Latinoamericanas* 13 (7): 62–72. https://repositorio.flacsoandes.edu.ec/bitstream/10469/4294/1/RFLACSO-LT13 -12-Acosta.pdf.

Adams, William (Bill), and Martin Mulligan. 2002. *Decolonizing Nature: Strategies for Conservation in a Post-colonial Era.* London: Routledge. https://doi .org/10.4324/9781849770927.

Alagona, Peter S., John Sandlos, and Yolanda F. Wiersma. 2012. "Past Imperfect: Using Historical Ecology and Baseline Data for Conservation and Restoration Projects in North America." *Environmental Philosophy* 9 (1): 49–70.

Alexandrakis, Othon. 2016. "Incidental Activism: Graffiti and Political Possibility in Athens, Greece." *Cultural Anthropology* 31 (2): 272–96. https://doi.org /10.14506/ca31.2.06.

Apostolopoulou, Evangelia, and William M. Adams. 2017. "Biodiversity Offsetting and Conservation: Reframing Nature to Save It." *Oryx* 51 (1): 23–31. https://doi .org/10.1017/S0030605315000782.

Archambault, Julie Soleil. 2016. "Taking Love Seriously in Human-Plant Relations in Mozambique: Toward an Anthropology of Affective Encounters." *Cultural Anthropology* 31 (2): 244–71. https://doi.org/10.14506/ca31.2.05.

Archer, Matthew. 2024. Unsustainable. New York: New York University Press.

Aristotle. 2004. *Politics.* Whitefish, MT: Kessinger.

Astrid, Arellano. 2021. "Víctor Guaillas: El defensor del agua y los páramos que fue asesinado en la cárcel mientras esperaba su liberación." Mongabay, December 7, 2021. https://es.mongabay.com/2021/12/victor-guaillas-defensor -del-agua-y-paramos-asesinado-en-ecuador/.

Atkinson, R., M. R. Gardener, G. Harper, and V. Carrion. 2012. "Fifty Years of Eradication as a Conservation Tool in Galápagos: What Are the Limits?" In *The Role of Science for Conservation*, edited by Matthias Wolf and Mark Gardener, 183–98. Oxon, UK: Routledge.

Baldwin, Frank, and Anne Allison. 2015. *Japan: The Precarious Future.* New York: New York University Press.

162 References

Barad, Karen. 2012. "On Touching—the Inhuman That Therefore I Am." *Differences* 23 (3): 206–23. https://doi.org/10.1215/10407391-1892943.

Bauman, Whitney A. 2015. "Climate Weirding and Queering Nature: Getting beyond the Anthropocene." *Religions* 6 (2): 742–54. https://doi.org/10.3390/re16020742.

Benitez-Capistros, Francisco, Jean Hugé, and Nico Koedam. 2014. "Environmental Impacts on the Galapagos Islands: Identification of Interactions, Perceptions and Steps Ahead." *Ecological Indicators* 38: 113–23.

Bensted-Smith, R. 2002. *A Biodiversity Vision for the Galápagos Islands: A Report for the Charles Darwin Foundation and WWF.* Puerto Ayora, Galapagos, Ecuador: Charles Darwin Foundation.

Berkes, Fikret, Carl Folke, and Johan Colding. 2000. *Rediscovery of Traditional Ecological Knowledge as Adaptive Management.* Cambridge: Cambridge University Press.

Biehl, João. 2013. *Vita: Life in a Zone of Social Abandonment.* Berkeley: University of California Press.

Biersack, Aletta, and James B. Greenberg. 2006. *Reimagining Political Ecology.* Durham, NC: Duke University Press.

Blake, Stephen, Anne Guézou, Sharon L. Deem, Charles B. Yackulic, and Fredy Cabrera. 2015. "The Dominance of Introduced Plant Species in the Diets of Migratory Galapagos Tortoises Increases with Elevation on a Human-Occupied Island." *Biotropica* 47 (2): 246–58. https://doi.org/10.1111/btp.12195.

Blaser, Mario. 2016. "Is Another Cosmopolitics Possible?" *Cultural Anthropology* 31 (4): 545–70. https://doi.org/10.14506/ca31.4.05.

Bocci, Paolo. 2017. "Tangles of Care: Killing Goats to Save Tortoises on the Galápagos Islands." *Cultural Anthropology* 32 (3): 424–49. https://doi.org/10.14506/ca32.3.08.

———. 2019. "Utopian Conservation: Scientific Humanism, Evolution, and Island Imaginaries on the Galápagos Islands." *Science, Technology, and Human Values* 45 (6): 1168–94. https://doi.org/10.1177/0162243919889135.

———. 2022. "'Rooting,' for Change: The Role of Culture beyond Resilience and Adaptation." *Conservation and Society* 20 (2): 103. https://doi.org/10.4103/cs.cs_7_21.

Bond, David. 2022. *Negative Ecologies: Fossil Fuels and the Discovery of the Environment.* Oakland: University of California Press.

Borras, Saturnino, and Jennifer C. Franco. 2013. "Global Land Grabbing and Political Reactions 'From Below.'" *Third World Quarterly* 34 (9): 1723–47. https://doi.org/10.1080/01436597.2013.843845.

Bowman, Robert. 1957. *A Biological Reconnaissance of the Galapagos Islands during 1957.* Paris: UNESCO.

Brandt, Kate. 2023. "I'm actively participating in the preservation of coral reefs from my desk. How? With @Google Arts & Culture's new interactive experiment." LinkedIn post, 2023. https://www.linkedin.com/posts/katebrandt_im -actively-participating-in-the-preservation-activity-7056086805367967744-yIGo/.

Brass, Tom. 2002. "On Which Side of What Barricade? Subaltern Resistance in Latin America and Elsewhere." *Journal of Peasant Studies* 29 (3–4): 336–99. https://doi.org/10.1080/03066150412331311109.

Braverman, Irus. 2009. *Planted Flags: Trees, Land, and Law in Israel/Palestine.* New York: Cambridge University Press.

———. 2023. *Settling Nature: The Conservation Regime in Palestine-Israel.* Minneapolis: University of Minnesota Press.

Bravo, Elizabeth, and Cecilia Chérrez, eds. 2012. *Sumak Kawsay o Plan Nacional del Buen Vivir: Qué está detrás del discurso?* Quito: Acción Ecológica.

Brockington, Daniel. 2002. *Fortress Conservation: The Preservation of the Mkomazi Game Reserve, Tanzania.* Bloomington: Indiana University Press.

Bubandt, Nils, ed. 2018. *A Non-Secular Anthropocene: Spirits, Specters and Other Nonhumans in a Time of Environmental Change: More-than-Human.* AURA Working Papers, vol. 3. Højbjerg, Denmark: Arhus University.

Büscher, Bram, and Robert Fletcher. 2019. "Towards Convivial Conservation." *Conservation and Society* 17 (3): 283–96.

———. 2020. *The Conservation Revolution: Radical Ideas for Saving Nature beyond the Anthropocene.* New York: Verso.

Büscher, Bram, Sian Sullivan, Katja Neves, Jim Igoe, and Dan Brockington. 2012. "Towards a Synthesized Critique of Neoliberal Biodiversity Conservation." *Capitalism Nature Socialism* 23 (2): 4–30. https://doi.org/10.1080/10455752.201 2.674149.

Callon, Michel. 1984. "Some Elements of a Sociology of Translation: Domestication of the Scallops and the Fishermen of St. Brieuc Bay." *Sociological Review* 32 (S1): 196–233.

Campbell, K. J., Greg S. Baxter, Peter J. Murray, Bruce E. Coblentz, and C. Josh Donlan. 2007. "Development of a Prolonged Estrus Effect for Use in Judas Goats." *Applied Animal Behaviour Science* 102 (1–2): 12–23. https://doi.org/10 .1016/j.applanim.2006.03.003.

Caria, Sara, and Rafael Domínguez. 2016. "Ecuador's Buen Vivir: A New Ideology for Development." *Latin American Perspectives* 43 (1): 18–33. https://doi.org /10.1177/0094582X15611126.

164 *References*

Carr, E. Summerson. 2015. "Occupation Bedbug, or, The Urgency and Agency of Professional Pragmatism." *Cultural Anthropology* 30 (2): 257–85.

Carrier, James G., and Paige West. 2013. *Virtualism, Governance and Practice: Vision and Execution in Environmental Conservation*. New York: Berghahn.

Carrion, Victor, C. Josh Donlan, Karl J. Campbell, Christian Lavoie, and Felipe Cruz. 2011. "Archipelago-Wide Island Restoration in the Galápagos Islands: Reducing Costs of Invasive Mammal Eradication Programs and Reinvasion Risk." *PLOS ONE* 6 (5): e18835. https://doi.org/10.1371/journal.pone.0018835.

Carroll, Clint. 2015. *Roots of Our Renewal: Ethnobotany and Cherokee Environmental Governance*. Minneapolis: University of Minnesota Press.

Cayot, Linda. 1996. "Alcedo Updates." *Noticias de Galapagos* 57: 14–17.

Ceballos, Gerardo, and Paul R. Ehrlich. 2023. "Mutilation of the Tree of Life via Mass Extinction of Animal Genera." *Proceedings of the National Academy of Sciences* 120 (39): e2306987120. https://doi.org/10.1073/pnas.2306987120.

Ceballos, Gerardo, Paul R. Ehrlich, Anthony D. Barnosky, Andrés García, Robert M. Pringle, and Todd M. Palmer. 2015. "Accelerated Modern Human–Induced Species Losses: Entering the Sixth Mass Extinction." *Science Advances* 1 (5): e1400253. https://doi.org/10.1126/sciadv.1400253.

Cetina, Karin Knorr. 1999. *Epistemic Cultures: How the Sciences Make Knowledge*. Cambridge, MA: Harvard University Press.

Chakrabarty, Dipesh. 2016. "Humanities in the Anthropocene: The Crisis of an Enduring Kantian Fable." *New Literary History* 47 (2): 377–97. https://doi.org/10.1353/nlh.2016.0019.

Chao, Sophie. 2022. *In the Shadow of the Palms: More-Than-Human Becomings in West Papua*. Durham, NC: Duke University Press.

Chao, Sophie, Karin Bolender, and Eben Kirksey. 2022. *The Promise of Multispecies Justice*. Durham, NC: Duke University Press.

Chrulew, Matthew. 2011. "Managing Love and Death at the Zoo: The Biopolitics of Endangered Species Preservation." *Australian Humanities Review*, no. 50: 137–57.

Clark, Jonathan L. 2015. "Uncharismatic Invasives." *Environmental Humanities* 6: 29–52.

Clark, Patrick. 2017. "Neo-Developmentalism and a 'Vía Campesina' for Rural Development: Unreconciled Projects in Ecuador's Citizen's Revolution." *Journal of Agrarian Change* 17 (2): 348–64. https://doi.org/10.1111/joac.12203.

Collard, Rosemary-Claire, Jessica Dempsey, and Juanita Sundberg. 2015. "A Manifesto for Abundant Futures." *Annals of the Association of American Geographers* 105 (2): 322–30. https://doi.org/10.1080/00045608.2014.973007.

Colloredo-Mansfeld, Rudi. 2009. *Fighting Like a Community: Andean Civil Society in an Era of Indian Uprisings*. Chicago: University of Chicago Press.

Comaroff, Jean, and John L. Comaroff. 2001. "Naturing the Nation: Aliens, Apocalypse, and the Postcolonial State." *Social Identities* 7 (2): 233–65.

Congreso Nacional. 1998. *Ley de regimen especial para la conservacion y desarrollo sustentable de la provincia de Galapagos*. Quito: Ministerio de Medio Ambiente, Programa de Manejo Ambiental para las Islas Galapagos.

Cons, Jason. 2018. "Staging Climate Security: Resilience and Heterodystopia in the Bangladesh Borderlands." *Cultural Anthropology* 33 (2): 266–94. https://doi.org/10.14506/ca33.2.08.

Crist, Eileen. 2013. "On the Poverty of Our Nomenclature." *Environmental Humanities* 3 (1): 129–47. https://read.dukeupress.edu/environmental-humanities/article/3/1/129/8096/On-the-Poverty-of-Our-Nomenclature.

Cronon, William. 1996. "The Trouble with Wilderness, or, Getting Back to the Wrong Nature." *Environmental History* 1 (1): 7–28.

———. 2011. *Changes in the Land: Indians, Colonists, and the Ecology of New England*. New York: Macmillan.

Cuvi, Nicholas. 2011. "'Dejen que el diablo haga lo demás': La promoción de productos complementarios en América Latina durante la década de 1940" ("Let the Devil Do the Rest": The Promotion of Complementary Products in Latin America during the 1940s). *Historia Crítica* 44 (May): 158–81. https://doi.org/10.7440/histcrit44.2011.08.

Dampier, William. 1699. *A New Voyage round the World*. London: J. Knapton.

Darwin, Charles. (1859) 1909. *The Origin of Species*. New York: P. F. Collier and Son.

———. (1839) 2001. *The voyage of the Beagle: Journal of researches into the natural history and geology of the countries visited during the voyage of HMS Beagle round the world*. New York: Modern Library.

Dave, Naisargi N. 2014. "Witness: Humans, Animals, and the Politics of Becoming." *Cultural Anthropology* 29 (3): 433–56. https://doi.org/10.14506/ca29.3.01.

de la Cadena, Marisol. 2015. *Earth Beings: Ecologies of Practice across Andean Worlds*. Durham, NC: Duke University Press.

de Vries, Tjitte. 1984. "The Giant Tortoises: A Natural History Disturbed by Man." In Key Environments: Galápagos, edited by R. Perry. Oxford: Pergamon Press.

Deleuze, Gilles. 1986. *Kafka: Toward a Minor Literature*. Minneapolis: University of Minnesota Press.

Deleuze, Gilles, and Félix Guattari. 1987. *A Thousand Plateaus: Capitalism and Schizophrenia*. Minneapolis: University of Minnesota Press.

Dembicki, Geoff. 2022. *The Petroleum Papers: Inside the Far-Right Conspiracy to Cover Up Climate Change.* Vancouver, BC: Greystone.

Dempsey, Jessica, and Daniel Chiu Suarez. 2016. "Arrested Development? The Promises and Paradoxes of 'Selling Nature to Save It.'" *Annals of the American Association of Geographers* 106 (3): 653–71. https://doi.org/10.1080/24694452.2016.1140018.

Des Informémonos. 2013. "Ecuador: Gobierno cierra Fundación Pachamama." *Des Informémonos*, May 12, 2013. https://desinformemonos.org/ecuador-gobierno-cierra-fundacion-pachamama-51213-servindi/.

Desender, Konjev, Leon Baert, Jean-Pierre Maelfait, and Peter Verdyck. 1999. "Conservation on Volcán Alcedo (Galápagos): Terrestrial Invertebrates and the Impact of Introduced Feral Goats." *Biological Conservation* 87 (3): 303–10. https://doi.org/10.1016/S0006-3207(98)00078-0.

Dhillon, Jaskiran, ed. 2022. *Indigenous Resurgence: Decolonialization and Movements for Environmental Justice.* New York: Berghahn Books.

Diver, Sibyl, Mehana Vaughan, Merrill Baker-Médard, and Heather Lukacs. 2019. "Recognizing 'Reciprocal Relations' to Restore Community Access to Land and Water." *International Journal of the Commons* 13 (1): 400–429. https://doi.org/10.18352/ijc.881.

Durham, William H. 2021. *Exuberant Life: An Evolutionary Approach to Conservation in Galápagos.* Oxford: Oxford University Press.

Eibl-Eibesfeldt, Irenäus. 1959. "Survey on the Galapagos-Islands." *UNESCO Mission Report* 8: 7–31.

El Confidencial. 2007. "Ecuador declara a las Islas Galápagos en emergencia." *El Confidencial*, April 11, 2007. https://www.elconfidencial.com/sociedad/2007-04-11/ecuador-declara-a-las-islas-galapagos-en-emergencia_473062/.

El Universo. 2021. "Hermandad es el nombre de la nueva área protegida en Galápagos; Hoy se firmó decreto." *El Universo*, October 1, 2021. https://www.eluniverso.com/noticias/politica/guillermo-lasso-firma-el-decreto-para-ampliar-la-reserva-marina-de-galapagos-nota/.

Enns, Charis, Brock Bersaglio, and Adam Sneyd. 2019. "Fixing Extraction through Conservation: On Crises, Fixes and the Production of Shared Value and Threat." *Environment and Planning E: Nature and Space* 2 (4): 967–88. https://doi.org/10.1177/2514848619867615.

Epler, Bruce. 2007. "Tourism, the Economy, Population Growth, and Conservation in Galapagos." Charles Darwin Foundation. http://cpps.dyndns.info/cpps-docs-web/planaccion/docs2011/oct/turismo_biodiv/doc.15.epler_tourism_report-en_5-08.pdf.

Escobar, Arturo. 2018. *Designs for the Pluriverse: Radical Interdependence, Autonomy, and the Making of Worlds.* Durham, NC: Duke University Press.

Etches, Robert J. 2014. "Chimeras and Transgenics: From Greek Mythology to Poultry Breeding." Paper presented to the Poultry Science Association, Champaign, Illinois, November 2, 2014. http://www.poultryscience.org/docs/pba/1952-2003/1997/1997%20Etches.pdf.

Fairhead, James, and Melissa Leach. 1996. *Misreading the African Landscape: Society and Ecology in a Forest-Savanna Mosaic.* Cambridge: Cambridge University Press.

Fairhead, James, Melissa Leach, and Ian Scoones. 2012. "Green Grabbing: A New Appropriation of Nature?" *Journal of Peasant Studies* 39 (2): 237–61. https://doi.org/10.1080/03066150.2012.671770.

Fara, Emmanuel. 2001. "What Are Lazarus Taxa?" *Geological Journal* 36 (3–4): 291–303. https://doi.org/10.1002/gj.879.

Fassin, Didier. 2012. *Humanitarian Reason: A Moral History of the Present.* Berkeley: University of California Press.

Fassin, Didier, and Richard Rechtman. 2009. *The Empire of Trauma: An Inquiry into the Condition of Victimhood.* Princeton, NJ: Princeton University Press.

Favini, John. 2023. "Fugitive Ecologies: Marronage and Invasive Species in Jamaica." *ACME: An International Journal for Critical Geographies* 22 (5): 1273–93. https://doi.org/10.7202/1107309ar.

Feldman, Gerald D., and Wolfgang Seibel. 2005. *Networks of Nazi Persecution: Bureaucracy, Business, and the Organization of the Holocaust.* Oxford, NY: Berghahn.

Ferdinand, Malcom. 2021. *Decolonial Ecology: Thinking from the Caribbean World.* Hoboken, NJ: Wiley.

Finn, Catherine, Florencia Grattarola, and Daniel Pincheira-Donoso. 2023. "More Losers than Winners: Investigating Anthropocene Defaunation through the Diversity of Population Trends." *Biological Reviews* 98 (5): 1732–48. https://doi.org/10.1111/brv.12974.

Flather, Curtis H., Gregory D. Hayward, Steven R. Beissinger, and Philip A. Stephens. 2011. "Minimum Viable Populations: Is There a 'Magic Number' for Conservation Practitioners?" *Trends in Ecology and Evolution* 26 (6): 307–16. https://doi.org/10.1016/j.tree.2011.03.001.

Fletcher, Robert. 2023. *Failing Forward: The Rise and Fall of Neoliberal Conservation.* Oakland: University of California Press.

Foucault, Michel. 2008. *The Birth of Biopolitics: Lectures at the Collège de France, 1978–1979.* Edited by Michel Senellart. Translated by Graham Burchell. Berlin: Springer.

168 References

Fry, Tom, Agnese Marino, and Sahil Nijhawan. 2022. "'Killing with Care': Locating Ethical Congruence in Multispecies Political Ecology." *ACME: An International Journal for Critical Geographies* 21 (2): 226–46.

Fujii, Lee Ann. 2009. *Killing Neighbors: Webs of Violence in Rwanda*. Ithaca, NY: Cornell University Press.

Galapagos Conservation Action. 2022. "El biocontrol de la mora." Galapagos Conservation Action, August 15, 2022. https://www.galapagosconservationaction .org/portfolio-items/morabiocontrol/.

García, María Elena. 2019. "Death of a Guinea Pig: Grief and the Limits of Multispecies Ethnography in Peru." *Environmental Humanities* 11 (2): 351–72. https:// doi.org/10.1215/22011919-7754512.

Gardener, Mark R. 2013. "The Management Framework in Practice—Can't See the Wood for the Trees: The Changing Management of the Novel Miconia–Cinchona Ecosystem in the Humid Highlands of Santa Cruz Island, Galapagos." In *Novel Ecosystems*, edited by Richard J. Hobbs, Eric S. Higgs, and Carol M. Hall, 185–88. Hoboken, NJ: Wiley. https://doi.org/10.1002/9781118354186.ch22.

Geertz, Clifford. 1973. *The Interpretation of Cultures: Selected Essays*. New York: Basic.

Ghosh, Amitav. 2016. *The Great Derangement: Climate Change and the Unthinkable*. Chicago: University of Chicago Press.

Ginn, Franklin, Uli Beisel, and Maan Barua. 2014. "Flourishing with Awkward Creatures: Togetherness, Vulnerability, Killing." *Environmental Humanities* 4: 113–23.

Giraud, Eva, and Gregory Hollin. 2016. "Care, Laboratory Beagles and Affective Utopia." *Theory, Culture and Society* 33 (4): 27–49. https://doi.org/10 .1177/0263276415619685.

Giunta, Isabella. 2018. "Soberanía alimentaria entre derechos del buen vivir y políticas agrarias en Ecuador." *Theomai* 38: 109–22.

Global Witness. 2019. "Enemies of the State?" *Global Witness*, July 30, 2019. https://www.globalwitness.org/en/campaigns/environmental-activists/enemies -state/.

———. 2021. "Hundreds of Fossil Fuel Lobbyists Flooding COP26 Climate Talks." *Global Witness*, November 8, 2021. https://www.globalwitness.org/en /press-releases/hundreds-fossil-fuel-lobbyists-flooding-cop26-climate-talks/.

Gómez-Barris, Macarena. 2017. *The Extractive Zone: Social Ecologies and Decolonial Perspectives*. Durham, NC: Duke University Press.

González, José, Carlos Montes, and Daniel Rodríguez. 2008. "Rethinking the Galapagos Islands as a Complex Social-Ecological System: Implications for Conservation and Management." *Ecology and Society* 13 (2): 13–26.

Goodyear-Kaʻōpua, Noelani. 2017. "Protectors of the Future, not Protestors of the Past: Indigenous Pacific Activism and Mauna a Wākea." *South Atlantic Quarterly* 116 (1): 184–94. https://doi.org/10.1215/00382876-3749603.

Graeter, Stefanie. 2017. "To Revive an Abundant Life: Catholic Science and Neo-extractivist Politics in Peru's Mantaro Valley." *Cultural Anthropology* 32 (1): 117–48. https://doi.org/10.14506/ca32.1.09.

Graham, Watkins, and Felipe Cruz. 2007. *'Galapagos at Risk': A Socioeconomic Analysis*. Puerto Ayora, Ecuador: Charles Darwin Foundation.

Grenier, Christophe. 2007. *Conservación contra natura: Las Islas Galápagos*. Quito: Abya Yala.

Groffman, Peter M., Jill S. Baron, Tamara Blett, Arthur J. Gold, Iris Goodman, Lance H. Gunderson, Barbara M. Levinson, et al. 2006. "Ecological Thresholds: The Key to Successful Environmental Management or an Important Concept with No Practical Application?" *Ecosystems* 9 (1): 1–13. https://doi.org/10.1007/s10021-003-0142-z.

Gudynas, Eduardo. 2009. "La dimensión ecológica del buen vivir: Entre el fantasma de la modernidad y el desafío biocéntrico." In *Debates sobre cooperación y modelos de desarrollo. perspectivas desde la sociedad civil en el Ecuador*, 83–102. Quito: Centro de Investigaciones CIUDAD y Observatorio de la Cooperación al Desarrollo.

Guerra, Pablo, Hugo Jácome Estrella, José Ramón Páez Pareja, María José Ruiz, Santiago Egüez, Manuel Mariño, Carlos Alonso Naranjo, and Geovanna Flores. 2016. *Contextos de la "otra economía."* Quito: Superintendencia de Economía Popular y Solidaria.

Gunn, Simon. 2019. "Malarial Subjects: Empire, Medicine and Nonhumans in British India, 1820–1909 by Rohan Deb Roy (Review)." *Journal of Colonialism and Colonial History* 20 (2). https://doi.org/10.1353/cch.2019.0023.

Guzmán, Juan Carlos, and José Enrique Poma. 2013. "Bioagriculture: An Opportunity for Island Good Living," *Galápagos Report* 6: 25–29.

Hall, Ruth, Marc Edelman, Saturnino M. Borras Jr., Ian Scoones, Ben White, and Wendy Wolford. 2015. "Resistance, Acquiescence or Incorporation? An Introduction to Land Grabbing and Political Reactions 'from Below.'" *Journal of Peasant Studies* 42 (3–4): 467–88. https://doi.org/10.1080/03066150.2015.1036746.

Hallett, Lauren M., Rachel J. Standish, Kristin B. Hulvey, Mark R. Gardener, Katharine N. Suding, Brian M. Starzomski, Stephen D. Murphy, and James A. Harris. 2013. "Towards a Conceptual Framework for Novel Ecosystems." In *Novel Ecosystems*, edited by Richard J. Hobbs, Eric S. Higgs, and Carol M. Hall, 16–28.

170 *References*

Hoboken, NJ: Wiley. http://onlinelibrary.wiley.com/doi/10.1002/9781118354186.ch3/summary.

Haraway, Donna J. 2008. *When Species Meet*. Minneapolis: University of Minnesota Press.

———. 2010. "Staying with the Trouble: Xenoecologies of Home for Companions in the Contested Zones." *Cultural Anthropology Online*. https://culanth.org/fieldsights/289-staying-with-the-trouble-xenoecologies-of-home-for-companions-in-the-contested-zones.

Head, Lesley. 2014. "Contingencies of the Anthropocene: Lessons from the 'Neolithic.'" *Anthropocene Review* 1 (2): 113–25. https://doi.org/10.1177/2053019614529745.

Hennessy, Elizabeth. 2013. "Producing 'Prehistoric' Life: Conservation Breeding and the Remaking of Wildlife Genealogies." *Geoforum* 49: 71–80.

———. 2018. "The Politics of a Natural Laboratory: Claiming Territory and Governing Life in the Galápagos Islands." *Social Studies of Science* 48 (4): 483–506. https://doi.org/10.1177/0306312718788179.

Hernandez, Jessica. 2022. *Fresh Banana Leaves: Healing Indigenous Landscapes through Indigenous Science*. Berkeley, CA: North Atlantic Books.

Heylings, Pippa, and Cruz Felipe. 1998. "Common Property, Conflict and Participatory Management in the Galapagos Islands." Paper presented at the Crossing Boundaries conference, Vancouver, BC, June 10–14, 1998. https://dlc.dlib.indiana.edu/dlc/items/5c786fb2-8837-4bcb-bbdc-7d9ocbc61459.

Hidalgo-Capitán, Antonio Luis, and Ana Patricia Cubillo-Guevara. 2018. "Orto y ocaso del buen vivir en la planificación nacional del desarrollo en Ecuador (2007–2021)." *América Latina Hoy* 78 (May). https://gredos.usal.es/handle/10366/137965.

Hill, Wendy, Jason Byrne, and Fernanda de Vasconcellos Pegas. 2016. "The Ecotourism-Extraction Nexus and Its Implications for the Long-Term Sustainability of Protected Areas: What Is Being Sustained and Who Decides?" *Journal of Political Ecology* 23 (1): 308–27. https://doi.org/10.2458/v23i1.20219.

Hinton, Alexander Laban. 2004. *Why Did They Kill?: Cambodia in the Shadow of Genocide*. Berkeley: University of California Press.

Hobbs, Richard J. 2013. "Grieving for the Past and Hoping for the Future: Balancing Polarizing Perspectives in Conservation and Restoration." *Restoration Ecology* 21 (2): 145–48. https://doi.org/10.1111/rec.12014.

Hobbs, R. J., and J. A. Harris. 2001. "Restoration Ecology: Repairing the Earth's Ecosystems in the New Millennium." *Restoration Ecology* 9 (2): 239–46. https://doi.org/10.1046/j.1526-100X.2001.009002239.x.

Hobbs, Richard J., Eric Higgs, Carol M. Hall, Peter Bridgewater, F. Stuart Chapin, Erle C. Ellis, John J. Ewel, et al. 2014. "Managing the Whole Landscape: Historical, Hybrid, and Novel Ecosystems." *Frontiers in Ecology and the Environment* 12 (10): 557–64. https://doi.org/10.1890/130300.

Hobbs, Richard J., Eric Higgs, and James A. Harris. 2009. "Novel Ecosystems: Implications for Conservation and Restoration." *Trends in Ecology and Evolution* 24 (11): 599–605. https://doi.org/10.1016/j.tree.2009.05.012.

Holden, Andrew. 2002. *Jehovah's Witnesses: Portrait of a Contemporary Religious Movement*. New York: Psychology Press.

Holmes, George. 2012. "Biodiversity for Billionaires: Capitalism, Conservation and the Role of Philanthropy in Saving/Selling Nature." *Development and Change* 43 (1): 185–203. https://doi.org/10.1111/j.1467-7660.2011.01749.x.

Hoover, Elizabeth. 2017. *The River Is in Us: Fighting Toxics in a Mohawk Community*. Minneapolis: University of Minnesota Press.

Hornborg, Alf. 2017. "Dithering while the Planet Burns: Anthropologists' Approaches to the Anthropocene." *Reviews in Anthropology* 46 (2–3): 61–77. https://doi.org/10.1080/00938157.2017.1343023.

Hribal, Jason. 2007. "Animals, Agency, and Class: Writing the History of Animals from Below." *Human Ecology Review* 14 (1): 101.

Hughes, David McDermott. 2010. *Whiteness in Zimbabwe: Race, Landscape, and the Problem of Belonging*. Berlin: Springer.

INEC. 2000. "Censo Nacional Agropecuario." Quito: Instituto Nacional de Estadística y Censo.

———. 2017a. "Censo Nacional Agropecuario." Quito: Instituto Nacional de Estadística y Censo.

———. 2017b. "Galápagos tiene 25.244 habitantes según censo 2015." Instituto Nacional de Estadística y Censo. http://www.ecuadorencifras.gob.ec /galapagos-tiene-25-244-habitantes-segun-censo-2015/.

Island Conservation. 2017. "Why Islands?" *Island Conservation* (blog). 2017. https://www.islandconservation.org/why-islands/.

Jacoby, Karl. 2014. *Crimes against Nature: Squatters, Poachers, Thieves, and the Hidden History of American Conservation*. Berkeley: University of California Press.

Jäger, Heinke. 2015. "Biology and Impacts of Pacific Island Invasive Species: 11. Cinchona Pubescens (Red Quinine Tree) (Rubiaceae)." *Pacific Science* 69 (2): 133–53. https://doi.org/10.2984/69.2.1.

———. 2018. "Quinine Tree Invasion and Control in Galapagos: A Case Study."

In *Understanding Invasive Species in the Galápagos Islands*, edited by Carlos F. Mena and María de Lourdes Torres, 51–74. Cham: Springer.

Jäger, Heinke, María José Alencastro, Martin Kaupenjohann, and Ingo Kowarik. 2013. "Ecosystem Changes in Galápagos Highlands by the Invasive Tree Cinchona Pubescens." *Plant and Soil* 371 (1–2): 629–40. https://doi.org/10.1007/s11104-013-1719-8.

Jäger, Heinke, Claudio Crespo, Francisco Abad, Alizon Llerena, and Paulina Couenberg. 2018. "Learning from Farmers: Invasive Species in the Agricultural Lands of Santa Cruz." *Galagagos Report 2017-2018*. https://www.galapagosreport.org/english/2019/6/29/learning-from-farmers-invasive-species-in-the-agricultural-lands-of-santa-cruz.

Jäger, Heinke, and Ingo Kowarik. 2010. "Resilience of Native Plant Community following Manual Control of Invasive Cinchona Pubescens in Galápagos." *Restoration Ecology* 18 (September): 103–12. https://doi.org/10.1111/j.1526-100X.2010.00657.x.

Jäger, Heinke, Ingo Kowarik, and Alan Tye. 2009. "Destruction without Extinction: Long-Term Impacts of an Invasive Tree Species on Galápagos Highland Vegetation." *Journal of Ecology* 97 (6): 1252–63. https://doi.org/10.1111/j.1365-2745.2009.01578.x.

Jäger, Heinke, Alan Tye, and Ingo Kowarik. 2007. "Tree Invasion in Naturally Treeless Environments: Impacts of Quinine (Cinchona Pubescens) Trees on Native Vegetation in Galápagos." *Biological Conservation* 140 (3–4): 297–307. https://doi.org/10.1016/j.biocon.2007.08.014.

Jasanoff, Sheila, and Sang-Hyun Kim. 2015. *Dreamscapes of Modernity: Sociotechnical Imaginaries and the Fabrication of Power*. Chicago: University of Chicago Press.

Jenkins, Willis. 2013. *Ecologies of Grace: Environmental Ethics and Christian Theology*. Oxford: Oxford University Press.

Johns, Loren. 2016. "The Apocalypse of John and Theological Ecosystems of Destruction and Escape." In *Rooted and Grounded: Essays on Land and Christian Discipleship*, edited by Ryan Dallas Harker and Janeen Bertsche Johnson, 77–94. Eugene, OR: Pickwick.

Jones, Andrew S. 1994. "The Global Environment Facility's Failure to Promote Sustainable Forestry in Ecuador: The Case of Ecoforest 2000." *Virginia Environmental Law Journal* 14: 507.

Keller, Catherine. 2007. "Eschatology, Ecology and a Green Ecumenacy." *Journal for the Study of Religion, Nature and Culture* 2. https://doi.org/10.1558/ecotheology.v1i2.84.

References 173

———. 2014. *Cloud of the Impossible: Negative Theology and Planetary Entanglement*. New York: Columbia University Press.

———. 2015. "A Democracy of Fellow Creatures." *Studia Theologica—Nordic Journal of Theology* 69 (1): 3–18. https://doi.org/10.1080/0039338X.2015.1033221.

Kirksey, Eben. 2012. "Living with Parasites in Palo Verde National Park." *Environmental Humanities* 1 (1): 23–55.

Kohler, Robert E. 1994. *Lords of the Fly: Drosophila Genetics and the Experimental Life*. Chicago: University of Chicago Press.

Kohn, Eduardo. 2013. *How Forests Think: Toward an Anthropology beyond the Human*. Berkeley: University of California Press.

Kothari, Ashish, Federico Demaria, and Alberto Acosta. 2014. "Buen Vivir, Degrowth and Ecological Swaraj: Alternatives to Sustainable Development and the Green Economy." *Springer Link* 57: 362–75. https://link.springer.com/article/10.1057/dev.2015.24.

Kueffer, Christoph, Curtis C. Daehler, Christian W. Torres-Santana, Christophe Lavergne, Jean-Yves Meyer, Rüdiger Otto, and Luís Silva. 2010. "A Global Comparison of Plant Invasions on Oceanic Islands." *Perspectives in Plant Ecology, Evolution and Systematics* 12 (2): 145–61. https://doi.org/10.1016/j.ppees.2009.06.002.

Laso, Francisco J., Fátima L. Benítez, Gonzalo Rivas-Torres, Carolina Sampedro, and Javier Arce-Nazario. 2020. "Land Cover Classification of Complex Agroecosystems in the Non-Protected Highlands of the Galapagos Islands." *Remote Sensing* 12 (1): 65. https://doi.org/10.3390/rs12010065.

Latorre, Octavio. 1999. *El hombre en las Islas Encantadas: La historia humana de Galápagos*. Self-published.

Latour, Bruno. 2007. *Reassembling the Social: An Introduction to Actor-Network-Theory*. Oxford: Oxford University Press.

Lavoie, C., F. Cruz, G. V. Carrion, K. J. Campbell, C. J. Donland, S. Harcourt, and M. Moya. 2007. "The Thematic Atlas of Project Isabela: An Illustrative Document Describing, Step-by-Step, the Biggest Successful Goat Eradication Project on the Galapagos Islands 1998–2006." Puerto Ayora, Ecuador: Charles Darwin Foundation.

Law, John. 2010. "Care and Killing: Tensions in Veterinary Practice." In *Care in Practice: On Tinkering in Clinics, Homes and Farms*, edited by Annemarie Mol, Ingunn Moser, and Jeannette Pols, 57–71. New York: Columbia University Press.

Le Billon, Philippe. 2021. "Crisis Conservation and Green Extraction: Biodiversity Offsets as Spaces of Double Exception." *Journal of Political Ecology* 28 (1): 854–88.

Lele, Sharachchandra, Oliver Springate-Baginski, Roan Lakerveld, Debal Deb, and Prasad Dash. 2013. "Ecosystem Services: Origins, Contributions, Pitfalls, and Alternatives." *Conservation and Society* 11 (4): 343–58.

Liboiron, Max. 2021a. "Decolonizing Geoscience Requires More than Equity and Inclusion." *Nature Geoscience* 14 (12): 876–77. https://doi.org/10.1038/s41561-021-00861-7.

———. 2021b. *Pollution Is Colonialism*. Durham, NC: Duke University Press.

Lidström, Susanna, Simon West, Tania Katzschner, M. Isabel Pérez-Ramos, and Hedley Twidle. 2015. "Invasive Narratives and the Inverse of Slow Violence: Alien Species in Science and Society." *Environmental Humanities* 7 (1): 1–40. http://environmentalhumanities.org/arch/vol7/7.1.pdf.

Lockwood, Julie L., Martha F. Hoopes, and Michael P. Marchetti. 2013. *Invasion Ecology*. Hoboken, NJ: Wiley.

Low, Tim. 1999. *Feral Future: The Untold Story of Australia's Exotic Invaders*. Chicago: University of Chicago Press.

Lyons, Kristina. 2016. "Decomposition as Life Politics: Soils, Selva, and Small Farmers under the Gun of the U.S.–Colombia War on Drugs." *Cultural Anthropology* 31 (1): 56–81. https://doi.org/10.14506/ca31.1.04.

———. 2018. "Chemical Warfare in Colombia, Evidentiary Ecologies and Senti-Actuando Practices of Justice." *Social Studies of Science*, March. https://doi.org/10.1177/0306312718765375.

Lyons, Kristina, Juno Parrenas, Noah Tamarkin, and Banu Subramaniam. 2017. "Engagements with Decolonization and Decoloniality in and at the Interfaces of STS." *Catalyst Feminism, Theory, Technoscience* 3 (3): 1.

Mabele, Mathew Bukhi, Judith E. Krauss, and Wilhelm Kiwango. 2022. "Going Back to the Roots: Ubuntu and Just Conservation in Southern Africa." *Conservation and Society* 20 (2): 92–102.

MacArthur, Robert H., and Edward O. Wilson. 2015. *Theory of Island Biogeography. (MPB-1)*. Princeton, NJ: Princeton University Press.

Maddox, Thomas, Pippa Howard, Jonathan Knox, and Nicky Jenner. 2019. *Forest-Smart Mining: Identifying Factors Associated with the Impacts of Large-Scale Mining on Forests*. Washington, DC: World Bank. https://doi.org/10.1596/32025.

Maier, Harry. 2010. "Green Milleniarism: American Evangelicals, Environmentalism and the Book of Revelation." In *Ecological Hermeneutics: Biblical, Historical and Theological Perspectives*, edited by David G. Horrell, Cherryl Hunt, Christopher Southgate, and Francesca Stavrakopoulou, 61–83. New York: Bloomsbury.

Malm, Andreas. 2016. *Fossil Capital: The Rise of Steam Power and the Roots of Global Warming*. London: Verso.

Mankekar, Purnima, and Akhil Gupta. 2017. "Future Tense: Capital, Labor, and Technology in a Service Industry (the 2017 Lewis Henry Morgan Lecture)." *HAU: Journal of Ethnographic Theory* 7 (3): 67–87. https://doi.org/10.14318 /hau7.3.004.

Mariscal, R. N. 1969. "Charles Darwin and Conservation in the Galápagos Islands." *Biological Conservation* 2 (1): 44–46.

Martin, Aryn, Natasha Myers, and Ana Viseu. 2015. "The Politics of Care in Technoscience." *Social Studies of Science* 45 (5): 625–41.

Martin, Laura J. 2022. *Wild by Design: The Rise of Ecological Restoration*. Cambridge, MA: Harvard University Press.

Martínez Novo, Carmen. 2018. "Ventriloquism, Racism and the Politics of Decoloniality in Ecuador." *Cultural Studies* 32 (3): 389–413. https://doi.org/10.1080 /09502386.2017.1420091.

Masco, Joseph. 2016. "Catastrophe's Apocalypse." In *The Time of Catastrophe: Multidisciplinary Approaches to the Age of Catastrophe*, edited by Christopher Dole, 1–36. London: Routledge.

McCullagh, Suzanne M., Luis I. Prádanos, Ilaria Tabusso Marcyan, and Catherine Wagner, eds. 2021. *Contesting Extinctions: Decolonial and Regenerative Futures*. Lanham, MD: Rowman and Littlefield.

Meadows, Donella H., Dennis L. Meadows, Joergen Randers, and William W. Behrens III. 1972. *The Limits to Growth*. London: Signet.

Mercer, Joyce. 2017. "Environmental Activism in the Philippines: A Practical Theological Perspective." In *Planetary Solidarity: Global Women's Voices on Christian Doctrine and Climate Justice*, edited by Grace Ji-Sun Kim and Hilda P. Koster, 287–310. Minneapolis: Fortress Press.

Merlen, Godfrey. 1999. *Restoring the Tortoise Dynasty: The Decline and Recovery of the Galapagos Giant Tortoise*. Quito: Charles Darwin Foundation.

Middleton, Townsend. 2021. "Becoming-After: The Lives and Politics of Quinine's Remains." *Cultural Anthropology* 36 (2): 282–311. https://doi.org/10.14506 /ca36.2.05.

Mignolo, Walter D., and Arturo Escobar. 2013. *Globalization and the Decolonial Option*. London: Routledge.

Ministerio Ambiente. 2022. *Rendición de Cuenta 2021*. Quito: Ministerio de Ambiente Ecuador.

Mol, Annemarie. 2008. *The Logic of Care: Health and the Problem of Patient Choice*. London: Routledge.

Mol, Annemarie, Ingunn Moser, and Jeannette Pols, eds. 2010. *Care in Practice: On Tinkering in Clinics, Homes and Farms*. Bielefeld: Transcript Verlag.

Moola, Faisal, and Robin Roth. 2019. "Moving beyond Colonial Conservation Models: Indigenous Protected and Conserved Areas Offer Hope for Biodiversity and Advancing Reconciliation in the Canadian Boreal Forest 1." *Environmental Reviews* 27 (2): 200–201. https://doi.org/10.1139/er-2018-0091.

Moore, Amelia. 2010. "Climate Changing Small Islands: Considering Social Science and the Production of Island Vulnerability and Opportunity." *Environment and Society* 1 (1): 116–31. https://doi.org/10.3167/ares.2010.010106.

Murphy, Devon. 2022. "A Bold Plan to Rewild the Galápagos Will Start with Floreana Island." Re:Wild, August 13, 2022. https://www.rewild.org/news/a-bold-plan-to-rewild-the-galapagos-will-start-with-floreana-island.

Nadasdy, Paul. 2007. "The Gift in the Animal: The Ontology of Hunting and Human–Animal Sociality." *American Ethnologist* 34 (1): 25–43.

Nading, Alex M. 2012. "Dengue Mosquitoes Are Single Mothers: Biopolitics Meets Ecological Aesthetics in Nicaraguan Community Health Work." *Cultural Anthropology* 27 (4): 572–96.

———. 2014. *Mosquito Trails: Ecology, Health, and the Politics of Entanglement.* Berkeley: University of California Press.

Nguyen, Vinh-Kim. 2010. *The Republic of Therapy: Triage and Sovereignty in West Africa's Time of AIDS*. Durham, NC: Duke University Press.

Novo, Carmen Martínez. 2014. "Managing Diversity in Postneoliberal Ecuador." *Journal of Latin American and Caribbean Anthropology* 19 (1): 103–25. https://doi.org/10.1111/jlca.12062.

Ogden, Laura A. 2021. *Loss and Wonder at the World's End*. Durham, NC: Duke University Press.

Olden, Julian D., Lise Comte, and Xingli Giam. 2018. "The Homogocene: A Research Prospectus for the Study of Biotic Homogenisation." *NeoBiota* 37 (June): 23–36. https://doi.org/10.3897/neobiota.37.22552.

O'Neill, Bruce. 2017. *The Space of Boredom: Homelessness in the Slowing Global Order*. Durham, NC: Duke University Press.

Ospina, Pablo. 2006. *Galápagos, naturaleza y sociedad: Actores sociales y conflictos ambientales en las islas Galápagos*. Quito: Corporación Editora Nacional.

Ospina, Pablo, and Cecilia Falconí. 2007. *Galápagos: Migraciones, economía, cultura, conflictos y acuerdos*. Quito: Corporación Editora Nacional.

Otis, Lindsay. 2023. "Zeroing in on Greenwashing: How Corporations Misuse Net Zero Pledges." *Carbon Market Watch*, March 9, 2023. https://carbonmarket

watch.org/2023/03/09/zeroing-in-on-greenwashing-how-corporations-misuse
-net-zero-pledges/.

Otto, Ilona M., Kyoung Mi Kim, Nika Dubrovsky, and Wolfgang Lucht. 2019. "Shift the Focus from the Super-Poor to the Super-Rich." *Nature Climate Change* 9 (2): 82–84. https://doi.org/10.1038/s41558-019-0402-3.

Pachamama Alliance. 2022. "An Alliance for the Amazon and the World." https:// www.pachamama.org/advocacy/fundacion-pachamama.

Packard, Randall M. 2007. *The Making of a Tropical Disease: A Short History of Malaria*. Baltimore: Johns Hopkins University Press.

Parque Nacional Galapagos. 2014. *Plan de manejo de las areas protegidas de Galapagos para el Buen Vivir*. Puerto Ayora, Ecuador: Dirección del Parque Nacional Galápagos.

Parreñas, Juno Salazar. 2018. *Decolonizing Extinction: The Work of Care in Orangutan Rehabilitation*. Durham, NC: Duke University Press.

Peluso, Nancy Lee, and Michael Watts. 2001. *Violent Environments*. Ithaca, NY: Cornell University Press.

Peñafiel, Natali Torres, and Pablo Enrique Fierro López. 2017. "Balance de la economía popular y solidaria en Ecuador." *Economía y Desarrollo* 158: 18.

Peretti, Jonah H. 1998. "Nativism and Nature: Rethinking Biological Invasion." Environmental Values 7 (2): 183–92.

Porter, David. 1815. *Journal of a Cruise Made to the Pacific Ocean, by Captain David Porter, in the United States Frigate Essex: In the Years 1812, 1813, and 1814*. Philadelphia: Bradford and Inskeep.

Postero, Nancy. 2017. *The Indigenous State: Race, Politics, and Performance in Plurinational Bolivia*. Berkeley: University of California Press.

Povinelli, Elizabeth A. 2011. *Economies of Abandonment: Social Belonging and Endurance in Late Liberalism*. Durham, NC: Duke University Press.

———. 2016. *Geontologies: A Requiem to Late Liberalism*. Durham, NC: Duke University Press.

Puar, Jasbir. 2017. *The Right to Maim: Debility, Capacity, Disability*. Durham, NC: Duke University Press.

Pugliese, Joseph. 2020. *Biopolitics of the More-Than-Human: Forensic Ecologies of Violence*. Durham, NC: Duke University Press.

Quiroga, Diego. 2009. "Crafting Nature: The Galapagos and the Making and Unmaking of a 'Natural Laboratory.'" *Journal of Political Ecology* 16 (1): 123–40.

Radford, Clare Louise. 2017. "Meaning in the Margins: Postcolonial Feminist Methodologies in Practical Theology." *Practical Theology* 10 (2): 118–32. https:// doi.org/10.1080/1756073X.2017.1302700.

Rammelt, Crelis F., Joyeeta Gupta, Diana Liverman, Joeri Scholtens, Daniel Cio-banu, Jesse F. Abrams, Xuemei Bai, et al. 2023. "Impacts of Meeting Minimum Access on Critical Earth Systems amidst the Great Inequality." *Nature Sustainability* 6 (2): 212–21. https://doi.org/10.1038/s41893-022-00995-5.

Reddekop, Jarrad. 2022. "Against Ontological Capture: Drawing Lessons from Amazonian Kichwa Relationality." *Review of International Studies* 48 (5): 857–74. https://doi.org/10.1017/S0260210521000486.

Redfield, Peter. 2013. *Life in Crisis: The Ethical Journey of Doctors Without Borders*. Berkeley: University of California Press.

Rentería B., Jorge Luis, and Carol Ellison. 2004. "Potential Biological Control of Lantana Camara in the Galapagos Using the Rust Puccinia Lantanae." *SIDA, Contributions to Botany* 21 (2): 1009–17.

Richardson, Katherine, Will Steffen, Wolfgang Lucht, Jørgen Bendtsen, Sarah E. Cornell, Jonathan F. Donges, Markus Drüke, et al. 2023. "Earth beyond Six of Nine Planetary Boundaries." *Science Advances* 9 (37): eadh2458. https://doi.org/10.1126/sciadv.adh2458.

Riofrancos, Thea. 2020. *Resource Radicals: From Petro-Nationalism to Post-Extractivism in Ecuador*. Durham, NC: Duke University Press.

Ripple, William J., Christopher Wolf, Thomas M. Newsome, Mauro Galetti, Mohammed Alamgir, Eileen Crist, Mahmoud I. Mahmoud, and William F. Laurance. 2017. "World Scientists' Warning to Humanity: A Second Notice." *BioScience* 67 (12): 1026–28. https://doi.org/10.1093/biosci/bix125.

Robbins, Paul, and Sarah A. Moore. 2013. "Ecological Anxiety Disorder: Diagnosing the Politics of the Anthropocene." *Cultural Geographies* 20 (1): 3–19. https://doi.org/10.1177/1474474012469887.

Rolston, Holmes. 1999. "Respect for Life: Counting What Singer Finds of No Account." In *Singer and His Critics*, edited by Dale Jamieson, 147–68. Oxford: Blackwell.

Rose, Deborah Bird. 2004. *Reports from a Wild Country: Ethics for Decolonisation*. Sidney: University of New South Wales Press.

———. 2008. "Judas Work." *Environmental Philosophy* 5 (2): 51–66. https://doi.org/10.5840/envirophil2008528.

Rossing, Barbara. 2017. "Reimagining Eschatology: Toward Healing and Hope." In *Planet Solidarity: Global Women's Voices on Christian Doctrine and Climate Justice*, edited by Grace Ji-Sun Kim and Hila P. Koster, 325–47. Minneapolis: Fortress.

Ruether, Rosemary Radford. 1996. *Women Healing Earth: Third World Women on Ecology, Feminism, and Religion*. Maryknoll, NY: Orbis.

Santos, Boaventura de Sousa, and Maria Paula Menseses, eds. 2020. *Knowledges Born in the Struggle: Constructing the Epistemologies of the Global South.* London: Routledge.

Santander, Tatiana, José Antonio González Novoa, Washington Tapia, Eddy Araujo, and Carlos Montes del Olmo. 2009. "Tendencias de la investigación científica en Galápagos y sus implicaciones para el manejo del archipiélago." In *Ciencia para la sostenabilidad.* Parque Nacional de Galápagos. https://repositorio.uam.es /handle/10486/3209.

Schlaepfer, Martin A., Dov F. Sax, and Julian D. Olden. 2011. "The Potential Conservation Value of Non-Native Species." *Conservation Biology* 25 (3): 428–37. https://doi.org/10.1111/j.1523-1739.2010.01646.x.

Scott, James C. 1985. *Weapons of the Weak: Everyday Forms of Peasant Resistance.* New Haven, CT: Yale University Press.

SENPLADES. 2009. *Plan Nacional para el Buen Vivir 2009–2013.* Quito: Secretaría Técnica de Planificacion y Desarrollo. https://www.planificacion.gob.ec/plan -nacional-para-el-buen-vivir-2009-2013/.

Shelton, Jo-Anne. 2004. "Killing Animals That Don't Fit In: Moral Dimensions of Habitat Restoration." *Between the Species* 13 (4): 3.

Sherwood, Stephen G., Alberto Arce, and Myriam Paredes. 2018. "Affective Labor's 'Unruly Edge': The Pagus of Carcelen's Solidarity and Agroecology Fair in Ecuador." *Journal of Rural Studies* 61 (July): 302–13. https://doi.org/10.1016 /j.jrurstud.2018.02.001.

Shinozuka, Jeannie N. 2022. *Biotic Borders: Transpacific Plant and Insect Migration and the Rise of Anti-Asian Racism in America, 1890–1950.* Chicago: University of Chicago Press.

Sideris, Lisa. 2020. "Grave Reminders: Grief and Vulnerability in the Anthropocene." *Religions* 11 (293).

Sieder, Rachel, and Emma Cervone. 2017. *Demanding Justice and Security: Indigenous Women and Legal Pluralities in Latin America.* New Brunswick, NJ: Rutgers University Press.

Simberloff, Daniel, Jean-Louis Martin, Piero Genovesi, Virginie Maris, David A. Wardle, James Aronson, Franck Courchamp, et al. 2013. "Impacts of Biological Invasions: What's What and the Way Forward." *Trends in Ecology and Evolution* 28 (1): 58–66. https://doi.org/10.1016/j.tree.2012.07.013.

Simpson, Audra. 2014. *Mohawk Interruptus: Political Life across the Borders of Settler States.* Durham, NC: Duke University Press.

Simpson, Leanne Betasamosake. 2016. "Indigenous Resurgence and Co-Resistance." *Critical Ethnic Studies* 2 (2): 19–34. https://doi.org/10.5749/jcritethnstud.2.2.0019.

Sodikoff, Genese Marie. 2012. *The Anthropology of Extinction: Essays on Culture and Species Death*. Bloomington: Indiana University Press.

Soulé, Michael E. 1985. "What Is Conservation Biology?" *BioScience* 35 (11): 727–34. https://doi.org/10.2307/1310054.

Steffen, Will, Wendy Broadgate, Lisa Deutsch, Owen Gaffney, and Cornelia Ludwig. 2015. "The Trajectory of the Anthropocene: The Great Acceleration." *Anthropocene Review* 2 (1): 81–98. https://doi.org/10.1177/2053019614564785.

Steffen, Will, Paul J. Crutzen, and John R. McNeill. 2007. "The Anthropocene: Are Humans Now Overwhelming the Great Forces of Nature?" *AMBIO: A Journal of the Human Environment* 36 (8): 614–21. https://doi.org/10.1579/0044-7447.

Stengers, Isabelle. 2013. "Introductory Notes on an Ecology of Practices." *Cultural Studies Review* 11 (1): 183–96.

———. 2015. *La vierge et le neutrino*. Paris: Média Diffusion.

Stott, Peter A., Nikolaos Christidis, Friederike E. L. Otto, Ying Sun, Jean-Paul Vanderlinden, Geert Jan van Oldenborgh, Robert Vautard, et al. 2016. "Attribution of Extreme Weather and Climate-Related Events." *WIREs Climate Change* 7 (1): 23–41. https://doi.org/10.1002/wcc.380.

Strathern, Marilyn. 2004. *Partial Connections*. Savage, MD: Rowman Altamira.

Subramaniam, Banu. 2001. "The Aliens Have Landed! Reflections on the Rhetoric of Biological Invasions." *Meridians: Feminism, Race, Transnationalism* 2 (1): 26–40.

———. 2014. *Ghost Stories for Darwin: The Science of Variation and the Politics of Diversity*. Urbana: University of Illinois Press.

Sulloway, Frank J. 1982. "Darwin and His Finches: The Evolution of a Legend." *Journal of the History of Biology* 15 (1): 1–53. https://doi.org/10.1007/BF00132004.

Swaisgood, Ronald R., and James Sheppard. 2011. "Hope Springs Eternal: Biodiversity Conservation Requires That We See the Glass as Half Full." *BioScience* 61 (6): 427–28. https://doi.org/10.1525/bio.2011.61.6.3.

TallBear, Kim. 2017. "Beyond the Life / Not Life Binary: A Feminist-Indigenous Reading of Cryopreservation, Interspecies Thinking and the New Materialisms." In *Cryopolitics: Frozen Life in a Melting World*, edited by Joanna Radin and Emma Kowal, 179–202. Cambridge, MA: MIT Press.

Taylor, Dan, and Larry Katahira. 1988. "Radio Telemetry as an Aid in Eradicating Remnant Feral Goats." *Wildlife Society Bulletin* 16 (3): 297–99.

Thompson, Kim-Ly, and Natalie C. Ban. 2022. "'Turning to the Territory': A Gitga'at Nation Case Study of Indigenous Climate Imaginaries and Actions." *Geoforum* 137 (December): 230–36. https://doi.org/10.1016/j.geoforum.2021.11.006.

Ticktin, Miriam I. 2011. *Casualties of Care: Immigration and the Politics of Humanitarianism in France*. Berkeley: University of California Press.

Traill, Lochran W., Corey J. A. Bradshaw, and Barry W. Brook. 2007. "Minimum Viable Population Size: A Meta-Analysis of 30 Years of Published Estimates." *Biological Conservation* 139 (1): 159–66. https://doi.org/10.1016/j.biocon.2007.06.011.

Tsing, Anna Lowenhaupt. 2015. *The Mushroom at the End of the World: On the Possibility of Life in Capitalist Ruins*. Princeton, NJ: Princeton University Press.

Tuck, Eve, and K Wayne Yang. 2012. "Decolonization Is Not a Metaphor." *Decolonization: Indigeneity, Education and Society* 1 (1): 1–40.

Turnhout, Esther, Claire Waterton, Katja Neves, and Marleen Buizer. 2012. "Rethinking Biodiversity: From Goods and Services to 'Living With.'" *Conservation Letters* 6 (3): 154–61. https://doi.org/10.1111/j.1755-263X.2012.00307.x.

Tye, Alan. 2006. "Can We Infer Island Introduction and Naturalization Rates from Inventory Data? Evidence from Introduced Plants in Galapagos." *Biological Invasions* 8 (2): 201–15. https://doi.org/10.1007/s10530-004-3574-2.

UN Environment Programme. 2021. *Ecosystem Restoration for People, Nature, and Climate*. Nairobi: United Nations.

UNESCO. 2007. "UNESCO Mission Confirms Threat to Galápagos Islands." UNESCO World Heritage Centre, April 16, 2007. https://whc.unesco.org/en/news/322/.

———. 2023. "UNESCO World Heritage Centre—State of Conservation (SOC 2021) Galápagos Islands (Ecuador)." UNESCO World Heritage Centre. https://whc.unesco.org/en/soc/4163/.

United Nations. 2023. "Hottest July Ever Signals 'Era of Global Boiling Has Arrived' Says UN Chief." UN News, July 27, 2023. https://news.un.org/en/story/2023/07/1139162.

van Dooren, Thom. 2011. "Invasive Species in Penguin Worlds: An Ethical Taxonomy of Killing for Conservation." *Conservation and Society* 9 (4): 286.

———. 2014. *Flight Ways: Life and Loss at the Edge of Extinction*. New York: Columbia University Press.

van Dooren, Thom, Eben Kirksey, and Ursula Münster. 2016. "Multispecies Studies Cultivating Arts of Attentiveness." *Environmental Humanities* 8 (1): 1–23. https://doi.org/10.1215/22011919-3527695.

van Elden, Sean, Jessica J. Meeuwig, Richard J. Hobbs, and Jan M. Hemmi.

2019. "Offshore Oil and Gas Platforms as Novel Ecosystems: A Global Perspective." *Frontiers in Marine Science* 6: 129–44. https://doi.org/10.3389/fmars.2019.00548.

Vanhulst, Julien. 2015. "El laberinto de los discursos del Buen vivir: Entre Sumak Kawsay y Socialismo del siglo XXI." *Polis: Revista Latinoamericana*, no. 40 (May). https://journals.openedition.org/polis/10727.

Villamil, Justin. 2023. "Ecuador's 'Blue' Bond Deal Won't Save the Galapagos." *Jacobin*, June 6, 2023. https://jacobin.com/2023/06/ecuador-blue-bond-deal-galapagos-debt-sustainability-conservation.

Vince, Gaia. 2011. "Embracing Invasives." *Science* 331 (6023): 1383–84. https://doi.org/10.1126/science.331.6023.1383.

Waddell, Robby. 2014. "A Green Apocalypse: Comparing Secular and Religious Eschatological Visions of the Earth." In *Blood Cries Out: Pentecostals, Ecology, and the Groans of Creation*, edited by A. J. Swoboda, 133–51. Eugene, OR: Wipf and Stock.

Wadiwel, Dinesh Joseph. 2016. "Fish and Pain: The Politics of Doubt." *Animal Sentience: An Interdisciplinary Journal on Animal Feeling* 1 (3): 31.

Walker, Jeremy, and Melinda Cooper. 2011. "Genealogies of Resilience: From Systems Ecology to the Political Economy of Crisis Adaptation." *Security Dialogue* 42 (2): 143–60. https://doi.org/10.1177/0967010611399616.

Walsh, Catherine E. 2022. *Rising Up, Living On: Re-existences, Sowings, and Decolonial Cracks*. Durham, NC: Duke University Press.

Wanderer, Emily Mannix. 2015. "Biologies of Betrayal: Judas Goats and Sacrificial Mice on the Margins of Mexico." *BioSocieties* 10 (1): 1–23.

Warren, Ben H., Daniel Simberloff, Robert E. Ricklefs, Robin Aguilée, Fabien L. Condamine, Dominique Gravel, Hélène Morlon, et al. 2015. "Islands as Model Systems in Ecology and Evolution: Prospects Fifty Years after MacArthur-Wilson." *Ecology Letters* 18 (2): 200–217. https://doi.org/10.1111/ele.12398.

Waters, Colin N., Jan Zalasiewicz, Colin Summerhayes, Anthony D. Barnosky, Clément Poirier, Agnieszka Gałuszka, Alejandro Cearreta, et al. 2016. "The Anthropocene Is Functionally and Stratigraphically Distinct from the Holocene." *Science* 351 (6269): aad2622. https://doi.org/10.1126/science.aad2622.

Webb, Campbell O. 2005. "Engineering Hope." *Conservation Biology* 19 (1): 275–77.

West, Paige. 2006. *Conservation Is Our Government Now: The Politics of Ecology in Papua New Guinea*. Durham, NC: Duke University Press.

Whyte, Kyle. 2017. "Indigenous Climate Change Studies: Indigenizing Futures, Decolonizing the Anthropocene." *English Language Notes* 55 (1): 153–62.

———, dir. 2023. *Kyle Whyte: Braiding Kinship and Time: Indigenous Approaches to Environmental Justice.* Seattle: University of Washington, Office of Public Lectures.

Willerslev, Rane. 2016. *Taming Time, Timing Death: Social Technologies and Ritual.* London: Routledge.

Wolf, Eric R. 1999. *Envisioning Power: Ideologies of Dominance and Crisis.* Berkeley: University of California Press.

Wolff, Matthias, and Mark Gardener, eds. 2012. *The Role of Science for Conservation.* London: Routledge.

Wood, Jamie R., Josep A. Alcover, Tim M. Blackburn, Pere Bover, Richard P. Duncan, Julian P. Hume, Julien Louys, Hanneke J. M. Meijer, Juan C. Rando, and Janet M. Wilmshurst. 2017. "Island Extinctions: Processes, Patterns, and Potential for Ecosystem Restoration." *Environmental Conservation* 44 (4): 348–58. https://doi.org/10.1017/S037689291700039X.

Wright, N. T. 2008. *Surprised by Hope: Rethinking Heaven, the Resurrection, and the Mission of the Church.* Grand Rapids, MI: Zondervan.

Ybarra, Megan. 2018. *Green Wars: Conservation and Decolonization in the Maya Forest.* Oakland: University of California Press.

Zaldívar, Víctor Bretón Solo de. 2017. "Three Divergent Understandings of Buen Vivir in the Ecuador of the Citizens' Revolution." *Latin American and Caribbean Ethnic Studies* 12 (2): 188–98. https://doi.org/10.1080/17442222.2017.1318541.

Zalucki, M. P., M. D. Day, and J. Playford. 2007. "Will Biological Control of Lantana Camara Ever Succeed? Patterns, Processes & Prospects." *Biological Control* 42 (3): 251–61. https://doi.org/10.1016/j.biocontrol.2007.06.002.

Index

Italicized page numbers refer to figures.

adaptation, xi

Agrarian Revolution, 82

agriculture: climate change impact on, 106; composting, 122; early settler dependence on, 109; as ecosystem threat, 107; employment shift to tourism, 114; expenses for, 105, 107; food sovereignty goal, 16–17, 80–81; green, 95–96; greenhouse use, 91–92, *92*; herbicides/pesticides, 121–22; hydroponic farming, 105–6, 147; impact of, 8; land ownership issues, 81–82, 157n1 (ch3); obstacles, 16–17; organic, 122; plan for, 80–81; productive, 80–81; soil health, 122; water and soil limitations, 105

Agriculture Ministry. *See* Ministry of Agriculture (MAGAP)

airline ticket pricing, residency status impact, 87

allopatric speciation, 12

Anthropocene, 132–36; Great Acceleration, *133*

anti-immigration rhetoric, 55, 114

Aristotle, 38

assemblages: more-than-human, 20–21; multispecies, 36, 42; reconfiguring, 42

Banco del Fomento (Development Bank), 89–90, 93

bank loans/bureaucracy: applicants, 91–94; documentation requirements, 90–91; presentation, 89–90; subsidies/loans to large landowners, 94; subsidies to small farmers, 81

bankruptcy, Ecuador (1999), 90

Belgica (farmer), 126

biblical names, church protest, 156n2 (ch1)

BID-FOMIN (Inter-American Development Bank), 81

biodiversity: isolation role in, 10–11; loss of, xiii, 24, 54–57; offset programs, 155n6

biogeography, 31

black rats, controlling, 67

Blake, Stephen, 73

Brandt, Kate, 159n2 (conclusion)

buen vivir: associations/workers' collectives role in, 94–95; bureaucracy, 82; goals/plans for, 4, 9; government use of, 155n2; harmonious well-being in, 34; local participation, xv; marginalization due to, 100; multilayered, xi; in policies for land stewardship and endemic species protection, x; principles of, 156n4

186 *Index*

buen vivir (*continued*)
(ch1); problems exacerbated by, 99;
socio-ecological, 13–17; subsidized
loans role in, 90; temporary and undocumented farmers under, 83–89
buen vivir insular, 80, 81, 82
buses (goats), police checks, 157n2
(intermezzo)

cacaotillo. See *Miconia robinsoniana*
caco trees, 125–26
cacti, 131
Campbell, Karl, 38
care: as lethal, 36; multispecies, 47
caring for the islands, opposing forms
of, 35–37
Carrión, Carlos, 1–2, 6, 7
cascarilla. See *Cinchona pubescens*
Cecilia (state agronomist), 95–96
Cedrela odorata, 119, 120
Celia: endemic gardens business,
130–31, 138; endemic harvest, *143*; as
Jehovah's Witness, 131–32, 140–41;
native plant collecting, 133–34
Charles Darwin Foundation: blackberry
control study, 60–62; Celia's time
at, 136–37; conservation approach,
137; establishment of, 32; funding
for, 1; goat eradication role, 33; hill
raspberry impact on *Scalesia* forest,
59; on hill raspberry seeds, 58; local
residents as allies/partners, 16; novel
ecosystems proposal, 52, 69, 150
Charles Darwin Station, xiv
Christian feminism, 135, 143–44
church protest over use of biblical
names, 156n2 (ch1)

Cinchona pubescens: beneficial impact
on endemic ferns, 53; blackberry
colonization after eradication, 63;
colonization after hill raspberry
eradication, 51; control challenges,
66–67; die-off from root fungus,
71; distribution of, 63; as ecosystem
engineer, 65; endangered in some
locations, 156n3 (ch2); as highly
invasive, 66; hybridization of, 156n2
(ch2); increased humidity as benefit, 53, 70–71; Indigenous use of,
64; as malaria treatment, 64;
post-eradication hill raspberry as
replacement, 67; synonyms for,
156n2 (ch2)
citizen participation, 4
Citizens' Revolution (Revolución
Ciudadana): marginalization due to,
15; resources for, 81; as surveillance
apparatus, 16
climate change: ENSO events fre-
quency, strength, and duration, 11;
global warming, xv, xii n6; industry
interests role in, 149, 159n2 (conclusion); species extinction from, xiii
climatic zones, 8
coexistence, alternative forms of, 22
compost facility, location considerations, 136–37
Consejo de Gobierno, 1, 155n1
conservation: blame placed on, 23; care
as lethal, 37; centered on what works,
24; contemporary market-based
approaches to, 111; as custodial and
exclusionary, x; Charles Darwin
Foundation approach, 137; decolo-

nizing, 151–52; deleterious effects of, 150–51; eradication as, 48; farmers' role in, 8–9; fortress approach, xiin3; funding for, 1; income flow from, ix–x; land alienated by, ix; leadership shortcomings, 138–39; mainstream, 155n5; millenarian beliefs in, 142–43; moral implications of, 41; more-than-human analysis of, 20; pledges for, 148; residents' contribution limitations, 16; residents disproportionally targeted by, 18; residents' role in, x; resilience in, 14; tourism as funding source, 12. *See also* novel ecosystems; restoration

conservation despair, 133

Conservation International, 1, 16

Constitution (1998), 83

constitutionally guaranteed "rights to nature," 14

contested ecologies, 20–25

cooperatives (associations), 94–100

Correa, Rafael: backlash against, 16; citizen participation agenda, 4; conservation steps taken by, 14–15; cycling passion, 79; on islands "at risk," 13; LOREG enforcement under, 83; meeting in Puerto Ayora, Santa Cruz, 79–82; oil drilling allowed by, 150; protest against, 79

corruption, non-refunded deposits, 88

dark-rumped petrel (*Pterodroma phaeopygia*): impact of invasive plants, 63, 67, 140; rebound in populations, 69

Darwin, Charles: theory of evolution, 31; visit to Galápagos Islands, xiv, 12

Deleuze, Gilles, 20–21, 109–10

dense present, 112

Development Bank (Banco del Fomento), 89–90, 93

DiCaprio, Leonardo, 148

Duque, Iván, 159n1 (conclusion)

Earl, Silvia, 159n1 (conclusion)

ecological barriers: factors in, 156n4 (ch2); goats' mobility, 29–30

ecologies: contested, 20–25; ENSO impact on, 11; eradication impact on, 51–52, 56–57; viable, xi, 17–20, 145. *See also* Proyecto Isabela

ecosystems: carbon storage capacity, xv; vulnerability of, 30–31. *See also* restoration; tourists/tourism

eco-theology, 135, 143–44

Ecuador: bankruptcy (1999), 90; on Galápagos Islands in crisis, xv, 83; increase in protected areas, 148; role in Marine Litter and Plastic Pollution Conference, Geneva, 149

El Niño–Southern Oscillation (ENSO), 11

endangered species care, 48

endemic species: climate change impact on, 11; collecting, for the end of the world, 141; conservation motivated by, 10; construction impact on, 129–32; extinction of, 31; humidity from *Cinchona* as benefit, 70–71; pledges for, 148; vulnerability to human impact, 11. *See also specific endemic species*

188 *Index*

Enlace Ciudadano (weekly radio/TV show), 79
ENSO (El Niño–Southern Oscillation), 11
environmental activism, violent state repression of, 149
environmental activists, assassination of, 149, 155n7
environmentalism: alternative, 151; among Jehovah's Witnesses, 136; eschatology reconciled with, 135
environmental organizations, view of novel ecosystems, 69
epistemic extractivism, 24
eradication: vs. genocide, 43; impact on other species, 51–52. *See also* Proyecto Isabela
ERAs (Schools of the Agrarian Revolution program), 95, 158n4
Ernesto (farmer), 123–26
Erythrina velutina trees, 159n2 (ch4)
eschatology: environmentalism reconciled with, 135; as precluding plans for the future, 133–34
ethnography, multispecies, 20
extinction: of endemic species, 31; increasing, xiii; of island species, 54; risk for tortoises, 31
extractive industries, funding from, 15

farmers: alternative living style, 151; assistance to, 16, 84; contributions of, 7; creativity in response to adverse conditions, 106–9; hill raspberry clearing, 4; identifying as mestizos, white, or other, 159n1 (ch4); irrelevance of associations, 97; marginalization, 82; needs, 6–7; poncho sym-

bolizing poverty and powerlessness, 157n1 (intermezzo); resilience and resistance, 112; temporary/undocumented residents, 83–89
farms: abandonment as setting for invasive species, 114; educational, 147–48, 152; productivity of, 151. *See also* bank loans/bureaucracy
FEIG (Galápagos Invasive Species Fund), 1
feminist theology, 144
fetishization of data, techno-optimism supported by, 159n2 (conclusion)
Floreana Island: habitation of, xv; hill raspberry presence on, 58; location of, 2
Floreana mockingbird, 148
food imports, as source of pathogens and invasive species, 9, 80–81, 95–96
food sovereignty, 16–17, 80–81

Gabriela (farmer), 49–50
Galápagos Invasive Species Fund (FEIG), 1
Galápagos Islands: areas of human occupation, 8, 10; as "at-risk" UNESCO World Heritage Site, xv, 13, 83; biodiversity, ix, 139; climate, 11; commercial uses of, xiv; as counterbalance to politics on the mainland, 149; geography of, 8, 10; inhabited islands, xv; maps, *xxiv*, 2; marine reserves, 10, 149, 159n1 (conclusion); politics on, 110; population of, 13; surrounded by extinction, 13; volcanic formation, 10. *See also* tourists/tourism

Galápagos Marine Reserve, expanding, 10, 149, 159n1 (conclusion)

Galápagos National Park: *Cinchona* presence in, 64, 66–67; conservation plan/goals, 14, 53, 150; founding of, xiv, 32; funding for, 1; Giant Tortoise Breeding Center, 42; goat eradication role, 33; hill raspberry removal, 3–6, 62–63; novel ecosystems proposal, 52, 69; painting outside, *134*; percent of the archipelago included in, xiv, 10, 29; pledges for, 148; protected and human areas integrated in conservation plan, 14; regrowth of vegetation, 44; residents as allies/partners, 13–16; socio-ecological systems (SES) used by, 14

Galápagos rail (*Laterallus spilonota*): impact of invasive plants, 63, 67; rebound in populations, 69

Gardener, Mark: on novel ecosystems, 52, 68, 70; on preservation of targeted species, 69

Geist, Dennis, 69

Geovanny (hunter), 57

giant tortoises, 13

global warming, xv, xii n6

goats: background, 29; body decomposition to return nutrients to soil, 48; chimeric, 40, 156n3 (ch1); death rates on Santiago and Isabela Islands, 38; eradication of, 32–33, 37–40, 42; eradication role similarity to Noah's ark, 47, 156n5; estrus lengthening, 34, 35, 39–40; Judas goats (looking for a new herd), 35, 38–40, 46, 156n2 (ch1); local residents' re-

lationship with, 48–50; meat from, 50; proliferation, 29–32; Proyecto Isabela impact on, 50; sterile females that could attract males, 34, 35. *See also* Proyecto Isabela

Great Acceleration (Anthropocene), 133

greenhouse agriculture, 91–92, *92*

greenhouse gas concentration, xiii, xv

greenhouses: to avoid fungal diseases, 147; impromptu, 76; improvised, 120–21; view of, *92*; water required for, 91

Guattari, Félix, 20–21, 109–10

guava (*Psidium guajava*), 114, 125

guayabillo trees, 125–26

Gutama, Víctor Joel Guaillas, assassination of, 149

health care: nationalized, 88, 158n3; quality of, 87–88

Helena (undocumented farmer), 101–3, 106–7, 127

herbicides: alternatives to, 122; ill effects of, 121; impact on species that feed on the targeted plants, 68; impact on warbler finches, 69; soil and water contamination, 68

Hermanedad (Brotherhood) marine reserve, 159n1 (conclusion)

Hibiscus tiliaceus trees, 159n2 (ch4)

hill raspberry (*Rubus niveus*): on abandoned farms, 114; background, 57; controlling, 125; eradication, 3–6, 59–60, 62; goats as control on, 51; local involvement in, x; locations of, 58; photo of, 59; resilience of, 57–58; seed dormancy of ten years, 58

Holden, Andrew, 133–34
housing: designed for additional stories, 118; Juan's house, Santa Cruz highlands, *117*
Humboldt Current, 10
hydroponic farming, 105–6, 147

IESP (Popular and Solidarity Economy), 81
immigration as contested issue, 113. *See also* undocumented residents
immigration law (1998), 16, 105, 113
Immigration Office, visa approvals, 84
Institute of the Popular Economy, cooperatives oversight by, 95
Inter-American Development Bank (BID-FOMIN), 81
invasive species: on abandoned farms, 114; acreage of, xv; anti-immigrant undertones in discussions about, 55; clearing with a machete, 124; controlling, 52, 125; cultivated land curbing the spread of, 108; definition of, 62; ethical dimensions of managing, 41; on fallow land, 94, 151; inadequate defenses against, 54; increase in, 139–40; local involvement in, x; management of, 54; novel ecosystem approach to, 52–53, 55; removal as counterproductive, 62; unexpected benefits of, 53; urbanization contributions to, 140. *See also* hill raspberry; *and specific invasive species*
irreversible thresholds, 68–69
Isabela Island: goat eradication on northern, 33–34; goats remaining on southern, 34; habitation of, xv; hill raspberry presence on, 58; location of, 2; percentage killed on northern, 38; Perry Isthmus, 2, 30
Island Conservation, 1, 148
island settings: ecosystem vulnerability, 30–31; extinctions on, 54

Jackson, Wes, xi
Jäger, Heinke: *Cinchona*/hill raspberry control, 67–68; *Cinchona* research, 65–66; plant species count, *61*
Jehovah's Witnesses: assistance provided by, 141–42; Celia's membership in, 131–32, 140–41; environmentalism present among, 134–35, 136; eschatology as precluding plans for the future, 133–34; philosophy of, 159nn1–3 (ch5)
Joel (farmer; temporary resident), visa application/renewals, 84–89, 157n2 (ch3)
Jorge (farmer), 123–26
José (association president), 97–99
Juan (farmer): farm work, 115–19; house, *117*
Juan (farm owner), 115–16, 117–18
Judas goats (looking for a new herd), 35, 38–40, 46, 156n2 (ch1)
Julie (farmer), 119–23

Keller, Catherine, 144
Kichwa traditions of beings of equal worth, 141

land ownership/land owners: farmers as anchor for, 118–19; skewed figures, 81–82, 157n1 (ch3); by undocumented residents, 101, 107–8

Lantana camara, 140

Lasso, Guillermo, 148, 159n1 (conclusion)

Law, John, 43

Law of Popular and Solidarity Economy (2011), 94

Lazarus taxa, 156n1

Ley Especial para Galápagos (LOREG). *See* LOREG

Ley Orgánica de Economía Popular y Solidaria y del Sector Financiero Popular y Solidario, 99

Lidia (farmer; loan applicant), 91–93, *92*

life uncertainties: bank loans/bureaucracy, 89–94; cooperatives (associations), 94–100; Correa's administration, 79–82; temporary resident visas, 83–89

Linnaeus, Carolus, 64

LOREG: economic interests reflected in, 113–14; enforcement under Correa, 83

Lucia (farmer): citizenship request, 82; as temporary resident, 75–77, 79–80, 99

Luisa (Celia's employee), 134

MAGAP. *See* Ministry of Agriculture

malaria treatment, 64, 65–66

Manrique, Gustavo, 159n1 (conclusion)

maracuya trees, 125–26

Marco (undocumented farmer), 101–3, 106–7, 127

marine currents, colonization role of, 10

Marine Litter and Plastic Pollution Conference, Geneva, 149

marine reserves, 10, 149, 159n1 (conclusion)

Mata Haris (sterile female goats with implanted hormones), 40

matazarno trees, 125–26

Mercer, Joyce, 144

Miconia robinsoniana (endemic shrub), 51, 53, 63

Migración (immigration), 84

millenarian beliefs, 142–43

Ministry of Agriculture (MAGAP): assistance provided by, 84; association registry, 95–96; credit for other people's work, 106; farmer signing log for field visits, *85*; goat eradication role, 33; Plan Piloto presentation by, 80; residents as allies/partners, 16; touting cooperatives, 94–95. *See also* bank loans/bureaucracy

Ministry of Environment (MAE), 80

minor thriving: Belgica (farmer), 126; concept of, 109–11; farmers' creativity, 106–9; hydroponic farming, 105–6; Jorge and Ernesto (farmers), 123–26, 127; Juan (farmer), 115–19, 127; Julio and Rosa (farmers), 119–23, *123*, 127; Marco and Helena (farmers), 101–3, 106–7, 127; resilience and resistance, 111–12; Vicente (farmer), 105–6

mora. See hill raspberry

mora thorns, 60, 61

Mother Nature (Pachamama), 16

multispecies ethnography, 20

Nading, Alex, 47

Noah's ark, goat eradication similarity, 47, 156n5

192 *Index*

nonnative (alien) species, positive effects of, 73

novel ecosystems: as adaptive management, 70–71; background, 68–71; invasive species proposal, 52–53, 55; for irreversible thresholds, 68–69; moderated intervention, 69; politics of, 71–72

oil drilling, *150*

Pachamama (environmental group), 16

Pachamama (Mother Nature), 16

Palo santo trees, 159n2 (ch4)

Panama Current, 10

Patricio, Don, 119–20

permanent residents, 83

Perry Isthmus, ecological communities separated by, 2, 30

pesticides: alternatives to, 122; ill effects of, 121

Philornis downsi (parasitic fly; invasive), 51–52, 69

PI. *See* Proyecto Isabela

pink iguana, 148

Pinta Island: goat eradication on, 33–34; location of, *2*

Piscidia carthagenensis trees, 159n2 (ch4)

Plan for Island Good Living, 16–17

Plan for Organic Agriculture on the Galápagos (Plan de Bioagricultura para Galápagos): benefits/intent of, 80–81; exclusion/marginalization of farmers, 99–100

Plan for the Buen Vivir Insular, 80

plan of *buen vivir* (2007–17), 4

Plan Piloto: benefits of, 80–81; farmers,

inclusion, 8–9; for hill raspberry clearance, 3–5, 7, 80

plant species count, *61*

police presence: checkpoints, 83, 107–8; checks of buses, 157n2 (intermezzo); minimal in the highlands, 109; notifications to Juan, 116–17

poncho, symbolizing poverty and powerlessness, 157n1 (intermezzo)

Popular and Solidarity Economy (IESP), 81

protected and human areas, feedback loops, 150

protests: against Correa, 79; modalities, 46

Proyecto Isabela (goat eradication, PI): as definitive solution, 32, 40–41; diminished/defiant presence afterwards, 50; eradication, 32–33, 37–40; goats replaced by hill raspberry, 57; justification for, 30; local resistance to, 45–46. *See also* goats

Puerto Ayora: conditions in, 137; construction in, 129–30; as headquarters for environmental organizations, 1; land swap, 129; waterfront degradation, 145

quinine, *Cinchona* as source, 64

Ramiro (farmer; loan applicant), 91–93

residents: as allies/partners, 13–16; disproportionate targeting by conservationists, 18; problems blamed on, 23

resilience: concept of, xi, 111–12; in conservation, 14, 15; residents' contributions limitation, 16 resistance, 21, 112

restoration: carbon storage resulting from, xv; as conservation practice, x, xv; as goal, 47–48, 52; historical baseline, 19; irreversible thresholds as obstacle, 68–69; Jehovah's Witnesses' outlook on, 131–32, 142; novel ecosystems vs., 52, 53–54, 68–69; pragmatic control measures, 69; unintended consequences, 53, 54. *See also* novel ecosystems

Re:wild, 148

"rights to nature" constitutionally guaranteed, 14

Rio Blanco mining project, 149

Rodrigo (local resident), 49

root fungus (*Phytophthora cinnamoni*), 71

Rosa (farmer), 113–14, 119–23, *123f*

Rose, Deborah Bird, xiii

Rossing, Barbara, 144

Rubus niveus. See hill raspberry

Sabatinas (weekly radio/TV show), 79

San Cristóbal Island: goats remaining on, 34; habitation of, xv; hill raspberry presence on, 58; location of, 2

Santa Cruz Island: *Cinchona* presence on, 64; goats remaining on, 34; habitation of, xv; hill raspberry presence on, 58; location of, 2; population of, 137

Santiago Island: goat eradication on, 33–34; hill raspberry presence on, 51, 58; location of, 2; percentage of goats killed on, 38

sauco macho, 108; on abandoned farms, 114; controlling,125

Scalesia cordata trees, 159n2 (ch4)

Scalesia peduncolata: blackberry domination over, 58–59; hill raspberry impact on, 59; photo of, *59*; preservation of, 62–63

Schools of the Agrarian Revolution program (Escuelas de la Revolución Agraria; ERAs), 95, 158n4

Scott, James: *Weapons of the Weak*, 46

socio-ecological systems (SES): challenging the static ecosystem model, 15; as conservation framework, 4, 14; in sustainable development, 155n1

species endemism. *See* endemic species

Stengers, Isabelle, 55–56

stewardship: as Kichwa tradition, 141; planetary, 133

Superintendencia de Economía Popular y Solidaria (SEPS), cooperatives registering with, 94–95

sustainable development draft, 155n1

techno-optimism, fetishization of data underpinning, 159n2 (conclusion)

temporary residents: discomfort with associations, 97–99; lobbying for, 79–80; status, 75–77; vulnerability/ marginalization, 88–89. *See also* police presence; visas

tortoises: caring for, 35, 37; extinction risk, 31; fertility practices at San Diego zoo, 42; Giant Tortoise Breeding Center, 42; goats impact on, 30; invasive plants as dietary benefit, 53, 73; species of, 13

194 Index

tourists/tourism: deleterious effects of, xiv, 13, 72, 150–51; evolution of, 118; experiences of, 17–18; fishers and farmers marginalized by, 36; as funding source, 12; immigration driven by, 114; impact of, 110; income flow from, ix–x, xiv; invasive species removal as benefit for, 62–63; as legal category, 83; political strength of, 113; as "protected species," 23

Tsing, Anna Lowenhaupt, 56

UN Climate Change Conference of the Parties, Glasgow, 149

undocumented residents: alternative survival modes, 109; construction workers as, 113; creative survival, 108; deportations, 17, 83; discomfort with associations, 97–99; farmers as, 83–89, 113–14, 115–19; job opportunity limitations, 108; land ownership challenges, 101, 107–8; lobbying for, 79–80. *See also* police presence

UNESCO, Galápagos Islands as "at-risk" World Heritage Site, xv, 13, 83

urbanization, invasive species increase with, 140

Urbino, Italy, 38, 155n1 (ch1)

van Dooren, Thom, 48

viable ecologies, xi, 17–20, 145

Vicente (farmer), 105–6, 147–48, 152

visas: approvals/renewals, 84; author's experience with, 157n2 (ch3); deposit requirements, 88; documentation requirements/bureaucracy, 84–89; sponsorship by a permanent resident, 84; work visas, 83

vivir. See *buen vivir*; life uncertainties

Walker trade wind, 10–11

Wallace, Alfred, theory of evolution, 31

Walsh, Catherine, 24

warble finches (endemic), eradication impact on food availability, 51–52, 69

Weapons of the Weak (Scott), 46

whooping cranes, insemination and breeding, 48

Whyte, Kyle, 110

wind patterns, 11

workers' collectives. *See* cooperatives (associations)

World Wildlife Fund, 1

Yasuní Indigenous territory (ITT): oil drilling allowed, *150*; oil drilling excluded, 14

CULTURE, PLACE, AND NATURE

Studies in Anthropology and Environment

Viable Ecologies: Conservation and Coexistence on the Galápagos Islands,
   by Paolo Bocci
Crafting a Tibetan Terroir: Winemaking in Shangri-La, by Brendan A. Galipeau
China's Camel Country:Livestock and Nation-Building in a Pastoral Frontier,
   by Thomas White
Sustaining Natures: An Environmental Anthropology Reader, edited
   by Sarah R. Osterhoudt and K. Sivaramakrishnan
Fukushima Futures: Survival Stories in a Repeatedly Ruined Seascape,
   by Satsuki Takahashi
*The Camphor Tree and the Elephant: Religion and Ecological Change in Maritime
   Southeast Asia,* by Faizah Zakaria
Turning Land into Capital: Development and Dispossession in the Mekong Region,
   edited by Philip Hirsch, Kevin Woods, Natalia Scurrah, and Michael B. Dwyer
*Spawning Modern Fish: Transnational Comparison in the Making of Japanese
   Salmon,* by Heather Anne Swanson
Upland Geopolitics: Postwar Laos and the Global Land Rush, by Michael B. Dwyer
*Misreading the Bengal Delta: Climate Change, Development, and Livelihoods
   in Coastal Bangladesh,* by Camelia Dewan
*Ordering the Myriad Things: From Traditional Knowledge to Scientific Botany
   in China,* by Nicholas K. Menzies
Timber and Forestry in Qing China: Sustaining the Market, by Meng Zhang
Consuming Ivory: Mercantile Legacies of East Africa and New England, by
   Alexandra C. Kelly
Mapping Water in Dominica: Enslavement and Environment under Colonialism,
   by Mark W. Hauser
Mountains of Blame: Climate and Culpability in the Philippine Uplands,
   by Will Smith
*Sacred Cows and Chicken Manchurian: The Everyday Politics of Eating Meat
   in India,* by James Staples

Gardens of Gold: Place-Making in Papua New Guinea, by Jamon Alex Halvaksz

Shifting Livelihoods: Gold Mining and Subsistence in the Chocó, Colombia,
by Daniel Tubb

Disturbed Forests, Fragmented Memories: Jarai and Other Lives in the Cambodian Highlands, by Jonathan Padwe

The Snow Leopard and the Goat: Politics of Conservation in the Western Himalayas, by Shafqat Hussain

Roses from Kenya: Labor, Environment, and the Global Trade in Cut Flowers,
by Megan A. Styles

Working with the Ancestors: Mana *and Place in the Marquesas Islands*,
by Emily C. Donaldson

Living with Oil and Coal: Resource Politics and Militarization in Northeast India, by Dolly Kikon

Caring for Glaciers: Land, Animals, and Humanity in the Himalayas,
by Karine Gagné

Organic Sovereignties: Struggles over Farming in an Age of Free Trade,
by Guntra A. Aistara

The Nature of Whiteness: Race, Animals, and Nation in Zimbabwe, by Yuka Suzuki

Forests Are Gold: Trees, People, and Environmental Rule in Vietnam,
by Pamela D. McElwee

Conjuring Property: Speculation and Environmental Futures in the Brazilian Amazon, by Jeremy M. Campbell

Andean Waterways: Resource Politics in Highland Peru, by Mattias Borg
Rasmussen

Puer Tea: Ancient Caravans and Urban Chic, by Jinghong Zhang

Enclosed: Conservation, Cattle, and Commerce among the Q'eqchi' Maya Lowlanders, by Liza Grandia

Forests of Identity: Society, Ethnicity, and Stereotypes in the Congo River Basin, by Stephanie Rupp

Tahiti Beyond the Postcard: Power, Place, and Everyday Life, by Miriam Kahn

Wild Sardinia: Indigeneity and the Global Dreamtimes of Environmentalism,
by Tracey Heatherington

Nature Protests: The End of Ecology in Slovakia, by Edward Snajdr

Forest Guardians, Forest Destroyers: The Politics of Environmental Knowledge in Northern Thailand, by Tim Forsyth and Andrew Walker

Being and Place among the Tlingit, by Thomas F. Thornton

Tropics and the Traveling Gaze: India, Landscape, and Science, 1800–1856,
by David Arnold

Ecological Nationalisms: Nature, Livelihood, and Identities in South Asia,
    edited by Gunnel Cederlöf and K. Sivaramakrishnan
From Enslavement to Environmentalism: Politics on a Southern African Frontier,
    by David McDermott Hughes
Border Landscapes: The Politics of Akha Land Use in China and Thailand,
    by Janet C. Sturgeon
Property and Politics in Sabah, Malaysia: Native Struggles over Land Rights,
    by Amity A. Doolittle
The Earth's Blanket: Traditional Teachings for Sustainable Living, by Nancy Turner
The Kuhls of Kangra: Community-Managed Irrigation in the Western Himalaya,
    by Mark Baker

Printed in the USA
CPSIA information can be obtained
at www.ICGtesting.com
CBHW021755111224
18608CB00002B/28